Essays on Toleration

ECPR Press

ECPR Press is an imprint of the European Consortium for Political Research in partnership with Rowman & Littlefield International. It publishes original research from leading political scientists and the best among early career researchers in the discipline. Its scope extends to all fields of political science, international relations and political thought, without restriction in either approach or regional focus. It is also open to interdisciplinary work with a predominant political dimension.

ECPR Press Editors

Essays on Toleration

Peter Jones

ecpr PRESS

ROWMAN &
LITTLEFIELD
——— INTERNATIONAL

London • New York

Published by Rowman & Littlefield International Ltd.
Unit A, Whitacre Mews, 26-34 Stannary Street, London SE11 4AB
www.rowmaninternational.com

In partnership with the European Consortium for Political Research, Harbour House, 6-8
Hythe Quay, Colchester, CO2 8JF, United Kingdom

Rowman & Littlefield International Ltd. is an affiliate of Rowman & Littlefield
4501 Forbes Boulevard, Suite 200, Lanham, Maryland 20706, USA
With additional offices in Boulder, New York, Toronto (Canada), and Plymouth (UK)
www.rowman.com

British Library Cataloguing in Publication Data
A catalogue record for this book is available from the British Library

ISBN: HB 978-1-78552-263-5

Library of Congress Cataloging-in-Publication Data Available

ISBN: 978-1-78552-263-5 (cloth : alk. paper)
ISBN: 978-1-78552-292-5 (pbk. : alk. paper)
ISBN: 978-1-78660-544-3 (electronic)

To the memory of Glen Newey

Contents

Acknowledgements

Peter Jones, 'Liberalism, Belief and Doubt'. In R. Bellamy, ed., *Liberalism and Recent Legal and Social Philosophy* (Stuttgart: Franz Steiner Verlag, 1989), 51–69.

'Toleration, the Rushdie Affair and the Perils of Identity', originally published in *Synthesis Philosophica* 9 (1994): 27–40.

Palgrave Macmillan grants permission for *Beliefs and Identities*.

'Toleration and Neutrality: Compatible Ideals?'. In Dario Castiglione and Catriona MacKinnon, eds., *Toleration, Democracy and Neutrality* (New York: Springer, 2003), 97–110, with permission of Springer.

Peter Jones, 'Toleration, Recognition and Identity', *Journal of Political Philosophy* 14 (2006): 123–43. Wiley. doi: 10.1111/j.1467-9760.2006.00246.

'Toleration, Value Pluralism, and the Fact of Pluralism'. *Critical Review of International Social and Political Philosophy* on August 18, 2006, available online: http://dx.doi.org/10.1080/13698230600655016.

Peter Jones, 'Making Sense of Political Toleration'. *British Journal of Political Science* 37 (2007): 383–402. Cambridge University Press. Reprinted with permission.

'Can Speech Be Intolerant?'. In Glen Newey, ed., *Freedom of Expression: Counting the Costs* (Cambridge: Cambridge Scholars Press, 2008), 9–29. Published with the permission of Cambridge Scholars Press.

'International Toleration and the "War on Terror"'. *Globalizations*, March 25, 2009, available at http:dx.doi.org/10.1080/14747730802692450.

Peter Jones, 'Legalising Toleration: A Reply to Balint'. *Res Publica* 18, 3 (2012): 265–70. With permission of Springer.

Peter Jones, 'Toleration, Religion and Accommodation'. *European Journal of Philosophy* 23 (2015): 542–63. Wiley. doi: 10.1111/j.1468-0378.2012.00549.

Preface

The essays making up this collection were written at different times during the past twenty-five years. In bringing them together in a single volume, I have as far as possible left the text of each as it was originally published. One consequence of my refraining from rewriting is that some of the essays have overlapping arguments, but another is that each essay should make sense as a stand-alone piece for those who want to read the volume selectively.

I have acquired many intellectual debts in working on toleration and many more, I am sure, than I have remembered to acknowledge in the essays. I am especially indebted to John Horton, Susan Mendus, and Matt Matravers, who for many years ran the Morrell programme on Toleration at the University of York to the great benefit of almost everyone working on the subject, but especially to the benefit of myself. I am also indebted to Ian O'Flynn and to Albert Weale for encouraging me to compile this volume, and to Madeleine Hatfield and Dhara Snowden of the ECPR Press and Rowman and Littlefield International partnership, for their patient assistance in preparing it for publication. As always I must thank my wife, Pat, for her encouragement and support and for putting up with my devoting so many hours to my intellectual obsessions. She has provided the illustration for the book's cover.

I dedicate the volume to the memory of Glen Newey. In so doing, I have to exonerate Glen of guilt by association since he took issue with much, though not all, of my thinking on toleration. I learned so much from his sceptical, challenging, and highly original work. His tragic and untimely death has robbed the study of toleration of one of its finest, wittiest, and most engaging scholars. I shall miss him greatly, as will so many others.

Introduction

The diverse make-up of modern societies has long been a major preoccupation of political philosophy. It has also been a prominent focus for public policy. How should a society provide for the differences exhibited by its population? Should it view them with indifference, or seek to diminish them in the interest of social cohesion, or view them as positive goods that it should facilitate or promote? The answer cannot be simple, partly because the differences captured by the terms 'difference' or 'diversity' are themselves so diverse. For example, how a society should respond to the different languages to be found amongst its population is likely to differ from the way in which it should respond to its population's different religious or other beliefs, which in turn will differ from its proper response to differences that arise from inequalities in the economic wellbeing or social status of its citizens. Nor are these merely intra-societal issues; given the global world in which we now live, they also arise as international or transnational issues.

The essays brought together in this volume focus on one sort of response to difference: toleration. They were written at different times and deal with different aspects of toleration, but they are characterised by a number of common themes.

One such theme concerns the idea of toleration itself. That idea has been analysed many times and I shall not present another formal analysis here. Fundamentally, we tolerate when we object to something but nevertheless refrain from impeding it. Religious faiths, for example, are conflicting as well as different in that they present rival bodies of belief. The adherents of one faith therefore have reason to disagree with and to disapprove of other faiths. Religious toleration requires those adherents not to prevent, or to seek to prevent, the practice of other faiths even though they have reason to disagree

1

with and disapprove of them. We tolerate when we refrain from impeding that to which we object; if we do not object, we have no occasion to tolerate.

Toleration is not therefore a response appropriate to every sort of difference. For example, we are often enjoined to celebrate cultural differences and that injunction can be entirely reasonable. Why should we not delight in rather than object to the music, literature, art, and cuisine of cultures other than our own? If we do respond to cultural differences with delight, they will make no call upon our toleration. Even if we do not positively approve of differences, we may respond to them with indifference. Others may possess preferences or pursue forms of life different from our own; why should that bother us? If we respond to differences with that sort of nonchalance, we shall again have no occasion to tolerate them. On the other hand, when cultures conflict rather than merely differ, as they sometimes do on matters of fundamental value, we may well find ourselves presented with questions of toleration. Moreover, what is an issue of toleration for some may not be for others. Same-sex relationships are matters of indifference for some and matters of dislike or disapproval for others. What *ought* to be a matter for toleration can be controversial simply because people have different views on what we can reasonably disapprove of or dislike. When differences present us with conflict rather than mere difference, they present us with more challenging instances of diversity and the idea of toleration is significant partly because it is a response to that more challenging case.

Contrary to the idea of toleration that I have outlined here, the terms 'toleration' and 'tolerant' are sometimes used nowadays in a more relaxed way. In this more generous usage, to tolerate is to accept. Tolerant people, rather than putting up with something to which they take exception, simply take no exception. They are open-minded and accepting of others, even though the beliefs and practices of others differ from her own. Rather than viewing people's differences negatively, they rejoice in them. That is not a conception of toleration I adopt. My reason is not that I reckon it to be linguistically mistaken; how can it be if it now figures in common usage? Rather I set it to one side because, if we remove disapproval or dislike from the idea of toleration, we lose what makes toleration distinctive, interesting, and demanding. In particular, we lose what is sometimes called the 'paradox of toleration': how can it be good or right not to prevent a preventable wrong? What is distinctive about toleration, traditionally conceived, is its combining two sorts of reason: reason to disapprove or dislike along with reason to refrain from impeding what we disapprove of or dislike.

What sort of reason, then, can be a reason for toleration? The answer to that question provides a second theme that runs through these essays. There are many different reasons why we might, or should, opt for toleration rather than intolerance. Some are prudential or strategic, such as an employee's reason to tolerate his superior's objectionable conduct if he wants to gain her support in seeking promotion, or a country's reason to tolerate the short-comings of other countries if it wants to retain them as allies. Some apply to interpersonal relationships rather than to politics, such as the way in which toleration can help sustain those relationships. My interest is primarily in moral reasons for toleration. Those reasons can also be several rather than singular. They can include consequentialist reasons and reasons that appeal to human well-being. However, the reason to which I appeal most frequently is deontological, that is, to the moral status possessed by persons and to the respect and equal respect that we owe one another as persons. Persons, in virtue of being persons, are entitled to pursue their preferred forms of life and others are duty-bound not to prevent their so doing. Thus, on this deontologi-cal view, a person has a right to the toleration of others and others have a duty to respond accordingly. This mode of moral thinking is peculiarly well-suited to the duality of reasons that figure in toleration, since the reason it gives for toleration—the *status* of the tolerated—differs in kind from the reason that appraises the object of toleration negatively—the *demerit* of the tolerated's conduct. There will, of course, be limits to how much toleration this deonto-logical thinking demands but, given the equal status of persons on which it relies, it endorses the general idea that people should possess equal liberty to live as they choose consistently with the right of others to do the same.

The idea of toleration as something to which people are equally entitled, and which should be mutual and reciprocal, is well-suited to the contempo-rary democratic age and therein lies a third theme of these essays. My concern has been to examine toleration as an idea that relates to the present. That is not because I think the past does not matter. Rather it is because I mean to resist the idea that toleration belongs only to the past. Historically, toleration has been most associated with religious differences and a quick glance around the world exposes the nonsense of supposing that the battle for religious tol-eration has been fought and won. Even in societies whose populations have largely embraced the idea of religious toleration, toleration still matters as a continuing state of affairs. Moreover, as many societies have moved from being multidenominational to being significantly multifaith, their commit-ment to religious toleration has been increasingly tested. As I indicate in chapter 4, the issue now is often not only *whether* the practices of a religious faith should be tolerated but also *how* they should be tolerated.

Religious faith is, of course, only one of many contemporary sites of toleration and intolerance. Another, which is frequently intertwined with religious difference, is cultural difference. Cultural differences, as I have already indicated, need not always raise issues of toleration but they do when they present us with conflicting norms of conduct. They may also raise those issues for less profound and more contingent reasons such as the aversion and suspicion with which people sometimes react to the unfamiliar and what they perceive as 'alien'. Consider too the importance of mutual toleration for the functioning of democratic political life or for peaceful coexistence both between societies and within them. Or consider how fundamentally important mutual toleration is for the conduct intellectual inquiry. Toleration may not be at issue in every case of difference, but it is no less relevant to the circumstances of the present than it was to those of the past.

A final theme that unites these essays is their focus on political or 'public' toleration. Their primary concern is with issues of toleration as these arise in the public life of societies rather than as they might arise in relationships between individual persons. The public/private distinction is notoriously difficult to draw satisfactorily and we run into that difficulty if we use it to distinguish different domains of toleration. We may readily describe as 'public' toleration that relates to law and to other institutions of the state, while toleration as it figures in one-to-one personal relationships may seem suitably described as 'private'. But how are we to categorize the toleration relevant to what are sometimes described as intermediate associations such as organized religions or universities or political parties, or to the looser but still highly significant associations that we often describe as 'communities'? If toleration is all of a piece so that political toleration is no different in character from person-to-person toleration, distinctions between different domains of toleration may be of little consequence. Toleration as it bears on the public life of a society is indeed frequently approached as though it were no more than an upscaled version of person-to-person toleration, so that we can understand 'public' toleration through the 'private' case. That, however, is an assumption I mean to question.

TOLERATION AND LIBERAL DEMOCRACY

The person-to-person model of toleration is not unsuited to all political circumstances. It is a model that translates easily to the political circumstances of early modern Europe. During that period, the prevailing form of government was monarchy and it was up to each monarch to decide whether he or she would tolerate subjects who practised a religion different from the monarch's own. The model does not transfer with similar ease to liberal democratic regimes. In a liberal democratic society, at least ideally conceived, citizens' religious freedom is not properly left at anyone's disposal, including a democratic majority or an elected government.

In chapter 1, I propose that, if we are to make sense of toleration as it figures in the idea of liberal democracy, we must abandon the ruler/subject model. We should conceive a liberal democratic society as one that instantiates the ideal of toleration. It does so through rules and arrangements that secure people's freedom to live as they wish, while simultaneously denying them the freedom to prevent *others* living as they wish. The rules and arrangements do not themselves 'tolerate' anyone or anything. They stand in a third-party, rather than a second-party, relation to the population whose lives they govern and the toleration they secure is 'horizontal' rather than 'vertical' in form. They require citizens to tolerate one another and they set out the terms on which they are to be mutually tolerant. Political toleration so conceived is consistent with the liberty and the equality that we associate with liberal democracy.

As well as setting out and defending that analysis, the chapter seeks to refute Glen Newey's suggestion that political toleration is all but impossible in a democratic society. Newey's thesis is that a democratic government typically faces competing groups, each of which insists that its demands should be met and those of its rivals frustrated. For that reason, a government cannot simply opt for tolerance rather than intolerance; in tolerating the demands of one group, it must fail to tolerate the demands of another. I aim to show, contrary to Newey's scepticism, that the choices between toleration and intolerance do not have to sum to zero and that a democratic government can choose between more or less tolerant arrangements.[1]

While the argument of chapter 1 is not tied to the idea of state neutrality, it clearly has an affinity with that idea. In chapter 2, I examine the relationship between toleration and neutrality more closely, with particular reference to the liberal political philosophy of John Rawls.[2] For Rawls, pluralism is an essential feature of modern democratic societies. The citizens of those societies subscribe to different 'comprehensive doctrines', philosophical, religious or moral, and to different 'conceptions of the good' emanating from those doctrines. How should a society deal with those differences? Rawls's answer is that, politically, the society should not attempt to judge which doctrine or which conception is right or best. Rather, its proper business is to secure a just distribution of freedoms and resources amongst its citizens and leave it to citizens themselves to decide which doctrine they should embrace and which conception of the good they should use their freedoms and resources to pursue.

Rawls's conception of the just society as one that remains neutral between people's different comprehensive doctrines and conceptions of the good would seem a model of the politically tolerant society. Yet several commentators have suggested that the association of neutrality with toleration is mistaken. Toleration requires us to refrain from preventing what we disapprove of or dislike but, if we remain neutral, we shall neither disapprove nor dislike and so will have no occasion to tolerate. Hence, the critics conclude, rather than instantiating political toleration, the neutral state makes it superfluous.

My principal response to that objection is that it gets the relationship between toleration and neutrality the wrong way round. It is not neutrality that gives rise to toleration but toleration that makes the case for neutrality. The doctrines and conceptions of the good of Rawls's citizens are conflicting rather than merely different; they therefore provide reasons for mutual disapproval. Suppose we believe that, even so, citizens should be mutually tolerant of one another's ways of life, especially in the political domain. How might we achieve that? For Rawls the answer is by establishing a regime in which citizens may not use *any* of the instruments of political power either to promote or to disadvantage a particular doctrine or conception of the good, which is to say that political power should, as far as possible, remain neutral between citizens' comprehensive doctrines and their conceptions of the good. Thus, so far from displacing toleration, the neutral state is the offspring of an unusually thorough commitment to toleration.

Peter Balint has argued that my attempt to make sense of liberal democratic toleration is unsuccessful.[3] In replying to his objections in chapter 3, I emphasize the difference between our two conceptions of a tolerant society. My conception involves a clear distinction between setting the rules of the game and actually playing it. The architects of the rules do not tolerate anybody; they simply instantiate the ideal of toleration. It is the citizens who, in playing by those rules, engage in toleration. Logically, the architect of the regime of toleration could be a monarch or someone who is not a member of the society, such as Rousseau's legislator. However, it is more consonant with the idea of liberal democracy that citizens should construct the arrangements under which they themselves live. But, if they do, we must distinguish between citizens as architects of the regime, in which role they are not engaged in tolerating anyone, from citizens as members of the society living in accordance with that regime, in which role they stand in a tolerant relation to one another.

My liberal democratic conception of political toleration does, however, depart from the orthodox account of toleration in a crucial respect. Imagine three societies. Society X conforms to my tolerant liberal democratic society, in which citizens are legally at liberty to live their preferred forms of life and legally debarred from depriving others of that liberty. Society Y deems only one form of life legitimate and compels its member to comply with that single form. Society Z falls in between X and Y. It does not impose a single form of life upon its members, but neither does it require them to tolerate one another's chosen forms. It leaves them to tolerate or not as they themselves see fit. Some citizens opt to be tolerant, but most do not; they use violence and whatever other means they can find to prevent or impede lives of which they disapprove. Which of these societies is the more tolerant? The obvious answer is society X. But, if we insist, along with the orthodoxy, that people tolerate only insofar as they remain legally free not to tolerate—that is, only insofar as they *choose* to tolerate—the answer must be society Z. Moreover, society X will rank as no more tolerant than society Y. Those conclusions are self-evidently absurd.

In chapter 4, I press the relevance of toleration to contemporary liberal democratic societies still further. Liberal democracies standardly ascribe to their citizens the right to freedom of religion. Yet what should be the precise make-up of that right remains controversial, especially in relation to religious accommodation. The term 'religious accommodation' generally describes an arrangement which takes account of features particular to a religious faith and makes special provision for them. The most conspicuous instances of religious accommodation are exemptions removing conflicts between laws and the demands of particular faiths. For example, many societies have laws requiring motorcyclists and construction workers to wear safety helmets. Those laws create difficulties for turban-wearing Sikhs and many societies remove those difficulties by exempting turban-wearing Sikhs from the relevant legislation. In European countries, the freedom to manifest one's religion or belief enunciated in article 9 of the European Convention on Human Rights has often been claimed as a ground for such accommodation. The US constitution's 'free exercise' clause has been invoked to similar effect. Another vehicle for accommodation is law providing against indirect religious discrimination in employment and in the provision of goods and services. A rule or practice is indirectly discriminatory when its effect, though not its purpose, is to disadvantage a group relative to others. A rule requiring employees to work at weekends, for example, discriminates indirectly against Orthodox Jews and Sabbatarian Christians; indirect discrimination law requires employers, unless they have adequate justification for doing otherwise, to exempt members of those religious groups from the rule. These various forms of exemption are, I argue, exercises in the toleration of religious differences, even though they are not commonly conceived in that way, and argument about whether they should exist and, if so, how generous they should be, is argument about the proper scope of religious toleration.

TOLERATION, BELIEFS, AND IDENTITIES

Toleration as a public issue arises most prominently in pluralist societies, that is, in societies characterized by what I have previously described as 'difference'. That pluralism includes differences in religious belief and in many other sorts of belief. Nowadays, however, the differences manifested by a population are frequently characterised in quite other terms: as differences of 'identity'. If we characterise a society's pluralism as a plurality of identities, how should that affect our thinking on toleration? Can we simply transpose our thinking on toleration from beliefs to identities, or does the shift to identities alter the kind of toleration there should be? Is it even appropriate to think of ourselves 'tolerating' identities?

In chapter 5, I examine the implications of recasting people's beliefs as identities. These are by no means straightforward. For example, we might suppose that ideas of the respect that is due to persons and of what matters to their wellbeing will provide even stronger protection if we conceive beliefs as constituents of people's identities. But those ideas might be used to opposite effect. If our respect for a person's identity turns on their beliefs and if we take a negative view of their beliefs, we shall take a negative view of their identity. Similarly, if people's identity is essential to their wellbeing and if someone's identity is grounded in beliefs that we reckon false, we may think we should do whatever we can to reshape their beliefs so that their identity becomes more conducive to their wellbeing.

Some commentators have suggested that, if we think of people's differences as differences of identity, we should treat those differences as public rather than private matters; our strategy should be democratic rather than liberal. I argue the opposite. The more we characterize beliefs as matters of identity, the more that pushes us towards privatizing belief. Of course, the privatizing of religious belief is a strategy commonly used for securing the toleration of those beliefs, but we need to be aware of differences in what 'privatizing' can mean. Liberal societies secure toleration by privatizing religious belief only in that, as far as possible, they keep religious belief out of the domain of public political decision making. People are then free to pursue whatever religious beliefs they embrace, which may be none, and they will not be subject to the political imposition of beliefs they do not share. That arrangement is quite consistent with religious beliefs remaining public in a different respect. Religious adherents are still free to preach and promote their faith to the world at large and nonadherents remain free to dispute their claims. If, however, we recast religious beliefs as identities, we make them matters that are entirely personal and private to their holders. An identity, unlike a belief, is not true or false, or plausible or implausible, and the make-up of an identity, unlike a belief, is not properly of concern to those who do not share it.

The principal normative thrust of my concern with the shift from beliefs to identities is the threat it poses to freedom of expression. Beliefs of the kind at issue here embody claims about what is true of the world and about the way in which we should conduct our lives. The content of those beliefs makes them everyone's business and suitable subjects for scrutiny and comment by anyone. But, if we reconstrue beliefs as identities, we make possible a potent argument—the 'identity argument'—for severely restricting freedom of expression. It runs as follows: My beliefs are essential to my identity, to the very person I am. Hence, if you attack my beliefs, you attack me. Such personal assaults are intolerable. Identities should be respected rather than attacked or eroded and assaults on identities should be deplored and discouraged, perhaps through the use of criminal law. Thus, by translating beliefs into identities, we can create a disturbing case for silencing critical commentary on beliefs, be they religious or nonreligious.

The identity argument was mobilized during the Rushdie Affair by Rushdie's critics, both Muslim and non-Muslim. In chapter 6, I examine its use in the context of that affair and indicate its sinister implications not only for those who, like Rushdie, want the freedom to question and criticize religious beliefs, but also for religious believers insofar as they demand that we take their beliefs seriously as beliefs. That demand is at odds with the notion that what really matters about beliefs is their impact on their holders' identities. Rushdie's *Satanic Verses* was published in 1988 and the affair it triggered has now passed into history, but the issues it raised are still with us, as is illustrated all too well by the furore sparked during 2005–2006 by the Danish cartoons of Muhammad and the murder in 2015 of journalists and others associated with the satirical magazine *Charlie Hebdo*.

The idea of identity is frequently combined with that of 'recognition'. An assertion of identity is typically accompanied by a call for positive public recognition of its status or value. Anna Elisabetta Galeotti has proposed that, in contemporary Western societies, we should reconceive toleration as recognition.[4] The kinds of minority that currently lack recognition and that, she argues, should receive it are Muslims in Western societies and homosexuals. Examples of measures she believes would bestow toleration as recognition, albeit symbolically, are legal changes enabling Muslim girls to wear hijabs while attending French state schools, and reforms instituting same-sex marriage and enabling openly gay people to join the military.

The idea of 'toleration as recognition' does, however, harbour a problem which I examine in chapter 7. As we have seen, toleration traditionally conceived entails a negative appraisal of whatever we tolerate and Galeotti means that negativity to remain part of her revised conception of toleration. Recognition, by contrast, requires positive endorsement of the identity we recognize. How, then, can we simultaneously tolerate and recognize? Does one not rule out the other?

I argue that we can square this circle only if our recognition takes a 'mediated' form. Suppose I am a Christian and I am called upon to accord recognition to Muslims. I cannot accord unmediated recognition to an Islamic identity, since I must believe it to be based on a false religion. I can, however, recognize that people who are Muslim are also, like me, persons or citizens and I can accept that, as persons or citizens, what matters to them should matter equally with what matters to myself. In other words, my recognizing them as persons or citizens provides reason for my recognizing that, as Muslims, they should enjoy the same civic status and the same rights as I do. That is how I, as a disapproving Christian, might accord recognition to those possessing a Muslim identity. For Galeotti, however, that sort of mediated recognition is not enough. She, like Charles Taylor,[5] insists that minorities should receive unmediated recognition; we should accord recognition to Muslims *as* Muslims and to gays *as* gays. But, in circumstances of disagreement and disapproval that create a need for toleration, that demand is unreasonable as is readily apparent if we combine Galeotti's two prime examples of unrecognised minorities. Given the negativity with which homosexuality is viewed within traditional Islam and in the orthodox versions of many other faiths, how can we insist that the adherents of those faiths must accord positive recognition to gays as gays? And, insofar as a gay identity is viewed negatively by a religious faith and its adherents, how can we expect gays to accord positive recognition to that faith and its adherents?

DOUBT, DISAGREEMENT, AND VALUE PLURALISM

Do we have reason to tolerate those with whom we disagree because, in that disagreement, they could be right and we could be wrong? John Stuart Mill certainly thought so.[6] Many defenders of toleration have, by contrast, shunned any suggestion that doubt or scepticism should figure in the justification of toleration. One reason for that shunning stems from the simple conceptual point that we tolerate x only if we believe x to be objectionable; if we refrain from preventing x because we are uncertain whether x is indeed objectionable, we are not really tolerating x. Another reason is that, if we found the case for toleration on scepticism, that scepticism may corrode the case for toleration itself. If we cannot be sure of anything, how can we be sure that we are right to be tolerant?

In spite of those objections, a degree of modesty about our own wisdom and others' lack of it can be part of a coherent case for toleration. That applies especially to the case of religious toleration. Many religious faiths are founded on 'revealed truths', which are usually truths said to be revealed in their sacred writings. Unfortunately, different religions lay claim to different revealed truths and, since we have little to go on apart from each religion's claim, we have no ready way of determining which revelation, if any, is correct. We therefore have reason to hold that no religion is sufficiently well-grounded epistemically to be justifiably imposed on those who reject it.

In chapter 8, I argue that the ideas of reasonable doubt and reasonable disagreement have a significant role to play in the dominant forms of contemporary liberal thinking. I preface that argument with a distinction between two kinds of conflict: conflicts of want and conflicts of belief. Insofar as a conflict is merely one of wants, it is not an epistemic conflict. All we have to determine is how the conflict can be fairly provided for. With beliefs it is a different matter. Beliefs are about what is true or false, right or wrong, prudent or imprudent, and so on. Beliefs are capable of being correct or incorrect, or more or less correct. Thus, people do not obviously have an interest in holding and acting on their beliefs merely because those beliefs are their own; they have a more obvious interest in holding and acting on correct beliefs. The appropriate collective response to a conflict of beliefs is not obviously therefore a liberal response. Believers have a more obvious interest in trying to establish which of their different beliefs is actually correct or best-founded. Only if they fail in that endeavour do they have reason to cast around for some other way of dealing with their differences. Thus, the presence of justified doubt and reasonable disagreement is crucial to the case for dealing with conflicting beliefs in a liberal fashion. I argue that that claim holds good whether the liberal solution on offer is the deontological liberalism associated with John Rawls and Ronald Dworkin or the perfectionist liberalism exemplified by the work of Joseph Raz.[7]

Even if scepticism can be mobilized in defence of toleration, there are other defences which can seem less hazardous. One such is value-pluralism. Value-pluralism is a theory about the nature of value. It holds that values are irreducibly plural and, in significant measure, uncombinable and incommensurable. It therefore rejects the idea that all that is of value can be reduced to a single ultimate value, such as utility, or that different values can be organized into a single correct hierarchy. It also holds that there are many good forms of life rather than only one and that, since many goods are uncombinable, not all them can be realized in a single life or even in a single society. Value-pluralism should not be confused with relativism or subjectivism. It does not deny the objectivity of values or that good can be distinguished from evil. It denies only that the good is singular and that one form of life is uniquely or supremely good.

Given its commitment to the diversity of values and good forms of life, value-pluralism would seem to yield a strong case for toleration. In chapter 9, I consider whether it does by examining the thought of John Gray, who has provided one of the most fully developed statements of value-pluralism, including its application to political life.[8] Gray argues that, given the truth of value-pluralism, differences and conflicts of value are unavoidable and that we can achieve peaceful coexistence, socially and globally, only by way of a modus vivendi based on compromise and toleration. However, the path from value-pluralism to toleration is less easily taken than Gray seems to suppose. If we manage to convince people of the truth of value-pluralism, they will not take a negative view of (good) forms of life other than their own and therefore will have no need to tolerate them. On the other hand, each of those people will commit to the goodness of a particular form of life and that specific commitment may be hard to combine with a general commitment to value-pluralism. In addition, value-pluralism is a theory about the plurality of *goods* rather than about the plurality of *conceptions* of the good, and it does not easily cater for conflict that stems not from the diversity of values but from people's diverse and conflicting judgements about what is of value. A theory of toleration needs to provide for what, following Rawls, I describe as 'the fact of pluralism': the fact that people subscribe to different and conflicting conceptions of the good, many of which are at odds with the claims of value-pluralism as an ethical or meta-ethical theory. Religious conceptions are an obvious case in point. It is difficult to see how people whose beliefs are at odds with value-pluralism might nevertheless embrace value-pluralism as a reason for toleration.

TWO SPECIAL CASES

The final two essays examine more specific issues, though still issues on which much depends. Chapter 10 considers whether speech can be intolerant. Chapter 11 examines how we might apply the idea of toleration to the international world.

Speech figures in discussions of toleration most commonly as a possible object of toleration. If we dislike or disagree with what others say, we confront the question of whether we should nevertheless tolerate their speech and, if we should, up to what point. Chapter 10 considers a quite different relationship between speech and toleration: whether speech itself can be an instrument of intolerance. Speech is often thought to be less capable than action of limiting the freedom of others and that is sometimes said to justify giving people greater freedom of speech than freedom of action. That, in turn, may suggest that speech is an unlikely instrument of intolerance. On the other hand, if one person denounces the conduct of another, that very denunciation may seem intolerant.

If speech expresses dislike or disapproval, should it be deemed intolerant merely for that reason? Given that we tolerate only what we disapprove of or dislike, it would be extravagant to hold that we are tolerant only if we never disclose our disapproval or dislike. But there are other ways in which speech might reasonably be deemed intolerant. It is, for example, if it is part of an effort to persuade legislators to prevent conduct of which the speaker disapproves. Speech might also be used deliberately to cause hurt and distress to those we disagree with or dislike, in which case it is intolerant because it aims to persecute rather than to impede. The cases on which it is more difficult to rule are social disapproval and proselytizing. Even if mere disapproval cannot itself be accounted intolerance, the sheer weight of social disapproval might inhibit people's conduct so that disapproval does function as an instrument of intolerance, whether justified or not. Proselytising is not normally deemed intolerant, even though it endeavours to change people's minds rather than settle for 'live and let live'. Yet proselytising might also take a form that amounts to intolerance. I suggest that we should look to the idea of autonomy for the test of what is and is not consistent with toleration. Proselytizing and expressing disapproval are consistent with toleration, but only so long as they take forms that do not subvert people's capacity to decide for themselves and to act as they decide.

The literature on toleration has focused overwhelmingly on either inter-personal relationships or domestic political arrangements. Only rarely has it turned to the case of international politics. In chapter 11, I examine how the idea of toleration might be deployed internationally. What distinguishes the international case is that the subjects and objects of toleration are corporate or collective entities: states or societies or peoples. The idea of *international* toleration is therefore different from that of *global* toleration which would focus on humanity as a whole without reference to political units.

There are plenty of reasons of a strategic kind why a society might opt to tolerate another society's objectionable conduct or arrangements, but my interest is in the application of moral rather than prudential reasons to the international case. More especially, I consider whether we might invoke the moral status of persons, and the respect they are due, as reasons for interna-tional toleration. Rawls is well known for grounding international toleration in that sort of deontological thinking.[9] However, for Rawls, the subjects and objects of international toleration are Peoples rather than persons. Peoples, as he conceives them, are not reducible to persons; they possess moral standing in their own right, a standing that is independent of the persons they encom-pass. Contrary to Rawls's thinking, I propose a conception of a People that is 'collective' rather than 'corporate'. According to that conception, the rights of a People are rights held jointly by the persons who constitute its members. The moral standing that underwrites those rights is that of the persons who jointly hold them rather than a standing that belongs to a People indepen-dently of its members. So understood, our reasoning about international toleration can be anchored in persons along with the status they possess and the respect they are owed.

A major subject of People-to-People toleration is cultural difference. If those differences are proper objects of toleration, why is that? People often turn to cultural relativism for an answer. Whether it yields an answer depends on the kind of relativism it is. A relativism that holds that there is no correct morality but only different sets of norms evolved by different segments of humanity can undermine intolerance by undermining the claim to correct belief on which that intolerance is based. But it provides no case against one culture's imposing itself upon another for other sorts of reason, such as a wish to dominate or to exploit. Appealing to the 'good' of different cultures is also ineffective insofar as cultures differ over what is good. The idea of person-hood provides a more compelling ground for international cultural toleration. Cultures matter primarily because they matter to those whose cultures they are and, insofar as we should tolerate cultures, the principal reason lies in the moral status of those who bear them rather than in the merits of the cultures themselves.

The idea of the equal status of persons, along with the equal respect they are due, does, of course, set limits to toleration; but those limits are, I argue, often drawn too closely. Respect for persons argues for government that pos-sesses popular legitimacy but not necessarily for democracy. Moreover, if a population sincerely embraces a system of belief in which its members pos-sess different statuses, the equal respect we owe them requires us to respect their system of belief, including arguably their beliefs about their differences in status.

Toleration is not an unmixed good simply because there are limits to what we should tolerate. Where precisely those limits should fall is often contro-versial, but the proposition that there should be no limits to toleration is inde-fensible. It equates with the claim that we should be free to do just anything, including to one another. We might defend the proposition by insisting that toleration remains toleration only so long as it is justified; we do not engage in toleration if we tolerate the intolerable. But that is no more than verbal duplicity. If we hold, for example, that people should not be free to engage in paedophilia, our stance, honestly stated, is that paedophilia is intolerable and should not be tolerated. Intolerance does not cease to be intolerance simply because it is justified.

Nowadays, the desirability of toleration is sometimes questioned in a less qualified and more fundamental way. Negativity, in the form of disapproval or dislike, is an essential feature of toleration traditionally conceived. Is that negativity not unfortunate and, if it is, should we not aim for something more and better than toleration? 'If tolerance is about objection, aversion, error, deviation, falsehood, I don't see how it gives you a positive notion of differ-ence', complains Wendy Brown.[10] But, if we were to dispense with toleration, we would find ourselves having to dichotomize the world between the good or the right, which we should embrace and promote, and the bad or the wrong, which we should reject and suppress. No space would remain for the possibil-ity that we can have reason to find something mistaken or objectionable but also reason not to prevent or impede it. As long as we continue to differ and to disagree, sincerely and reasonably, it is hard to see how we can do better than take seriously the case for toleration. Without it, disputants can reach too easily for the words of Bishop Bossuet: 'I have the right to persecute you because I am right and you are wrong'.[11]

NOTES

1. For further comment on this issue, see Glen Newey, 'Political Toleration: A Reply to Jones', *British Journal of Political Science* 41 (2011): 223–27, and Peter Jones, 'Political Toleration: A Reply to Newey', *British Journal of Political Science* 41 (2011): 445–47. Newey went on to develop a fuller critique of the sort of position I adopt in his *Toleration in Political Conflict* (Cambridge: Cambridge University Press, 2013), especially chapter 5.

2. The fundamental place occupied by toleration in Rawls's thinking is most readily apparent in his *Political Liberalism*, expanded edition (New York: Columbia University Press, 2005).

3. Peter Balint, 'Not Yet Making Sense of Political Toleration', *Res Publica* 18 (2012): 259–64. For Balint's more comprehensive thinking on toleration, see his *Respecting Toleration* (Oxford: Oxford University Press, 2017).

4. Anna Elisabetta Galeotti, *Toleration as Recognition* (Cambridge: Cambridge University Press, 2002).

5. Charles Taylor, *The Ethics of Authenticity* (Cambridge, MA: Harvard University Press, 1992) and 'The Politics of Recognition', in Amy Gutman, ed., *Multiculturalism: Examining the Politics of Recognition* (Princeton, NJ: Princeton University Press, 1994).

6. Especially in his *On Liberty*, chapter 2.

7. John Rawls, *A Theory of Justice*, revised edition (Cambridge, MA: Harvard University Press, 1999) and *Political Liberalism*; Ronald Dworkin, *A Matter of Principle* (Oxford: Clarendon Press, 1986) and *Sovereign Virtue* (Cambridge, MA: Harvard University Press, 2000); Joseph Raz, *The Morality of Freedom* (Oxford: Clarendon Press, 1986).

8. See especially, John Gray, *Two Faces of Liberalism* (Cambridge: Polity Press, 2000).

9. John Rawls, *The Law of Peoples* (Cambridge, MA: Harvard University Press, 1999).

10. Wendy Brown and Rainer Forst, *The Power of Tolerance: A Debate*, edited by Luca Di Blasi and Christopher F. E. Holzhey (New York: Columbia University Press, 2014), 67.

11. Quoted in Susan Mendus, *Toleration and the Limits of Liberalism* (Basingstoke: Macmillan, 1989), 7.

Chapter 1

Making Sense of Political Toleration[*]

Toleration is a political ideal with which we are very familiar. We commonly suppose that some societies and some political regimes are more tolerant than others. Liberal democratic societies, in particular, conceive themselves as tolerant and suppose that a commitment to toleration is present in the design and operation of their institutions. Yet a moment's reflection on the nature of toleration shows that it is not an idea that can be readily transposed from the political circumstances of the sixteenth and seventeenth centuries to those of contemporary liberal democracies.

Consider the paradigm case of religious toleration. In the centuries immediately following the Reformation, rulers, in their official capacity as rulers, typically endorsed either Catholicism or a form of Protestantism. They had then to decide what to do about those of their subjects who were committed to something other than the officially approved religious faith. Rulers were tolerant if they permitted dissenters to practise their dissenting faith and intolerant if they did not. Consider now the same issue in the context of liberal democracy. Typically, nowadays, it would be thought quite improper for a liberal democratic regime either to endorse or to deprecate any religious faith

---

[*] Earlier versions of this chapter were presented to the Workshop on Toleration, organized by John Horton and Monica Mookherjee for the Political Theory conference held at Manchester Metropolitan University in 2005 and to the annual conference of the Association of Legal and Social Philosophy, 2005. I am grateful to the participants in both events for sharpening up my thinking. I have also benefited greatly from the detailed comments of my fellow political theorists at Newcastle, Derek Bell, Thom Brooks, Graham Long, and Ian O'Flynn, and from those of John Horton, Shane O'Neill, Albert Weale, and *The British Journal of Political Science*'s anonymous referees. I must also acknowledge my debt to Glen Newey; although I spend much of this article taking issue with Newey, I am greatly indebted to his original and penetrating work on toleration for stimulating much of my own thought on the subject. This chapter was written during my tenure of a Leverhulme Research Fellowship and I am very grateful to the Leverhulme Trust for its support.

or any particular denomination within a religious faith. For those who wield political power in liberal democratic societies, religious faith, as such, is simply off limits. But if a liberal democratic regime adopts no official view on the rights or wrongs of different religious faiths, how can it engage in religious toleration? If religious matters fall outside its jurisdiction, it is in no position either to tolerate or not to tolerate its citizens' diverse religious commitments. Thus, it might seem that religious toleration, either as a political principle or as a political practice, has become obsolete. It is a relic of a bygone age that has been superseded by, rather than instantiated in, liberal democratic institutions. That, in turn, implies that the many imposing arguments for toleration that have been developed during the last five centuries are misapplied if they are urged in defence of contemporary political regimes. They may retain their force as arguments for 'nonpolitical' toleration amongst individuals or groups but they are misdirected if they are mobilized in defence of liberal democratic arrangements.[1]

Yet there is something strangely counterintuitive about that conclusion. Rather than seeing the 'hands-off' approach to religious diversity, associated with liberal democratic regimes, as delivering something other than toleration, we might be more inclined to regard it as a full and final endorsement of the ideal of religious toleration. In this chapter, I examine and try to make sense of toleration as a contemporary political idea and as a feature of liberal democratic arrangements ideally conceived. I shall argue that 'tolerant' and 'intolerant' are qualities that we can still ascribe to political regimes and that arguments concerning toleration have lost none of their salience for political life.

Two standard conceptual features of toleration are particularly relevant to this exercise. First, toleration in its orthodox sense entails disapproval or dislike.[2] We tolerate only that to which we object; if we find something unobjectionable, we have no occasion to tolerate it. Thus, when people conform to the model case of toleration, they are usually thought to possess two sorts of reason: (a) a reason for objecting to and so for preventing x and (b) a reason for not preventing x. Their reason not to prevent x overrides their reason to prevent it; hence they tolerate x.

Secondly, we can tolerate only what we are able to prevent. If we object to x, but are powerless to prevent it, we cannot tolerate x. Toleration exists only when intolerance is an option. We can adopt a tolerant stance or possess a tolerant disposition even though we are powerless; that is, we might resolve not to prevent x even if we could. But, strictly, we actually tolerate x only if we are actually able to prevent x but opt not to do so.

The phrase 'political toleration' might be used to describe toleration exercised within a political process. We might observe, for example, that, since disagreement, debate, and contestation for power are essential features of democracy, so too is political toleration, even though, curiously, the give-and-take that is essential to a democratic process is rarely considered under the heading of toleration. Here, however, I mean 'political toleration' to have a broader meaning. It describes toleration secured through the apparatus of the state. Thus, for example, both religious toleration and cultural toleration fall within the compass of political toleration in so far as they are forms of toleration secured by the state. We might describe political toleration in this sense as 'public' toleration since it is toleration secured by and through a society's public authority and public arrangements. Thus 'private' toleration is toleration afforded by one individual or group to another without its being routed through the state. If, for example, a household plays loud music which neighbouring households find objectionable but which they nevertheless resolve to endure, their toleration is 'private'. Their toleration is 'public' in the sense that both the objectionable noise and the toleration goes beyond a private household, but it is not 'public' in the sense intended here in that it is not secured by way of public authority.

CAN THERE BE LIBERAL DEMOCRATIC TOLERATION?

With these simple features of the concept of political toleration in place, we can consider how different sorts of political regime might exhibit toleration. Consider again a simplified version of the absolute monarchy that characterized many European societies during the early modern era. Suppose that a monarch possessed more or less absolute power, and embraced a particular religious faith as the officially approved faith of her realm. Suppose, for example, that the monarch was a Catholic and made Catholicism the approved religion of her kingdom but that amongst her subjects she had some who were avowed Protestants. In these circumstances, the possibility of political toleration or political intolerance is readily evident. The ruler had the power either to permit or to disallow the practice of the Protestantism of which she disapproved. The monarch displayed toleration if she permitted Protestant subjects to practise their faith and intolerance if she did not.

If we carry that idea of political toleration forward to contemporary democratic societies, who or what is the equivalent of the tolerant monarch? The most obvious equivalents are the elected governments that wield power in modern indirect democracies. So should we now conceive political toleration as a toleration that elected governments might extend to the populations they govern, just as unelected monarchs once decided whether to tolerate their dissenting subjects? That cannot be right. For one thing, as we have already noted, there are many matters relating to toleration that fell within the authority of early modern monarchs, such as ruling on the 'right' religious faith, that liberal democratic thinking places outside the proper competence of elected governments. But, more generally, the notion that an elected government might tolerate its electors inverts the proper democratic relationship. An elected government stands to its electorate as agent to principal and it cannot be for an agent to decide whether it shall indulge its principal. On the contrary, in democratic theory, it is the people as principal who should wield ultimate power over its government as agent.

Of course, in modern democratic reality, popular controls over elected governments are so limited and so crude that governments have ample opportunity to act as agents free from the thrall of their electors. Nor do governing parties merely transmit popular preferences. They develop strongly approving or disapproving views of their own which may or may not align with popular attitudes. Witness, for example, the conduct of British Labour MPs in securing a ban on hunting with dogs or the stance of the Bush presidency on embryo research and gay marriage. If 'political toleration' means toleration by government, real-life democratic political systems still offer some scope for toleration that takes a ruler–subject form.

Yet, if political toleration is to occupy a significant place in liberal democratic thinking and institutions, it cannot be confined to the occasions when governments break free of democratic control and gain an opportunity to behave like indulgent autocrats. So where else might we locate democratic toleration? An obvious answer is in the conduct of democratic majorities. In simple democratic contexts, a majority can wield power over minorities and is therefore able to tolerate minorities by allowing them to behave in ways that the majority dislikes or deprecates. Powerless minorities, just because they are powerless, cannot reciprocate that toleration. But that asymmetric conception of toleration is also deeply unsatisfactory as a democratic ideal and is particularly unsuited to *liberal* democratic thinking. The citizens of a democratic society should stand on an equal footing and that equality is at odds with the unequal power relations that the traditional conception of toleration seems to presuppose.

It is not altogether surprising, therefore, that some commentators have concluded that toleration belongs to the politics of a bygone age. It may have been welcome in hierarchical societies in which the freedom of subjects depended upon the grace of their rulers, but it is has no place in a society of self-ruling citizens, each of whom enjoys equal status and equal rights. It may remain an important virtue in people's personal lives, but as a political ideal toleration is now otiose. That dismissal of political toleration is, I shall argue, unwarranted and stems from a misconception of the role of political authority in relation to toleration.[3]

FROM RULERS TO RULES

It is clear that, if toleration is to figure significantly in liberal democratic thinking and arrangements, it must take a more symmetrical form than those we have so far considered. It must be consistent with a democratic conception of citizens as people who enjoy equal status and equal rights as members of a common political community. That points to the error of trying to make sense of political toleration in contemporary circumstances by finding some individual, group, or entity that is the contemporary equivalent of an early modern monarch. Rather than locating political toleration in the dispositions and vagaries of governments or majorities, we should locate it in a society's legal and political arrangements. We need to explore the idea of the tolerant society rather than the tolerant ruler.

In describing a society as 'tolerant', we might refer to either or both of two things. First, we might refer to the personal qualities of its population. We might mean that, in significant number and in significant measure, members of the society are committed to the rightness or goodness or desirability of toleration and that, accordingly, they display toleration in their relations with one another. Secondly, we might mean that the public arrangements of the society embody a commitment to toleration and secure toleration for the society's members. It is this second conception of a tolerant society that I shall equate with 'political toleration' and which, I shall argue, is a feature of liberal democracy ideally conceived. Of course, these two respects in which a society might be described as tolerant are likely to be found together, especially in democratic circumstances. Tolerant political and legal arrangements are likely to be put in place only if they enjoy reasonable support amongst the relevant population, and they may be sustainable only if there is a limit to the weight of popular intolerance that they have to contain. But, if we are to make good the claim that some political regimes can properly be described as tolerant, that claim has to rely upon more than the supposition that they are staffed and supported by tolerant people.

If we shift our focus from rulers to rules and institutions, that still does not render the idea of political toleration immediately intelligible. For one thing, rules and arrangements regulate and restrain people's conduct, and restraint implies intolerance rather than tolerance. For another, it is not clear that the disapproval, that is essential to the idea of toleration, can be a feature of rules and arrangements. Inanimate human creations, such as rules and institutional structures, cannot entertain feelings of dislike or form disapproving judgements. They may, of course, express the dislike or disapproval of their architects. Yet instruments of people's dislike and disapproval are precisely what we think the rules and institutions of a tolerant society should *not* be.

UPHOLDING AN IDEAL OF TOLERATION

The solution I propose to this conundrum is that we should conceive political toleration not as toleration extended by a society's rules and institutions to the population they regulate. Rather, rules and institutions can be adjudged tolerant because and in so far as they uphold an ideal of toleration. They secure an order of things in which people can live their lives as they see fit, unprevented by disapproving others who might otherwise impede them. Thus, for example, a tolerant political order will allow neither Christians to prevent Muslims living as Muslims, nor Muslims to prevent Christians living as Christians; nor will it allow either to suppress atheists, or atheists to suppress either. I do not mean, of course, that a tolerant political order will secure people's freedom to do just anything; there must be limits. But, in general, a tolerant regime should be understood as tolerant in virtue of its preventing the censorious from using political power to suppress the objects of their censure.

A tolerant political arrangement is, then, one that upholds an ideal of toleration rather than one that itself engages in toleration. Now I must acknowledge what might seem a paradoxical, and perhaps incoherent, feature of this way of understanding a tolerant political order: it is an order in which no one need actually behave tolerantly. Suppose that A wants to do x, that B disapproves of and wishes to prevent her doing x, and that G, the government or institutional cum legal order, upholds toleration by prohibiting B from acting in ways that thwart A's freedom to do x.[4] None of the three parties, A, B, and G, engages in toleration. A, as the beneficiary of the arrangement, is the putatively tolerated, rather than tolerating, party. G, the government or institutional cum legal order that prevents B from interfering with A, may be motivated by an ideal of toleration but it clearly does not tolerate B's intended conduct. Nor does G tolerate A's conduct. G acts to safeguard A's freedom, but it would misdescribe G's act to say that G itself 'tolerates' A's conduct.[5] Finally, we might suppose that B is made to behave tolerantly towards A but, since B's noninterference is a product not of his own volition but of external restraint imposed by G, B cannot properly be said to 'tolerate' A.

Of course, while B may be rendered legally unfree to interfere with A, B's noninterference need not be a product of that legal restraint. B may have his own firmly held nonlegal reasons for believing that he should not prevent A from doing x even though B disapproves of x. To that extent, B's subjection to legal prohibition does not preclude B behaving tolerantly towards A. As I noted earlier, we might expect a tolerant political regime to be supported by a tolerant political culture, so that, in significant measure, people will refrain from suppressing one another's conduct, not out of fear of legal penalty or a sense of merely legal obligation, but because they believe they would be wrong not to tolerate it. A tolerant regime may, therefore, check intolerance that is more possible than real.

Nevertheless, if it turns out that, in a tolerant political arrangement, none of the actors, A, B, or G, engages in toleration, what can justify its description as 'tolerant'? The answer is simply that it secures a state of affairs in which A is unprevented from doing *x* by intolerant others. It is tolerant not because it provides an arena within which people can engage in acts of toleration but because it holds intolerance at bay.

How satisfactory we find that answer may well depend upon how we conceive the value of toleration. If we find the 'good' of toleration principally in the virtue of tolerance, our focus will be on acts of tolerance, for the virtue of tolerance will be realized only in so far as people can and do engage in acts of tolerance.[6] On this view, it matters very much that people should have significant opportunities to be tolerators. Hence, for those who hold that view, my account of political toleration may be deeply unsatisfying. If, by contrast, we believe (as I do) that we should look for the good of toleration not towards the tolerator but towards the tolerated, we may think very differently. On this view, what is important about toleration is the value to A herself, or to others, of A's being free to do *x*, in spite of others finding something to dislike or to disapprove of in A's doing *x*. What matters therefore is that A's conduct should not be not tolerated, rather than that it should be the object of an act of toleration. An arrangement that secures for A the freedom to do *x*, by holding at bay those whose disapproval of *x* would otherwise lead them to impede A, secures what is valuable about toleration. The value of that freedom is neither removed nor diminished because it is secured by legal restraint of the intolerant rather than by the self-restraint of the tolerant.[7]

DISAPPROVAL AND NEUTRALITY

Given this understanding of political toleration, we should not look for the disapproval that is essential to the idea of toleration within the rules and institutions of the tolerant society. Rather, that disapproval will be located in the population whose lives the rules and institutions regulate. Of course, those rules and institutions are not likely to make explicit reference to either disapproval or toleration. They may stipulate only what people are permitted and not permitted to do in relation to one another. The rules that properly distribute freedom amongst a population might be the same rules irrespective of whether people do, or do not, disapprove of the use that others make of their freedom. But those rules still provide for toleration in that they uphold an ideal of toleration; they safeguard a society's members against the possible intolerance of others.

Absence of official disapproval might suggest political neutrality and, although the liberal democratic arrangements that I am associating with toleration do not presuppose a neutral state, I want here to comment on the relationship between toleration and political neutrality. Neutrality is often thought to be incompatible with toleration for the simple reason that, in so far as a state or government or body of citizens remains neutral, it refrains from taking either an approving or disapproving stance on the matter at hand. In so far as it refrains from disapproval, it cannot engage in toleration for, as we have seen, disapproval is an essential ingredient of toleration. Neutrality, therefore, precludes toleration, and those who suppose that the neutral state is a vehicle for toleration would seem to be in the grip of a misconception.

Although this view is often stated,[8] it rests upon a mistaken understanding of the relationship between toleration and neutrality. It is not neutrality that, *per impossibile*, spawns toleration. Rather, it is a particular sort of commitment to toleration that yields a case for neutrality. I shall use John Rawls's political liberalism to explain and justify this claim, though I believe the thought of many other deontological liberals, such as Charles Larmore, Thomas Nagel, and Brian Barry, might be used to make the same point.[9]

Rawls's political liberalism is designed for a society whose members subscribe to different and conflicting comprehensive doctrines and to different and conflicting conceptions of the good grounded in those doctrines. In so far as people recognize the 'burdens of judgement', they will recognize that at least some of the doctrines of others are 'reasonable' even though they believe them to be mistaken. Rawls aims to find a just way of providing for that reasonable pluralism. He aims, that is, to discover political arrangements that would regulate fairly the lives of people who possess different and conflicting conceptions of the good. He does so by drawing upon certain ideas that he takes to be fundamental to the public culture of a democratic society, particularly the ideas of society as a fair scheme of cooperation and of persons as free and equal. Those ideas he takes to be independent of any particular conception of the good, so that he is not drawing on any particular conception of the good in devising principles and institutions that will regulate the lives of people who possess different conceptions of the good.

Through reasoning that I shall not reproduce here, he arrives at his celebrated two principles of justice. But, more generally, he arrives at an order of things in which citizens may not use political power either to advance their own conceptions of the good or to discriminate against the rival conceptions of others. In reasoning about and in deciding upon 'political' matters,

Rawlsian citizens will not draw upon—and in that respect will remain politically neutral among—particular conceptions of the good. But if Rawlsian individuals, in their political role as citizens, are to conduct themselves in that scrupulously neutral fashion, how can they be politically tolerant? The answer is, of course, that Rawlsian individuals are not only citizens. They are also fully fledged persons possessed of different and conflicting comprehensive doctrines who, in the absence of Rawls's political conception of justice, would have ample reason to impose their conceptions of the good upon one another. The institutional constraints that Rawlsian individuals and groups have to observe as political actors are grounded in the principle that it is unjust for citizens to use political power to impose their rival conceptions upon one another. Good Rawlsian citizens manifest their commitment to toleration through their commitment to political arrangements that are designed neither to favour their own conception of the good nor to disadvantage the conflicting conceptions of others.

As an argument for toleration, the reasoning associated with the neutral state is historically novel. That reasoning also provides an unusually strong form of argument for toleration. If we owe others our toleration as a matter of justice, any hint of largesse or condescension disappears from toleration. The novelty of this reasoning for toleration has placed it beyond the comprehension of some commentators. So, for example, John Gray writes:

> Toleration as a political ideal is offensive to the new liberalism—the liberalism of Rawls, Dworkin, Ackerman and suchlike—because it is decidedly non-neutral in respect of the good. For the new liberals, justice—the shibboleth of revisionist liberalism—demands that government, in its institutions and policies, practise *neutrality*, not toleration, in regard to rival conceptions of the good life.[10]

Gray supposes that political toleration must be something dispensed by governments that are disapproving rather than neutral. What that view misses is an egalitarian conception of toleration in which the members of a society, each of whom is 'decidedly non-neutral in respect of the good', extend toleration to one another and establish and support political institutions appropriate to that toleration. Gray also suggests that political neutrality goes beyond toleration in rejecting as unjust not merely the coercive imposition of a particular conception of the good but also any attempt to favour a way of life through 'education, subsidy, welfare provision, taxation or legal entrenchment'.[11] But that fails to notice that, if we are committed to toleration as a matter of justice or fairness, we should refrain from using *any* of the instruments of political power to promote our own conception of the good or to disadvantage the rival conceptions of others. Toleration can certainly take, and historically has taken, much less generous and even-handed forms than that. But theories that treat toleration as a matter of justice do not transform it into something else. They simply make the case for political toleration's assuming a thorough-going form.

Of course, all of this leaves untouched the long-running debate about whether the idea of a neutral state is sustainable.[12] That debate is not my concern here. My concern has been to indicate only how rules and arrangements that aim to deal neutrally with an issue can still embody a commitment to toleration. That point has significance not only for red-blooded proponents of the neutral state. It also has relevance for anyone who thinks that—for whatever reason—there are *some* matters on which the state should assume a neutral posture and which it should, therefore, either regulate without taking sides or treat as beyond the reach of legitimate political power.

CAN A STATE PROMOTE TOLERATION?

A neutral state that is grounded in a commitment to toleration cannot be neutral on the issue of toleration itself. It must be committed to the promotion and maintenance of an ideal of toleration. But is it possible for a state to promote toleration? Glen Newey has crafted the most extensive and trenchant contemporary critique of the idea of political toleration.[13] He does not reject that idea altogether, since he accepts that it made perfect sense in the early modern political circumstances that I have previously described. But, he argues, once a government is expected to stand in a third-party relation to disputes amongst its population, the idea of political toleration becomes incoherent.

Suppose that, as before, A wishes to do x (e.g., have an abortion, hunt with dogs, eat meat, attend a Catholic mass, engage in ritual slaughter) while B objects to, and seeks to prevent, A's doing x. B appeals to G, the government, to intervene on his behalf and to prevent A from doing x. A similarly appeals to G to intervene on her behalf and to prevent B from interfering with her conduct. Each finds the conduct of the other intolerable and each calls upon G to prohibit the conduct it finds intolerable. Thus G confronts competing demands for intolerance and can respond to those demands only by promoting intolerance. If it responds to A's complaint against B, it prohibits B's conduct and, if it responds to B's complaint against A, it prohibits A's conduct. G therefore, rather than being faced with a choice between tolerance and intolerance, can choose only between different combinations of tolerance and intolerance. It can decide how tolerance and intolerance are to be distributed between A and B, but its decision cannot simply promote tolerance at the expense of intolerance.

To exemplify his claims, Newey points to the dispute in Northern Ireland surrounding the Orange Order's march from Drumcree church in Portadown along the Garvaghy Road, which runs through a mainly Nationalist area.[14] The Orangemen find it intolerable that they should be unfree to march along the Garvaghy Road and accuse the Nationalist community of intolerance in seeking to prevent their parade. The Nationalist community finds it intolerable that the Orangemen should intrude into their community and accuses the Orangemen of intolerance in persisting with their parade. Each calls upon the government to prohibit what it dislikes, leaving the government with no obviously tolerant option. If it provides for the march to take place, it licenses Orange intolerance of the Nationalists' wishes and, if it prohibits the march, it licenses Nationalist intolerance of the Orangemen's wishes.

Newey reads the Rushdie Affair in a similar fashion.[15] The typical liberal reading of that affair was that Rushdie was the standard-bearer for tolerance while his Muslim opponents acted intolerantly in seeking to have the *Satanic Verses* banned. But, Newey argues, Rushdie and his supporters behaved no less intolerantly in assaulting the Islamic faith and in not respecting the wishes of Muslims that sacred aspects of their faith should not be subjected to obscene and disrespectful treatment. Once again, therefore, the issue that faced government was not whether it should uphold toleration, but rather how it should apportion tolerance and intolerance between the competing parties to the dispute.

One implication that Newey pulls out of his analysis of political toleration is that 'tolerating the intolerant' is not an issue that should be located, where it usually is, at the margins of political toleration. Rather, politically, tolerating the intolerant is the normal state of affairs. When disputes arise amongst a population, the parties to the dispute typically regard one another's demands as intolerable and, when government responds to their conflicting demands, it inevitably indulges the intolerance of one or other party.[16] But Newey claims more than that. He also claims that the circumstances of political toleration are such as to render it impossible. If A wishes to do something of which B disapproves but which B is nevertheless willing to tolerate, that raises no issue for the public authorities. If B is unwilling to tolerate A's act but A yields to B's disapproval and does not perform the act, again no issue arises for the public authorities. An issue arises for government only if B is unwilling to tolerate A's act and appeals to the government to prevent it and only if A responds by appealing to the government not to concede B's demand. The government then confronts demands from both A and B that it should not tolerate the other and no tolerant option is available to it.[17] That is why the circumstances of *political* toleration seem to render it impossible.[18]

The central thrust, then, of Newey's analysis of political toleration is that it is an idea that makes no sense in contemporary democratic circumstances. It makes no sense precisely for those liberal democratic societies that conceive themselves as embodiments of the ideal of toleration. Rather than engage in toleration, the real task of government in those societies is to decide what they should *not* tolerate. 'Democratic toleration' is a 'rubber duck'.[19]

My more inclusive conception of political toleration, which takes in general political arrangements as well as particular acts of government, is no less vulnerable to Newey's claim that toleration and intolerance are but two sides of a single coin. If that claim is correct, the supposition that we can identify a particular type of society as 'tolerant', or as 'more tolerant' than another, must be an illusion. Every instance of political toleration must have intolerance as its flip-side.

In considering how we might meet this challenge, I want to begin by setting aside an obvious but, I think, unsatisfactory way of responding to it. 'Tolerant' and 'toleration' are frequently used as commendatory terms, while 'intolerant' and 'intolerance' are often used pejoratively. Perhaps then we should accept that the language of toleration is inescapably value-loaded and that 'tolerant' cannot be used merely to *describe* a society; rather, 'tolerant' is a term we should use only if we mean to *endorse* it. Thus, we might say, Newey's claim would be true if the language of toleration were merely descriptive. But the reality is, and should be, that we identify as instances of 'toleration' only those protected freedoms that we think people should enjoy and not those to which they have no proper claim. Equally, we characterize, and should characterize, as 'intolerant' only those limits on freedom that we mean to condemn and not those that we believe rightly constrain our conduct.

The trouble with this 'moralized' approach is that the identity of what we applaud is swallowed up by the fact that we applaud it. We cannot argue over whether a tolerant society is good or bad, right or wrong, desirable or undesirable, because those evaluative judgements are already at work in determining what counts as a tolerant society. I do not mean to deny that 'tolerant' is frequently used in a favourable sense, nor that those who use the phrase 'tolerant society' typically suppose that a society is better for being tolerant. But we want to use the term 'tolerant society' to describe a particular state of affairs; we may very well want to applaud that state of affairs but we do not want 'tolerant society' to signify nothing more than our applause. If we come up with reasons for valuing a tolerant society, we intend those to be reasons for valuing a society that we can identify as tolerant independently of our reasons for valuing it. Moreover, it is not actually true of our usage that 'toleration' must always signify approval and 'intolerance' condemnation. We can describe people as 'tolerating' acts that we think they should not tolerate, and as being 'intolerant' of things of which they are rightly intolerant.[20] More generally, a resort to value-loading threatens to reduce the term 'tolerant society' to a mere tool of rhetoric, since it invites each party to a conflict to load its own values into the terms 'tolerant' and 'intolerant'.

AGENTS, OBSERVERS, AND TOLERATION

How else then might we fend off Newey's claim? The situation we are to contemplate is one in which A wants to do x; B disapproves of, and wishes to prevent, A's doing x. Accordingly, B appeals to the government to prevent A from doing x. Similarly, A appeals to the government not to respond to B's appeal and so not to allow B to prevent her doing x. Is Newey right to portray A and B as 'symmetrically' situated here with respect to toleration?

A and B are symmetrically situated only if we treat as equivalent (i) B's not tolerating A's conduct and (ii) A's not tolerating B's objection to, and intolerance of, A's conduct. But that seems plainly unsatisfactory. The intolerant party here is clearly B. A wants to do x, and B wants to stop her. A is very likely to resist B's wish to stop her and to appeal to those with political power to stop B from stopping her. But to treat (ii) A's intolerance of B's intolerance of A, as no different from (i) B's intolerance of A, is decidedly odd. If we do treat these as no different, it will of course follow that every demand for tolerance will also be a demand for intolerance. But, in our ordinary thinking about political toleration, we would treat intolerance of intolerance as something that a commitment to toleration itself requires rather than just one more form of intolerance that it should condemn.

What this points to is that, in thinking of a tolerant society, we should think of toleration as something that we extend to 'agents' rather than to 'observers', to actors rather than to those who observe and assess the actions of others. Toleration concerns what people themselves wish to do or not to do and their being unprevented from doing or not doing it by censorious others. It does not include responding positively to the wishes of those who disapprove of, and who seek to prevent, what *others* wish to do. Although we can quite intelligibly speak of 'tolerating' B's intolerance of A's conduct, we cannot incorporate that usage into the toleration that we impute to the tolerant society and the tolerant political order without making a nonsense of those ideas.

In limiting the objects of toleration to 'agents' and 'actions', I use those as terms of art which are to be understood generously in two respects. First, we can disapprove of and tolerate not only what people do but also what they fail to do. Thus I intend the 'action' that I distinguish from 'observation' to include inaction, and 'agents' to include those who might act but who choose not to. Secondly, I intend 'agency' to include being and believing as well as doing, as in being gay or straight or believing in Christianity or Islam. Very often, for purposes of toleration, the distinction between being, believing,

and doing will be insignificant, since being and believing will manifest
themselves through doing and intolerance of being or believing will function
through intolerance of doing. But the distinction will be significant if we take
intolerance to include persecution as well as prevention, since intolerance can
then reach beyond preventing active expressions of being and believing.[21]

Should we allow that A behaves tolerantly towards B if she refrains from
acting in ways of which B would disapprove, and intolerantly if she does
not? Again, ordinary usage does not debar that. So a teenager might be said
to tolerate her parents' wish that she should not practise body-piercing, or
a husband might be said to tolerate his wife's wish that he should not drink
alcohol, while she might be said to tolerate his wish that she should not smoke
tobacco.[22] But if, in trying to characterize a tolerant society, we follow a
usage in which 'toleration' applies equally to A's wishes about what A should
do and to B's wishes about what A should (not) do, we shall render nugatory
the very notion of a tolerant society.

Indeed, in political contexts we do not normally use the terms 'toleration'
and 'intolerance' with that degree of generosity. Suppose that A, a pro-choice
individual, believes that she is morally at liberty to have an abortion and
wishes to have an abortion. B, a pro-life individual, believes that A would be
wrong to have an abortion. If B is able to, but does not, prevent A's having
an abortion, B tolerates A's conduct. If B is able to, and does, prevent A's
having an abortion, B does not tolerate A's conduct. But suppose that B is
simply unable to prevent A's having an abortion: whether A has an abortion
is entirely in A's hands. In those circumstances, we would not normally say
that A, in having an abortion, is acting intolerantly towards B since B wishes
her not to have an abortion. That holds even if we believe that A is wrong to
have the abortion, for that wrong is not a wrong of intolerance. The toleration
of a tolerant society is directed at A's wishes, rather than B's wishes, about
what A should do.

If we do not limit the idea of political toleration in these ways, we shall
be driven to some very odd conclusions. Consider a society whose population includes both Christians and Muslims. The Christians, because they are
Christians, object to Muslim practices, and the Muslims, because they are
Muslims, object to Christian practices.[23] Thus the circumstances of toleration
take the following form: A believes it is right to do x and wrong to do y; B
believes it is right to do y and wrong to do x. Now consider two ways in which
the arrangements of a society might provide for these circumstances.

1. The rules respond to Christians' desire to live as Christians and to Muslims' desire to live as Muslims, and so allow each group to pursue its own
   faith. The rules concede no ground to Christians' desire to suppress Islam,
   nor to Muslims' desire to suppress Christianity.

2. The rules respond to Christians' desire to suppress Islam and to Muslims' desire to suppress Christianity, and so prohibit the pursuit of both faiths. The rules concede no ground to Christians' desire to live as Christians, nor to Muslims' desire to live as Muslims.

The obvious description of these two arrangements is that the first instantiates mutual toleration while the second instantiates mutual intolerance.[24] But if A is deemed to act intolerantly not only when A prevents B from acting according to B's wishes, but also when A acts contrary to B's wishes, we cannot say that the second arrangement is less tolerant than the first. The two arrangements would seem to score equally on the counts of tolerance and intolerance. Moreover, if we accept that view, we have also to accept the implication that each group would fully tolerate the other only by adopting the other's preferred form of life. To be fully tolerant of Muslims, Christians would have not only to allow Muslims to live (as Christians see it) wrongly; they themselves would have to commit (for them) the double wrong of ceasing to live as Christians and living as Muslims. The fully tolerant Muslim would be identically placed. The fully tolerant society would therefore be one in which each group lived according to the other's faith. That *reductio* indicates not the incoherence of the idea of a tolerant society or of political toleration, but the unsatisfactory nature of a concept of toleration that treats failure to defer to another's wishes as intolerance.

AGENTS, PATIENTS, AND INTOLERANCE

What then are we to say of the two major examples Newey uses in casting doubt upon the possibility of political toleration: the dispute at Drumcree and the Rushdie Affair? I have suggested that we should treat people as possible objects of toleration if they are agents but not if they are observers. The simple implication of that view would seem to be that, in the dispute at Drumcree, it is the Orangemen who are candidates for toleration rather than the Nationalists. The Orangemen are the agents and the Nationalists are the observers. The fact that the Orangemen wish to do something of which the Nationalists disapprove makes them possible objects of Nationalist toleration. The fact that the Nationalists disapprove of what the Orangemen wish to do and seek to block their action does not make them possible objects for Orange tolerance or intolerance. Thus, if the government is to favour the tolerant option, it should provide for the march to take place. That is not, of course, to say that the Orangemen are right and the Nationalists wrong and that the march should indeed take place. On the contrary, what I have said is quite consistent with holding that the Orangemen are wrong to persist with their march and the Nationalists right to find it intolerable.

Similarly, in the Rushdie Affair, it was Rushdie who was the agent and his critics who were the observers. Thus, in so far as toleration was at issue in the Rushdie Affair, it was Rushdie's publication of *The Satanic Verses* that was eligible for toleration and not the outraged reactions of his Muslim critics. Once again, that is not to say that Rushdie was right and his critics wrong; it is to insist only upon an accurate and nonduplicitous description of what took place.

Yet there is reason to be less than wholly satisfied with the simple analysis presented in the previous two paragraphs, even if we accept that the language of tolerance and intolerance does not prejudge the rights and wrongs of these conflicts. Newey's two prime cases do seem to relate ambiguously to toleration. Is there not more than a whiff of intolerance about the Orangemen's behaviour at Drumcree? Is there not some substance to Muslims' complaints that they were objects of intolerance in the Rushdie Affair? Are these not cases in which, as Newey says, the opposing parties register conflicting demands for tolerance and intolerance rather than conflicts in which one party calls for tolerance and the other for intolerance? If so, how can we make sense of that?

The answer I believe lies not in the simple fact that the Orangemen want to do something to which the Nationalists object or that Rushdie did something to which Muslims took exception. Rather the answer lies in the fact that, in these examples, the Nationalists and Muslims might claim to be patients rather than mere observers.

Let us take the Rushdie Affair first. In that affair, Muslims did not conceive themselves as mere onlookers. On the contrary, it was *their* faith that Rushdie had subjected to obscene and disrespectful treatment. It was their Prophet he had insulted and their sensibilities he had assaulted. If Rushdie was the agent, Muslims were his patients: they were victims of the affair and, as victims, they could properly complain of intolerant treatment at the hands of Rushdie and his supporters.

However, there are a number of reasons why we should hesitate before making the leap from patienthood to intolerance. First, whether Muslims were right to conceive themselves as patients rather than observers of Rushdie's authorship is moot. Rushdie would claim that he merely wrote a novel and that it was no part of his intention to insult or upset Muslims. He was not aiming to do something *to* Muslims. Muslims may, as a matter of fact, have been offended and upset by what he wrote, but Rushdie could still question the reasonableness of their reaction and deny that he should be held responsible for the outrage and distress they experienced. Part of the difficulty in controversies of this sort is people's ability to transform themselves from observers into patients by claiming to be offended by conduct of which they disapprove. I do not mean that to claim offence is to dissemble, although that may sometimes be an issue[25]; rather, my point is that, even if people genuinely experience offence, there is often room for disagreement over whether they can rightly hold others responsible for the offence they feel.

Secondly, even when patienthood takes a negative form, it need not constitute intolerance. People are victims of intolerance only if their conduct is curtailed because others dislike or disapprove of their conduct. If I am physically assaulted by someone seeking to steal my wallet, it would be odd to describe that assault as an act of intolerance and equally odd to explicate the wrongness of the act by reference to intolerance. Not all wrongs are intolerant, just as not all intolerance is wrong.

Thirdly, and most significantly for my argument, even if people are patients, they can properly complain of intolerance only if their agency is curtailed. To suffer intolerance is to suffer a loss of freedom. Thus, if we take the Rushdie Affair again, Muslims can be properly said to have suffered intolerance at Rushdie's hands only if we can plausibly maintain that, in publishing the *Satanic Verses*, he in some way removed or reduced Muslims' freedom either to be, or to live as, Muslims. Their demands should be understood as demands for toleration only in so far as their agency was at stake—where agency includes manifesting a particular identity, holding particular beliefs and pursuing of a particular way of life—and only if and because Rushdie's conduct constituted an intervention that impaired their freedom to bear that identity, hold those beliefs or pursue that way of life. If their patienthood did not take that form, they were not victims of intolerance. I must add again that, even if we deny that Muslims were victims of intolerance, we need not deny that they were victims of any sort. For example, Rushdie might stand accused of failing to show the respect that is due to others' most cherished beliefs and that failure may be judged intolerable. But a wrong can be a wrong, and be intolerable, without being intolerant.[26]

Much the same reasoning applies to the Drumcree dispute. This is also a case in which people's status as observers or patients is controversial. Doubtless, the Orangemen would protest that they wish merely to engage in a march that has become an established part of their traditions. They are not seeking to do anything *to* the Nationalist community and Nationalists who seek to frustrate the march are merely censorious observers seeking to prevent an activity they dislike. Many Nationalists, however, see the march as a triumphalist assault upon their community designed to remind Nationalists of their subordinate position in Northern Ireland. They see themselves as the actual and intended patients of the Orangemen's act.

If they are patients, can they complain that they are victims of intolerance? Once again, that will be sustainable only if the Orange Lodge's march can be plausibly represented as an impediment to the agency of the Nationalists, where agency includes manifesting an identity and holding beliefs as well as engaging in action in an ordinary sense. It is not enough that they take exception to, and justifiably take exception to, what the march symbolizes. If their agency is not at stake, they may still have reason to complain that they are the victims of a wrong perpetrated by the marchers, but that wrong will have to be explicated with reference to something other than intolerance.

TOLERATION AND COMPOSSIBILITY

We should not suppose that every difference of view amongst people admits of a politically tolerant solution. That is not because there are cases in which we can choose only between different sorts of intolerance. It is because it is wrong to assume that tolerance and intolerance are at stake in every instance of conflict. Suppose that the march along the Garvaghy Road is absolutely central to the way of life of the Orangemen and that its absence is absolutely central to the way of life of the Nationalists. Doubtless that overstates the reality of either case, but, for the sake of argument, let that pass. If we do suppose this, we have a conflict between two ways of life—and a conflict that is not about which way of life is best or right but a conflict between the actual living of two ways of life. The two ways of life are incompossible.[27] Under these circumstances, the issue spawned by this conflict is arguably not one of political toleration at all. The standard circumstances of mutual toleration are those in which group A wishes to live life x and disapproves of life y and group B wishes to live life y and disapproves of life x. Mutual toleration is possible only if x and y are compossible, so that A's living life x does not preclude B's living life y, and vice versa.[28] But if each way of life *does* preclude the other, that would seem to take political toleration off the agenda.

In fact, it would not preclude an extreme form of toleration. Either A or B could willingly sacrifice its way of life for the sake of the other. But that degree of sacrifice goes beyond the kind of toleration that we think it reasonable to expect or to require in political contexts. As I have indicated above, our model of political toleration is one in which A allows B to live as B wishes and B allows A to live as A wishes. It is not one which allows either A to dictate how B shall live or B to dictate how A shall live.

It is perhaps unusual for the sorts of thing that we mean by 'ways of life' to be wholly incompossible in all possible circumstances. The exceptional case is where it is intrinsic to one group's way of life that it should dominate or displace the life of another group.[29] But there are many political issues which oblige us to choose between x and y rather than permit us to provide for both x and y. One such issue, which is closely associated with toleration, is that of domains. Suppose that two ways of life are in general compossible but that, at their edges, they rub up against each other in ways that generate conflicting demands. We have then to decide where the boundary should fall that defines each group's legitimate domain. That decision will set the terms of toleration for each group. But it cannot be a decision that tolerates the conflicting demands of both groups concerning where the boundary should be set. The boundary has to be set at some specific point; it cannot be located at the two different points demanded by the two competing groups.

The Drumcree conflict might be seen as just such a boundary conflict. The conflict might be seen, that is, as a dispute over the legitimate domains of the two parties to the conflict. If we do see it in that way, it will be inappropriate to represent it as an issue that is eligible for solution by a policy of toleration. Each party might very well insist that it is entirely willing to tolerate the other's way of life and that its tolerance or intolerance is not the issue. Rather, the issue concerns the terms on which each should live alongside the other. It concerns where the boundary should be set that defines the legitimate domain within which each group can pursue its way of life, and *that* has to be a decision between x and y; it cannot provide for both x and y.[30]

The Rushdie Affair might also be represented as a domain dispute. Many Muslims clearly conceived Rushdie as intruding wrongly into a 'space' that was properly theirs. In so far as the conflict between Rushdie and his opponents was a dispute about where the boundary should fall between freedom of speech and protection from offence, that was a dispute that forced a choice between x and y rather than one that allowed there to be both x and y. However, here we need to tread carefully. What I have just said is to observe no more than that the boundary between free speech and protection from offence cannot be drawn simultaneously in two different places. But that is not to say that disputes over *that* boundary are without consequence for political toleration. Tolerance is forced off the agenda only in so far as a political choice has to be a choice between the incompossible conduct of two agents. But, in so far as the publication of *The Satanic Verses* did not remove or diminish Muslims' freedom to be, and to live as, Muslims, the Rushdie Affair did not present a choice of that sort. Permitting Rushdie to publish his book was compossible with providing for Muslims to pursue an Islamic form of life, and choosing between free speech and preventing offence was not the same as drawing a line between the domains of two rival *actors*.[31]

To that extent, it misdescribes the Rushdie Affair to present it as a conflict between two parties each of whom could properly complain of the intolerance of the other and in which all of the choices on toleration summed to zero. As I have previously insisted, even if we think that Rushdie was wrong to give offence and so wrong that his offensive conduct was intolerable, that need not imply that his conduct was intolerant.

The presence of compossibility amongst the circumstances of political toleration helps to explain why it is that we think of some matters as suitable subjects for toleration and others as not. Toleration becomes a candidate for policy only when we think that it is possible, and that it can make sense, for different people to follow different paths.[32] It is a candidate when there can be both *x* and *y* rather than only *x* or *y*. So it is no accident that religious faith, cultural differences, sexual conduct, and lifestyle issues are nowadays amongst the standard fare of political toleration. However, the 'compossibility' at stake here is often more than merely logical or physical. Frequently, it is appropriate or acceptable compossibility. Consider taxation. People possess strongly conflicting views on just taxation. We could respond to those conflicting views by allowing each person to pay taxes in accordance with his or her own conception of what justice requires. But there are all sorts of reason why that would be a wholly unsatisfactory arrangement and why we think that matters of taxation should be decided publicly for an entire public. The same applies to decisions concerning matters such as war and peace, the provision of public services, and penal policy.[33] Thus, tolerance and intolerance are at stake only in a limited range of political issues. We should not look for them in every case in which people hold conflicting beliefs or desires, nor should we describe as 'intolerant' every instance in which the beliefs or desires of some prevail politically over those of others.

CONCLUSION

In this chapter I have tried to make sense of political toleration in contemporary liberal democratic circumstances. I have done so by proposing that we understand a tolerant regime as one that upholds an ideal of toleration rather than one that itself tolerates the population whose lives it regulates. All of the traditional considerations that argue for toleration argue for a regime of that sort, just as they once argued for the tolerant ruler. Toleration is, therefore, neither redundant nor superseded as a political ideal in our time and it would be most surprising if it were. I have also indicated how this understanding of a tolerant regime is consistent with the nontraditional ideal of the neutral state. Indeed, the idea of the neutral state as it figures in deontological liberalism is, in part, a conception of how toleration should be realized under contemporary conditions of democracy and diversity, although it is not the only possible conception of liberal democratic toleration. However, if this idea of political toleration is to remain coherent, we must limit its possible objects. Toleration must be something that is secured for agents rather than observers: it provides for people's own deeds, beliefs, and identities, but not for their ambitions to curb the deeds, beliefs, and identities of others. Even when agents have patients, their agency need not always be a source of intolerance. Finally, political toleration is an option only when the actions at stake are compossible. If, as political decision makers or institutional architects, we have to choose between incompossible options, our choice should not be represented as a choice between toleration and intolerance, nor even between different possible combinations of toleration and intolerance. In the absence of compossibility, a political issue is not an issue of toleration at all.

The idea of political toleration and the associated ideal of a tolerant society remain highly unspecific notions. They indicate a predisposition to allow people to conduct their lives as they themselves see fit and to secure them against the intolerance of disapproving others, but that leaves the details of the toleration people should and should not enjoy still to be specified. It would be absurd to say that a society is always better for being more tolerant. A society that permits and protects active paedophilia is, in that respect, more tolerant than one that does not, but it is not therefore a better society. Nor should we pretend that rightful intolerance is always and only intolerance of intolerance, so that intolerance is justified only if and because it protects toleration. Part of my concern has been to resist overextended complaints of intolerance, in which groups or individuals juggle with the idea of toleration so that they can represent themselves as victims of intolerance. Most of the conduct that we do not tolerate, routinely and rightly, has nothing to do with intolerance. Murder, rape, assault, intimidation, theft, and exploitation are not, in the ordinary run of cases, expressions of intolerance. We should not, therefore, feel obliged always to characterize the intolerable as intolerant.

Modern European thinking on toleration, both as a practice and a principle, has its roots in the Reformation of the sixteenth century. Since that time, political structures have changed; so too (although not wholly) has the make-up of the human diversity that makes toleration a pressing issue both socially and globally. But those changes do not signal the demise of toleration as a proper political concern; they simply require us to think about toleration in new ways.

NOTES

1. For important statements of this view, see Glen Newey, *Virtue, Reason and Toleration* (Edinburgh: Edinburgh University Press, 1999), especially chapters 4 and 5, and his 'Is Democratic Toleration a Rubber Duck?', *Res Publica* 7 (2001): 315–36, reprinted in Dario Castiglione and Catriona McKinnon, eds., *Toleration, Neutrality and Democracy* (Dordrecht: Kluwer, 2003), 143–58; Hagut Benbaji and David Heyd, 'The Charitable Perspective: Forgiveness and Toleration as Supererogatory', *Canadian Journal of Philosophy* 31 (2001): 567–86; David Heyd, 'Is Toleration a Political Virtue?', in Melissa S. Williams and Jeremy Waldron, eds., *Toleration and Its Limits*

(*Nomos*, 48) (New York: New York University Press, 2008), 171–94. For an analysis of toleration that carries similar implications, see Adeno Addis, 'On Human Diversity and the Limits of Toleration', in Ian Shapiro and Will Kymlicka, eds., *Ethnicity and Group Rights* (*Nomos* 39) (New York: New York University Press, 1996), 112–53, at 119–26. The view that toleration is something political institutions should supersede rather than instantiate is not confined to the recent past. Thomas Paine observed that the French Declaration of the Rights of Man and Citizen, 1789, in establishing universal rights of conscience, 'hath abolished or renounced *toleration*, and *intoleration* also'; Bruce Kuklick, ed., *Thomas Paine: Political Writings* (Cambridge: Cambridge University Press, 1989), 94. Kant too remarked that an enlightened prince, who considered it his duty to allow his people complete freedom in religious matters, would decline to accept 'the presumptuous title of *tolerant*'; Hans Reiss, ed., *Kant: Political Writings* (Cambridge: Cambridge University Press, 1991), 58.

2. 'Toleration' is now sometimes used in a more generous sense to mean a readiness to accept and positively to value social diversity, rather than merely a willingness to endure what one finds objectionable. For examples of this usage of toleration, see Karl-Otto Apel, 'Plurality of the Good? The Problem of Affirmative Tolerance in a Multicultural Society from an Ethical Point of View', *Ratio Juris* 10 (1997): 199–212; Michael Walzer, *Toleration* (New Haven, CT: Yale University Press, 1997), 11–12; and Ingrid Creppell, *Toleration and Identity* (London: Routledge, 2003), 3–4.

3. Both Newey and Heyd, who take this view, do not exclude altogether the possibility of a role for toleration in political life. Newey argues that there remains some scope for politicians to exercise the virtue in character of tolerance in the limited areas of discretion that democratic principles do not preempt; *Virtue, Reason and Toleration*, 167–83. Heyd argues that a tolerant attitude can be politically important as a background value, especially in pluralistic societies, since it can promote solidarity, social bonding and trust; see 'Is Toleration a Political Virtue?'. But both reject the idea that toleration is something that can inhabit liberal democratic arrangements themselves.

4. To avoid confusion of pronouns, I shall suppose in referring to A and B that A is female and B is male.

5. I say G does not tolerate A since G's toleration would imply that G itself disapproves of A's conduct, whereas I suppose that G itself need take no view on the merits of A's conduct; it upholds toleration merely by not allowing the disapproving B to impede A. That is most clearly the case where G is not a person or body of persons but an established rule apportioning freedom and unfreedom amongst the members of a society and an apparatus for upholding that rule. If G stands for a government and if we think of that government as a set of persons, those persons might, of course, take a disapproving view of A's conduct. But equally, in their role as G, they may see their task as simply to maintain an order of freedom amongst citizens and not, *qua* G, to assess the merit or demerit of the use that particular citizens make of that freedom.

6. I refer particularly to Glen Newey's account of tolerance as a virtue of character. For his aretaic analysis of tolerance, see *Virtue, Reason and Toleration*, pp. 85–114, and, for his development of that analysis to provide an account of tolerance as a political virtue, see pp. 171–97. For a variety of views on toleration as a virtue,

see David Heyd, ed., *Toleration: An Elusive Virtue* (Princeton, NJ: Princeton University Press, 1996). Susan Mendus has suggested that, contrary to the contemporary orthodoxy, we might do better to follow the example of Locke and give primacy to the duty to tolerate rather than to the right to be tolerated; *Toleration and the Limits of Liberalism* (Basingstoke: Macmillan, 1989), 37–41. That suggestion may also seem to run counter to the thrust of my argument here, even though I make no claim specifically about the *right* to be tolerated. Mendus's distinction would seem to have significance only if we ground the duty to tolerate in something other than the good or the right of the tolerated. But what might that ground be? The duty might be conceived as one owed to a third party, such as God, rather than to its immediate beneficiary. Alternatively, it might be goal-based, where the goal is something other than the good of the tolerated party. But, even in that case, what is likely to be critical for realizing the goal is A's not being not tolerated rather than B's freely refraining from intolerance, so that the point of B's duty is not thwarted by its becoming a legal requirement.

7. For the sake of clarity, I state this point starkly and perhaps too starkly. I concede that, as well as giving independent value to A's freedom, we might find reason to prefer a state of affairs in which others willingly respect A's freedom to one in which they respond only to the restraints of law. But I have already indicated that legal protection of A's freedom does not mean that others cannot respect A's freedom for reasons other than merely legal obligation or threat of legal penalty. Thus the order of things I describe does not render people incapable of possessing and exercising the virtue of tolerance.

8. See, for example, Newey, *Virtue, Reason and Toleration*, 123–24, 128–30, 131, 142, 154, 186; 'Is Democratic Toleration a Rubber Duck?', 325–26; John Horton, 'Toleration as a Virtue', in Heyd, ed., *Toleration*, 36; Saladin Meckled-Garcia, 'Toleration and Neutrality: Incompatible Ideals?', *Res Publica*,7 (2001): 293–313, reprinted in Dario Castiglione and Catriona McKinnon, eds., *Toleration, Neutrality and Democracy* (Dordrecht: Kluwer, 2003), 77–95; Robert Paul Churchill, 'Neutrality and the Virtue of Toleration', in Castiglione and McKinnon, eds., *Toleration, Neutrality and Democracy*, 65–76, especially p. 72. I consider the relationship between neutrality and toleration at greater length in chapter 2. For Meckled-Garcia's reply to my argument (by which I remain wholly unpersuaded), see Castiglione and McKinnon, eds., *Toleration, Neutrality and Democracy*, 181–85.

9. John Rawls, *Political Liberalism* (New York: Columbia University Press, 1993); Thomas Nagel, *Equality and Partiality* (Oxford: Oxford University Press, 1991), especially pp. 154–68; Charles Larmore, *Patterns of Moral Complexity* (Cambridge: Cambridge University Press, 1987) and *The Morals of Modernity* (Cambridge: Cambridge University Press, 1996); Brian Barry, *Justice as Impartiality* (Oxford: Clarendon, 1995).

10. John Gray, *Enlightenment's Wake: Politics and Culture at the Close of the Modern Age* (London: Routledge, 1995), 19.

11. Gray, *Enlightenment's Wake*, 19–20.

12. For a critique of the ideal of neutrality specifically in relation to toleration, see Mendus, *Toleration and the Limits of Liberalism*, chapters 4 and 5.

13. Newey, *Virtue, Reason and Toleration*, especially chapters 4 and 5, and Newey, 'Is Democratic Toleration a Rubber Duck?'.

14. Newey, *Virtue, Reason and Toleration*, 76, 83, 129, 160–61. Newey also considers the Drumcree issue in 'Discourse Rights and the Drumcree Marches: A Reply to O'Neill', *British Journal of Politics and International Relations* 4 (2002): 75–97. However, his concern there is not directly with toleration but with Shane O'Neill's use of Habermas's discourse theory of rights to find a way through the Drumcree dispute. See Shane O'Neill, 'Liberty, Equality and the Rights of Cultures: The Marching Controversy at Drumcree', *British Journal of Politics and International Relations* 2 (2000): 26–45; and, for his response to Newey, 'Democratic Theory with Critical Intent: Reply to Newey', *British Journal of Politics and International Relations* 4 (2002): 98–114.

15. Newey, *Virtue, Reason and Toleration*, 13–14, 166, 188; and Newey, '*Fatwa* and Fiction: Censorship and Toleration', in John Horton, ed., *Liberalism, Multiculturalism and Toleration* (Basingstoke: Macmillan, 1993), 178–92.

16. Newey, *Virtue, Reason and Toleration*, 147, 152, 160, 161–62, 165, 167; and Newey, 'Is Democratic Toleration a Rubber Duck?', 320–21.

17. Thus Newey observes, 'the *political* problem of toleration is always one of intolerance. That is, the political question is whether to tolerate the intolerance of those who regard others' activities as being intolerable' (*Virtue, Reason and Toleration*, 152). However, given Newey's conception of conflicting popular demands upon government as conflicting demands for intolerance, the political question would seem to be not whether to tolerate intolerance but which intolerance to tolerate. Unless a government simply refuses to confront and resolve a conflict, it can opt only for the intolerance of one or other party to the conflict, or perhaps for a compromise solution that concedes something to each party's intolerance.

18. Newey, *Virtue, Reason and Toleration*, 138, 144, 154–55, 162, 165, 180; 'Is Democratic Toleration a Rubber Duck?', 319–21; and *After Politics: The Rejection of Politics in Contemporary Liberal Philosophy* (Basingstoke: Palgrave, 2001), 51.

19. A 'rubber duck' exemplifies an object whose description renders it not that object: if a duck is a rubber duck, it cannot be a (real) duck. Thus the analogous claim is that, if toleration is democratic, it cannot really be toleration. Cf. Frances Howard-Snyder, 'Rule Consequentialism is a Rubber Duck', *American Philosophical Quarterly* 30 (1993): 271–78.

20. Newey himself rejects this normative approach; see 'Is Democratic Toleration a Rubber Duck?', 323. He is, however, willing to moralize toleration for other purposes; see *Virtue, Reason and Toleration*, 22.

21. For purposes of this article I treat the opposite of toleration as prevention rather than persecution. 'Persecution' may, of course, be a form of prevention, but it need not be: suffering may be inflicted upon those who are perceived as evil-doers not in order to prevent or deter them but simply because they deserve to suffer. While the paradigm case of intolerance is straightforward prevention, intolerance also admits of degree and can take the form of disincentives or disadvantages such as penal taxation. For example, a society that imposes penal taxation upon tobacco is less tolerant of smoking than one that does not, but more tolerant than a society that prohibits the smoking of tobacco.

22. The following example, given by Newey, also has this structure: my tolerance of vegetarianism requires that 'I do not merely refrain from force-feeding vegetarians with meat, but also [that I myself] forgo the pleasures of veal or beef when I invite them to my home for dinner' ('Is Democratic Toleration a Rubber Duck?', 317).

23. I recognize that reasons can be found within Christianity and Islam for tolerating other faiths. In order to deal graphically with the notion of *political* toleration, I suppose here that Christians and Muslims each want to suppress the other and that a political community or government has to decide how it should respond to their wishes. However, as I have previously argued, even if Christians and Muslims are committed to tolerating one another, we can still describe a political arrangement that prohibits each from not tolerating the other as politically 'tolerant' in that it upholds an ideal of toleration. Endorsement of that tolerant arrangement by Christians and Muslims would not convert it into something other than, or less than, political toleration; it would simply make it the object of an 'overlapping consensus'. See further, chapter 2.

24. Not all contemporary instances of toleration need be mutual. Often they are lopsided in having the following form: A believes that we have no duty not to do *x*; in other words, that we are at liberty to do *x*; B believes that we are duty-bound not to do *x*; this means that B may object to, and so have occasion to tolerate, A's conduct, while A will not object to, and therefore have no occasion to tolerate, B's conduct. Suppose that A is prohunting and B antihunting. B will object to A's hunting, but A will not object to B's not hunting (assuming that A believes that we have no obligation to hunt as well as no obligation not to hunt). Thus A's conduct can present an issue of toleration for B, without B's conduct presenting a similar issue for A. Toleration on matters such as abortion, meat-eating, pornography, and the recreational use of drugs will be similarly lopsided.

25. The following view has become widely accepted in liberal societies. If you do *x*, which I believe to be wrong but which you do not, my believing *x* to be wrong has no force as a reason why you should not do *x*. But if your doing *x* causes me offence, that places your act in the other-regarding domain and my offence should be factored into the decision on whether you should be free to do *x*. Thus, if I believe *x* to be wrong and wish to stop to it, I have an incentive to claim that I am offended by *x*, and to talk up the extent to which I am offended. So, for example, in the recent controversy over *Jerry Springer the Opera*, members of the organization Christian Voice stressed the degree to which they were offended, even though their primary concern was clearly and properly (what they believed to be) the opera's wrongful treatment of Jesus Christ. Similarly, much emphasis was placed upon the offence caused to Muslims by the cartoons of Muhammad published by the Danish newspaper, *Jyllands-Posten*, even though the principal concern of Muslims themselves was the wrongfulness of representing Muhammad pictorially and, more particularly, of portraying him in an unfavourable light. That case was complicated by Muslims' also conceiving the cartoons as insults to themselves, but the character and wrongfulness of an insult is not reducible to the offended feelings it may cause. The point of my remarks here is not to dismiss the concerns of Christians and Muslims in controversies of this sort nor even to deny the reality of offended sensibilities, but to question

whether we should treat offence, understood as a painful or disagreeable psychologi-cal condition, as the primary consideration. I suggest an alternative to the offensive-ness approach in 'Respecting Beliefs and Rebuking Rushdie', *British Journal of Political Science* 20 (1990): 415–37.

26. In *'Fatwa* and Fiction', Newey presents the Muslim complaint against Rush-die as one grounded in the principle of equal respect. Rushdie behaved intolerantly because he failed to accord Muslims the respect to which they were entitled; so the Muslim complaint of intolerance could be grounded in the very principle to which liberals were inclined to appeal in opposing censorship. But, as I argue here, to claim that Rushdie behaved disrespectfully is not necessarily to claim that he behaved intolerantly.

27. For the idea of compossibility, see Hillel Steiner, *An Essay on Rights* (Oxford: Blackwell, 1994), 86–101. Jeremy Waldron has also deployed the idea of compos-sibility in relation to toleration. However, while I appeal to compossibility here only as a necessary condition for political toleration, Waldron considers it in relation to the liberal ambition to establish arrangements in which everyone has adequate scope to pursue their ends. See Jeremy Waldron, 'Toleration and Reasonableness', in Catriona McKinnon and Dario Castiglione, eds., *The Culture of Toleration in Diverse Societies* (Manchester: Manchester University Press, 2003), 13–37. I claim here that compos-sibility is a condition for *political* toleration, not that it is a condition for toleration in all cases. Political toleration entails the use of political authority to create or promote a state of affairs in which more toleration prevails over less; for example, by securing freedom to do both x and y rather than only x or y. But if two individuals confront each other with intended actions that are incompossible, one can tolerate the other simply by refraining from acting on his original intention.

28. In the lopsided cases of toleration that I describe in fn. 24, y will be equivalent to not-x. But x and not-x are compossible in these cases in that A's doing x is compos-sible with B's doing not-x (though not, of course, with satisfying B's demand that A should also do, or be made to do, not-x).

29. The Northern Ireland conflict does have some features of this exceptional case.

30. Rather than being a decision that adopts either x or y, it might be one that concedes something to each of x and y, where x and y represent the content of each group's demands. But, although a decision that concedes something to both x and y may seem to have a greater affinity with toleration than one that concedes everything to one or other side, it would be a mistake to represent that as a tolerant solution. It may be a fair or fairer solution but it is not a solution in which tolerance prevails over intolerance.

31. For a different view, see Waldron, 'Toleration and Reasonableness', especially pp. 27–31.

32. I say only a 'candidate' for policy since, even if toleration is an eligible option, we may not always think it the right option.

33. There may be scope for 'pockets' of toleration in policy matters of this sort. An example is provision for conscientious objection in time of war. But I know of no society that has required only those of its citizens who favour a war to prosecute and pay for it, while exempting all opponents of the war from military service and from paying taxes raised to fund it.

Chapter 2

Toleration and Neutrality

*Compatible Ideals?**

The relationship between toleration and liberalism has not been one of mutual entailment. Historically, many who have favoured toleration have not been liberals. The liberal who does not favour toleration has been a rarer specimen. Given societies as we know them, most liberals have regarded some form of toleration as both necessary and desirable. That would seem as true of present as of past liberal theorists and no less true of those contemporary liberal theorists who are commonly identified as 'neutralists'. John Rawls is a clear example. For Rawls, religious toleration is one of the 'settled convictions' from which he develops his political liberalism; it constitutes a 'fixed point' that 'any reasonable conception must account for'.[1] His political liberalism generalizes that settled conviction by applying 'the principle of toleration to philosophy itself'.[2] One of his principal concerns is to establish the grounds of toleration in modern democratic societies[3] and toleration figures in a pivotal way in the political conception of justice that he goes on to construct. Accordingly, he ranks tolerance as one of the 'great political virtues' that a well-ordered society should cultivate amongst its citizens.[4] The theories developed by other neutralist liberals, such as Nagel, Larmore, and Barry, would seem equally hospitable to the idea of toleration.[5]

Yet, despite this ready association of toleration with neutrality, a number of writers, most notably Saladin Meckled-Garcia,[6] have challenged the compatibility of neutrality and toleration. In this chapter, I shall try to meet that challenge. I shall argue that the ideals of neutrality and toleration are indeed compatible, by which I mean that both can figure coherently in a single political theory.

---

* I am grateful to Derek Bell for his helpful comments on an earlier draft of this chapter.

I do not claim either that toleration must entail neutrality or that neutrality must entail toleration. Clearly a political system may be tolerant of beliefs and practices without being neutral amongst them. Historically, a religiously tolerant state has commonly been one that has *not* been neutral in that it has been officially committed to a particular religion; it has nevertheless been tolerant in that it has permitted the practice of more than just its officially approved religion. More generally, a state may be tolerant without being neutral in that it may appraise and treat some conceptions of the good more favourably than others but still permit the pursuit of those conceptions it disfavours. Toleration does not have to be even-handed.

Equally, a political system can be neutral without being tolerant. Imagine a society whose members wish to live different forms of life but each of whom regards the different forms pursued by others as reflecting no more than their different preferences. People's preferred forms of life are diverse, but that diversity neither reflects nor generates disagreement. No one finds reason to object to anyone else's chosen form. In such a society there could still be a place for neutrality: it might be thought right that political power should not be used to advantage or disadvantage some people's preferred ways of life. But there would be no place for toleration, for there would be nothing objectionable for anyone to tolerate.

My claim will not be, therefore, that neutrality and toleration *must* go together. Rather it will be that neutrality and toleration *can be* compatible ideals and that they *are* compatible in the political liberalism of John Rawls.

TOLERATION AND NEUTRALITY: MUTUAL EXCLUSION?

One way in which toleration and neutrality may be thought mutually exclusive is implicit in what I have already said. Toleration entails not preventing something of which we disapprove. Now if a state adopts a position of neutrality with respect to different conceptions of the good, it remains officially agnostic on the relative merit of those conceptions: it neither approves of some, nor disapproves of others. But if there are no conceptions of the good of which it disapproves, there is none that it can tolerate. Neutrality therefore precludes toleration.[7]

The answer to this claim is easily made. To observe that a state cannot act at once neutrally and tolerantly is to look at the relationship between neutrality and toleration in the wrong way. The ideals of neutrality and toleration do not function on the same plane. Toleration comes first and neutrality second: the members of a liberal state have reason to tolerate one another's different and conflicting conceptions of the good and the establishment of a neutral state is the outcome of their commitment to toleration.[8] So we should look for toleration not in the immediate functioning of a neutral state but in the reasons for that state's functioning in a way that is neutral amongst conceptions of the good. It is because we have reason to tolerate one another's different and conflicting conceptions of the good that we should establish political arrangements that are neutral in respect of those conceptions.

It is specifically on the score of *reasons*, however, that Meckled-Garcia argues that the attempt to combine neutrality and toleration must fail. The neutralist ideal, Meckled-Garcia points out, must encompass citizens as well as institutions. In a neutralist society, neutrality is a virtue required of citizens as well as of institutions. But if citizens, or other decision makers, approach and resolve political issues in accordance with a principle of neutrality, they cannot simultaneously engage in toleration.

More specifically, Meckled-Garcia's argument runs as follows. He defines toleration such that it entails having both a first-order reason to repress a view or practice and a second-order reason not to repress that view or practice.[9] This combination of first- and second-order reasons he sees as essential to toleration since, if we are to be properly described as 'tolerating' x, it is essential that we continue to find x objectionable even though we refrain from preventing it. If our reasons for allowing x were such as to cancel its objectionable character, we would no longer be tolerating x. Thus, 'toleration requires us to both believe that we have reasons for repressing a view and that we have reasons not to act on those reasons'.[10]

Meckled-Garcia seeks to prise apart neutrality and toleration at the level of citizenship by insisting that the reasons that citizens must act upon *qua* citizens of a neutral state are incompatible with the reasons they would need to act upon if they were to be tolerant.[11] As we have seen, if our reason for refraining from repressing x were such as to cancel the reason we had to repress x, we should be left with nothing to tolerate. That, according to Meckled-Garcia, is what happens when we move to a neutralist position. Rather than recognizing two sorts of reason—a first-order reason to repress and a second-order reason not to repress—neutralism presents us only with a first-order reason not to repress: 'neutrality gives us a first-order reason not to repress or seek repression as well as not to seek favours from the state'.[12] What is missing from the neutralist's account is any reason for repression over which that neutralist reason prevails. So, for example, if I am a consistent neutralist, I refrain from repressing your religion not because I have a second-order reason that prevails over an initial first-order reason I possess for repressing your religion. I have no reason, initial or otherwise, to repress your religion. I regard it as simply unreasonable to use state power to repress or favour religious views.

In what follows I take issue with Meckled-Garcia on three counts. First, I question his claim that toleration requires a combination of first- and second-order reasons. Certainly, our tolerating x requires that we have both reason to disapprove of x and reason not to repress x but those reasons, I shall argue, can be merely competing first-order reasons. Secondly, I argue that the members of a Rawlsian society do have reason to repress one another's views as well as countervailing reason not to engage in that repression. In other words, I argue that Rawlsian individuals can possess the duality of reasons that toleration requires. Thirdly, although I show that a tolerant position does not have to be one that combines first- and second-order reasons, I argue that toleration as it figures in Rawls's political liberalism conforms closely to the combination of first- and second-order reasons set out in Meckled-Garcia's model of toleration.

FIRST- AND SECOND-ORDER REASONS

The distinction between first- and second-order reasons derives from the work of Joseph Raz.[13] Raz distinguishes two ways in which reasons can conflict. First, two conflicting reasons may be of the same order. How then do we decide which should prevail? Reasons are not always of equal importance; some matter more than others. Thus we attribute weight or strength to reasons and, when two or more reasons conflict, we assess their relative strengths and allow the stronger to override the weaker. For example, I may have reason to help Jim and reason to help John, but I cannot help both of them. So I assess the relative weights of these reasons and find that I have greater reason to help Jim than to help John. My reason to help Jim therefore outweighs and overrides my reason to help John. This does not mean that I cease to have reason to help John; whatever reason I have to help him remains.[14] It means simply that I should not act on that reason because it is overridden by my reason to help Jim.

Raz describes the reasons at issue here as conflicting first-order reasons since they operate on the same level; one reason simply outweighs and overrides the other. In other cases, however, conflicting reasons can be of a different order. Raz characterizes a second-order reason as a reason to act for a reason or to refrain from for a reason'.[15] As this definition indicates, second-order reasons can be either positive (reasons to act for a reason) or negative (reasons not to act for a reason).[16] We can disregard here the case of positive second-order reasons, since it is negative second-order reasons that are significant for the analysis of toleration.[17] Raz describes negative second-order reasons as 'exclusionary' reasons since they function by excluding rather than by merely overriding conflicting first-order reasons. Suppose, for example, that I promise to mow your lawn at regular intervals while you are away. Having made that promise, I have an exclusionary reason to do what I have promised. My promise is not just one more first-order reason that should weigh along with other first-order reasons in determining whether I should or should not mow your lawn. Promising gives me a reason of a special kind, a reason that excludes or preempts reasons that would otherwise figure in an on-balance calculation of whether I should mow your lawn. In particular, the reasons for keeping a promise are not reducible to the reasons for making it in the first place. Or consider what is involved in being subject to authority. A superior officer commands a soldier to fire on an enemy position. If the soldier responds to this command as an authoritative command, the soldier will not assess the intrinsic merits of what he or she has been told to do and respond accordingly. The mere fact that the soldier has received a command will provide a reason for doing what he or she has been ordered to do and a reason which excludes reasons that would otherwise determine whether the soldier should or should not fire on the enemy position. Exclusionary reasons are not limited to promises and authoritative instructions; they are also an essential feature of mandatory norms, rules of thumb, and decisions, as well as of some nonmandatory norms and all prescriptions that are not norms.[18]

In some cases, a reason's being an exclusionary reason will make no difference to what I should do; that is, what I should do once I have an exclusionary reason may be no different from what I would have had overriding reason to do without that exclusionary reason. Having promised to do x, I have an exclusionary reason to do x; but, even without that promise, the balance of reasons may still have dictated that x was the right thing for me to do. In other cases, however, the introduction of an exclusionary reason will alter not only my reasons but also what I should do. Having promised to do x, I have an exclusionary reason to do x; but, if I were to disregard the exclusionary character of the promise and engage in a simple on-balance calculation of the best thing to do, I may discover that the balance of reasons favours my not doing x. Hence, we sometimes find that keeping a promise or complying with an authoritative command or abiding by a rule requires that we do something other than what, on the balance of first-order reasons, would seem the best thing to do.[19] One well-known manifestation of this point is the inability of simple consequentialism to do justice to the way in which promises, authority, rules, rights, and the like figure in our practical reasoning.

There are two further features of exclusionary reasons that we should note. First, a promise or authoritative instruction or mandatory norm provides us with a first-order reason as well as an exclusionary reason. Thus, having promised to do x, I have both a first-order reason to do x and a second-order reason that excludes reasons that would otherwise weigh for or against my doing x. Similarly, if I am ordered to do x by someone who has authority over me, that order constitutes both a first-order reason for my doing x and a second-order reason that excludes reasons that would otherwise determine whether I should or should not do x. In these cases I have exclusive reason to act on a particular first-order reason. Raz describes first-order reasons that are immured by exclusionary reasons variously as 'protected' or 'peremptory' or 'pre-emptive' reasons.[20]

Secondly, exclusionary reasons need not be unlimited in scope. Rather than excluding all other reasons, they may exclude only some. Thus, while a promise must have the exclusionary or preemptive character that I described above, there may be some countervailing considerations that it does not exclude. The exclusionary scope of my promise to do x may stop short of excluding a conflicting reason that I have to do y; that conflicting reason may then outweigh and override my reason to do what I have promised. That is how it can sometimes be right to break a promise. Likewise, an order from someone who has authority over me constitutes an exclusionary reason but not necessarily a reason that excludes every possible other reason that bears upon what I am ordered to do. It may not exclude, for example, concerns about human rights such that I can have reason to defy an order commanding me to violate another person's human rights.[21]

TOLERATION AND ORDERS OF REASON

How then does all this apply to toleration? Meckled-Garcia claims that the logical structure of a tolerant position is one in which the tolerant person has a first-order reason to repress x but a second-order reason (an exclusionary reason) not to act on that first-order reason. But does our reason for being tolerant have to be of that exclusionary kind? Cannot toleration be required simply by a first-order reason that overrides whatever first-order reason we have for repression? Suppose I am disposed to repress all but (what I believe to be) the one true religion. Consider the following reasons that I might be presented with to persuade me not to act on that repressive disposition:

1. If I attempt to repress other religions, I shall meet stiff resistance which will issue in bloodshed and strife. That bloodshed and strife is too high a price to pay for eliminating false religions.
2. I believe that my faith is correct, but sane and sensible people who subscribe to other faiths are no less convinced of the correctness of their beliefs. Hence there is scope for reasonable doubt and disagreement about what is the one true faith. That gives me reason to refrain from enforcing what I nevertheless reckon to be the correct faith.

3. We should give weight to people's own beliefs about how they should live. That weight is sufficient to give me reason not to coerce people into complying with the one true religion even though lives lived in accordance with that religion are better than those that are not.

Each of these arguments for toleration is entirely intelligible as an argument that functions through a first-order reason. In each case, if the argument for toleration wins out, that is because it outweighs my reason for repression. It neither excludes nor cancels the reasons I have for enforcing the one true religion; it simply overrides those reasons.

Consider now the remarks of Raz on a different sort of toleration. We might find someone's deliberate manner of speech or their slow and methodical way of considering every issue frustrating and annoying. Nevertheless, these irritating features of a person may be inevitable accompaniments of characteristics that we value. The reason people lack certain virtues or accomplishments may be, and often is, that they possess other incompatible virtues and accomplishments. When we tolerate the limitations of others, we may be aware that these are but the other side of their virtues and personal strengths. This may indeed be the reason why we tolerate them.[22] The rationale for toleration that Raz offers here is, again, one that conforms to the model of conflicting first-order reasons. We find people's failings objectionable but we appreciate that those failings are simply the flip-side of their virtues and the value of those virtues provides adequate reason to tolerate the failings. The virtues provide us with sufficiently strong first-order reason, rather than with an exclusionary second-order reason, for tolerating the failings.

Finally, consider an example given by Meckled-Garcia himself.[23] Some people engage in a freely chosen way of life that does not harm other humans but does involve animal cruelty. I have reason to repress views and practices that involve animal cruelty. But I also have reason to encourage people freely to choose their way of life and, in this instance, my repression of animal cruelty may set an example that militates against encouraging people freely to choose their way of life. I consider this reason important enough not to act on my reason to prevent animal cruelty. Meckled-Garcia identifies my reason to repress animal cruelty as a first-order reason and my reason to encourage people freely to choose their way of life as a second-order reason. But, again, the most obvious reading of this example is that it is one in which I have conflicting first-order reasons of unequal strength. I have a first-order reason to prevent animal cruelty and a competing and stronger first-order reason to allow someone to live the non-human-harming form of life that they have freely chosen. My concern for freedom simply outweighs my objection to animal cruelty.

It is certainly possible to characterize the respect that we should have for people's choice over their form of life as an exclusionary reason. If, for

example, they have a *right* to live the form of life they have chosen for themselves, that constitutes an exclusionary reason for their not being prevented
from living that form of life.[24] But there is no obvious exclusionary reason
in the example as Meckled-Garcia sets it out. Raz's formal definition of a
second-order reason—'any reason to act for a reason or to refrain from acting
for a reason'[25]—is potentially misleading. An overriding first-order reason
could be described as a reason for refraining from acting for an overridden
first-order reason. But that is clearly not what Raz intends his definition of
a negative second-order reason to describe. A clearer brief description is 'a
reason to exclude reasons and not to act for them'.[26]

TOLERANT PERSONS AND NEUTRAL CITIZENS

All of this is, of course, of no significance for Meckled-Garcia's attempt to
prise apart the concepts of toleration and neutrality if he is right in claiming
that neutralists, like Rawls, provide us only with first-order reasons for being
neutral rather than with conflicting reasons whose resolution results in a case
for toleration which, in turn, requires neutrality. So do Rawls's citizens need
to practise toleration?

Rawls aims to provide us with reasons why people should enjoy fairly distributed liberties, opportunities, and resources to pursue their conceptions of
the good. He is not in the business of persuading us that we should use political power to prevent or impede people's pursuit of their conceptions of the
good. Thus, if we are in search of reasons for repression, *A Theory of Justice*
and *Political Liberalism* will not be good places to find them. Nevertheless,
Rawls's neutralist theory is clearly designed for a society in which people
have different and conflicting beliefs and a society in which, in the absence of
his political conception of justice, people could find reason to resort to state
power to promote their own conceptions of the good and to repress the conceptions of others. Rawls is at pains to emphasize that the pluralist society for
which he provides is one whose members are 'profoundly divided by reasonable though incompatible religious, philosophical, and moral doctrines'.[27] He
describes the doctrinal beliefs of his citizens variously as 'conflicting', 'irreconcilable', 'incompatible', 'incommensurable', 'deeply divided', 'deeply
opposed', and as offering 'no prospect of resolution'.[28] He traces the origins
of liberalism in general, and of political liberalism in particular, to the Reformation of the sixteenth century and to the religious divisions that emerged
from it.[29] Noting the 'clash' of conceptions of the good that developed after
the Reformation, he observes that political liberalism 'starts by taking to heart
the absolute depth of that irreconcilable latent conflict'.[30] Thus the world for
which Rawls provides is one characterized by deep doctrinal conflict and one

in which, without his political conception of justice, people could find ample reason to use political power to repress doctrines with which they disagreed and ways of life of which they disapproved.

It is precisely because his citizens subscribe to such different and conflicting comprehensive doctrines that Rawls tries to provide a theory of justice to which they can subscribe in spite of their doctrinal differences. That is, he seeks to find a theory of justice, including a reason for citizens to tolerate one another's conflicting doctrinal allegiances, that is independent of those doctrinal differences. Hence we have his idea of a specifically 'political' liberalism that uses a form of 'political' constructivism to generate a 'political' conception of justice. Hence too his concern to develop that conception as a 'freestanding view'. It is neither a comprehensive doctrine nor derived from a comprehensive doctrine; instead it is drawn from ideas implicit in the public political culture of a democratic society.[31] In the same spirit, the quality that Rawls claims for his political conception of justice is not 'truth' but 'reasonableness' so that, rather than competing with comprehensive doctrines, it can be seen to function on a different plane from them.[32]

Thus Rawls's political conception of justice is designed to leave in place, rather than to displace, the various (reasonable) comprehensive doctrines held by his citizens. So whatever reasons those comprehensive doctrines give their adherents for objecting to conflicting doctrines held by others will continue to be reasons for them in Rawls's just society. That is why Rawlsian citizens are called upon to engage in toleration. While they may have good reason (from within their own doctrines) for objecting to and repressing the doctrines and ways of life of others, Rawls gives them strong, countervailing, nondoctrinal reason not to use political power to act on these doctrinal reasons. He hopes, of course, that tension between comprehensive doctrines and his political conception of justice will disappear over time and be replaced by an overlapping consensus. I shall consider the implications of that idea for toleration in a moment but, in the first instance at least, there is ample scope for Rawlsian individuals to object to one another's doctrines and conceptions of the good and therefore ample opportunity for them to engage in toleration.

One thing that helps to obscure this simple feature of Rawls's society is his constantly addressing the members of his society as 'citizens'. Now to be a citizen is, for Rawls, to assume a 'political' role and, when an individual conscientiously assumes that role, he or she will act only on 'political' reasons. Thus, in their role as citizens, individuals will be guided by the political conception of justice and by public reason, rather than by the 'nonpublic reason' of their different comprehensive doctrines.[33] In making political decisions as citizens, they will take no account of whatever reasons for repression their comprehensive doctrines may contain; rather they will simply deliberate and decree—as justice requires—in a way that is neutral between comprehensive doctrines. That is why Rawlsian citizens might seem to exhibit a commitment to neutrality that is bereft of toleration. But, of course, Rawls's individuals are not only citizens; they are also full persons possessed of comprehensive doctrines and it is as full persons that they exhibit toleration. Their toleration is manifest in their willingness, in spite of their doctrinal commitments, to limit their use of political power (as citizens, but in other political roles as well) in the ways that Rawls prescribes.

RAWLSIAN TOLERANCE AND SECOND-ORDER REASONS

This separation between the political and the nonpolitical, the public and the nonpublic, takes us on to the question of whether the reason Rawls gives for toleration is a first- or a second-order reason. To my knowledge, Rawls nowhere refers to Raz's distinction between these different types of reason or shows any indication of using it self-consciously to structure his theory. Nevertheless, he does present his conception of justice as one that should function in political decision making in an exclusionary way. It matches Raz's idea of a 'protected' or 'peremptory' reason. It is a first-order reason in that it prescribes how we should settle fundamental political matters, but it is also a second-order reason in that it provides that, in dealing with those political matters, other sorts of reason—reasons drawn from our comprehensive doctrines—should be excluded from consideration. Similarly, in political matters the associated idea of public reason operates in an exclusionary way. In their role as citizens, just individuals do not engage in political decision making by weighing both public and nonpublic reasons and letting the balance fall where it may. Rather, they exclude nonpublic reasons from consideration and attend only to public reasons.[34] Thus, given that Rawls's argument for toleration forms part of his political conception of justice, there is a clear case for holding, *pace* Meckled-Garcia, that it provides us with a negative second-order reason for toleration. That is, on public or 'political' matters, it provides us with a reason for refraining from acting on reasons of another sort.

This interpretation of the logic of Rawls's position is not without complication. When he confronts the question of why we should settle issues of constitutional essentials and of basic justice by reference to political values alone, he answers that political values 'normally have sufficient weight to override all other values that may come into conflict with them'.[35] His use of the language of 'outweighing' and 'overriding' suggests that political values and values stemming from comprehensive doctrines relate to one another as competing first-order reasons rather than as reasons of a different order. Even so, that is consistent with my claim that, for the citizens of Rawls's society, the political conception of justice functions as an exclusionary reason. In dealing with constitutional essentials and matters of basic justice, including questions of toleration, citizens are to attend only to political values. But those citizens can also take a step back and ask why they should give those political values that exclusionary status. In other words, they can ask why the political conception of justice should constitute an exclusionary reason and it is at that point that it is appropriate to answer that the 'values of the political are very great values and hence not easily overridden'.[36] We should distinguish between a reason's functioning as an exclusionary reason and the reason for its being an exclusionary reason.

I have previously argued that the distinction between first- and second-order reasons is not critical for toleration. The duality of reasons that is essential for toleration can be competing first-order reasons, and in most instances of toleration probably is. But suppose we accept that the reason that Rawls's citizens have for being tolerant is, indeed, a second-order reason. Should that lead us to invert the logic of Meckled-Garcia's analysis and hold that this reason cannot count as a reason for *toleration* precisely because it is an *exclusionary* reason? In excluding rather than outweighing whatever countervailing first-order reason we might have for intolerance, it might be thought to deprive us of the duality of competing reasons that is essential if we are to have a genuine instance of toleration. But that would be a thought too far. An exclusionary reason does not eradicate other reasons. It simply preempts them in determining what we should do. Thus, even if Rawls's principles of justice have an exclusionary character, they can still be reasons for toleration.[37]

Finally, there is the matter of overlapping consensus. The primary concern that has driven Rawls to reformulate his liberalism as political liberalism has been his concern for stability. Stability is achieved when the various reasonable comprehensive doctrines to which the members of a society subscribe overlap in supporting the political conception of justice. In some cases that may be achieved negatively. A comprehensive doctrine may be less than fully comprehensive in that it may be silent on matters that are the concern of the political conception of justice. In that case, the political conception can simply occupy the 'gap' or 'leeway' left by the comprehensive doctrine.[38] In other cases, stability may be achieved more positively. A comprehensive doctrine might come to be understood by its adherents as fully endorsing the political conception of justice so that they can find positive reason, within their comprehensive doctrine, for embracing that conception. By whichever of these routes overlapping consensus is achieved, it will remove conflict between the demands of an individual's comprehensive doctrine and the demands of the political conception of justice. Does that mean that, even if there is a place for toleration in Rawls's political liberalism, it is merely provisional: that, once the goal of overlapping consensus has been achieved, toleration will become redundant?

That does not follow. Where a citizen finds that his or her comprehensive doctrine endorses the political conception of justice, that citizen has both public and nonpublic reason to be tolerant. The need for toleration does not disappear simply because it is required by a comprehensive doctrine. The duality of conflicting or competing reasons necessary for toleration can occur within a comprehensive doctrine as well as between a doctrine and an external principle. Consider, for example, Locke's celebrated *Letter on Toleration*. Locke does not seek to neuter Christianity by pretending that Christians have no reason to object to heresy or infidelity. Rather, he produces a series of reasons, several of them specifically Christian reasons, why Christians should not persecute or coerce those whose religious beliefs and conduct they view, quite properly, as wrongful. So Locke's message is not that Christians should urge others to tolerate what they themselves find unexceptionable. Rather, his message is that they, as Christians, have reason to tolerate what they, as Christians, have reason to condemn. Toleration therefore needs to be internal to Christianity itself. Thus the Christian who finds reason within his comprehensive doctrine for endorsing Rawls's political conception of justice does not lose the need to be tolerant; he simply discovers a congruence of reasons for being tolerant.

THE SIGNIFICANCE OF DEMOCRATIC TOLERATION

Set in the context of the long history of political toleration, both the circumstances of toleration that Rawls contemplates, and the main justification he gives for toleration, are unusual. Historically, political toleration has commonly taken the form of a state's officially subscribing to a doctrine, typically a religious faith or denomination, but nevertheless refraining from coercing or persecuting those who subscribe to other doctrines. Thus, there has been a clear distinction between the state that tolerates and the subjects who are tolerated. In Rawls's democratic society, tolerators and tolerated are not dichotomized in that way. Toleration is multilateral rather than unilateral: all democratic citizens are committed to tolerating one another's different and conflicting but reasonable comprehensive doctrines and the ways of life based upon them. Thus, everyone simultaneously tolerates and is tolerated. Historically, Rawls's multilateral model of toleration may not have been the norm, but it is nonetheless entirely coherent as a model of toleration.

It is this democratic model of toleration that some of Rawls's critics seem unable to comprehend. John Gray, for example, writes

Toleration as a political ideal is offensive to the new liberalism—the liberalism of Rawls, Dworkin, Ackerman and such like—because it is decidedly non-neutral in respect of the good. For the new liberals, justice—the shibboleth of revisionist liberalism—demands that government, in its institutions and policies, practise *neutrality*, not toleration, in regard to rival conceptions of the good life.[39]

Gray supposes that political toleration can be exhibited only by governments and only if those governments identify certain beliefs or practices as 'bad'. What he overlooks is the further possibility that the citizens of a democratic society, each of whom is 'decidedly non-neutral in respect of the good', can engage in mutual toleration by refraining from using political power to impose or privilege their particular conceptions of the good. In this democratic model, the neutrality of a government manifests the tolerance of its citizens.

Why should democratic citizens behave in this mutually tolerant way? Rawls's main answer is: because that is what justice as fairness requires. To use political power to repress reasonable comprehensive doctrines, or otherwise to disadvantage people because of their doctrinal affiliations, is to behave unfairly. He arrives at that answer by taking ideas implicit in the public culture of a democratic society—particularly the ideas of society as a fair system of cooperation and of persons as free and equal—and applying them to the fact of reasonable pluralism. Now once again, this way of arguing for toleration has not figured prominently in the catalogue of reasons that have been used, in the past, to plead the case for toleration. It provides us nevertheless with an entirely intelligible and cogent case for toleration. For Rawls, it is a peculiarly strong case; indeed, reasons of justice are peculiarly strong for most of us. But it would be perverse to hold that Rawls, in providing us with a peculiarly strong reason for being tolerant, somehow removes the need or occasion for toleration.

It is because Rawls locates toleration within fairness that he gives it such a far-reaching and thorough form. Gray protests that the neutralism of Rawls goes far beyond a policy of toleration since it rules out as wrong or unjust not only the coercive imposition of a favoured conception of the good, but also governmental encouragement of particular ways of life through education, subsidy, taxation, welfare provision, and the like.[40] But for Rawls, citizens who extend toleration fairly to one another will not use *any* of the levers of political power to privilege or disadvantage particular conceptions of the good. Political toleration can, of course, take less generous forms than this and Gray is right to point out the contrast between Rawls's policies and the more parsimonious forms of toleration exhibited by past 'tolerant' regimes. Even so, the generous and inclusive approach to toleration that we find in Rawls is still fully intelligible as a policy of toleration.

Finally, we might ask whether toleration has any special value or significance for a neutralist like Rawls. After all, Meckled-Garcia does not seek to
criticize those who (as he sees it) substitute neutrality for toleration. On the
contrary, he holds that a neutralist position is superior to one of toleration
and argues that neutralists can dispense with the value of toleration without
loss.[41] Toleration can, indeed, seem second best. Those who are tolerated
would prefer to be accepted; they would prefer not to be objected to by their
tolerators and so not to stand in need of their toleration. Those who tolerate
would prefer that they did not have to: they tolerate only what they object to
and they must surely prefer that what they object to did not exist. For both
parties in the relationship therefore, toleration can seem unfortunate. It may
be the best they can achieve in the given circumstances but, for each, it falls
short of their most desired condition.

Rawls does not share this pessimistic view of toleration. The pluralism
that he believes a democratic society should accommodate is not any sort of
pluralism but reasonable pluralism—a plurality of reasonable comprehensive
doctrines. Rawls is not wholly clear about what it is that makes a doctrine
'reasonable'. Sometimes it seems to be the doctrine's epistemic qualities,[42]
sometimes if and because it does not reject the essentials of a democratic
regime,[43] sometimes both of these,[44] sometimes its recognizing the burdens of
judgement,[45] and sometimes its actually supporting the political conception of
justice.[46] I do not want to pursue that matter here. Clearly Rawls thinks that
the fact that doctrines can be various yet reasonable contributes importantly
to the case for toleration. Disagreement amongst reasonable persons arises
because of the burdens of judgement. Reasonable persons will recognize
those burdens and be willing to accept their consequences, including their
consequences for the legitimate exercise of political power.[47] One such consequence is that there is a limit to what we can reasonably justify to others
and that, in turn, makes it unreasonable to use political power to repress comprehensive doctrines that we do not share.[48] The burdens of judgement are,
therefore, 'of first significance for a democratic idea of toleration'.[49]

Rather than excavate further the justificatory link between toleration and
the reasonableness of pluralism, I want here to fasten on a related aspect of
Rawls's thinking. Reasonable pluralism for Rawls arises from 'the work of
free practical reason within the framework of free institutions'.[50] It is 'the normal result of the exercise of human reason within the framework of the free
institutions of a constitutional democratic regime'.[51] As such, it is a normal
and enduring feature of a democratic society. The multiplicity of doctrines
and conceptions of the good that we find in modern democratic societies is
not something that we should regret, nor something that we can reasonably
hope will disappear over time, and certainly not something that we should try
to eradicate or even discourage.

Now, if reasonable pluralism is an enduring feature of a democratic society, so must be toleration. Disagreement remains disagreement even when it is reasonable: people engaged in reasonable disagreement still have reason to regard one another's doctrines as wrong. It is crucial to Rawls's position that we can regard the doctrines of others as reasonable yet wrong, and our own doctrine as uniquely true if not uniquely reasonable. Thus, the reasonableness of pluralism does not diminish the need for toleration. On the contrary, as long as we are confronted with reasonable pluralism, we have both occasion and reason to respond to it tolerantly. Hence, if a diversity of reasonable comprehensive doctrines is not a contingent and temporary characteristic of a modem democratic society but 'a permanent feature of the public culture of democracy',[52] toleration must also be an enduring feature of a democratic society. For Rawls, then, toleration is not second-best. It is neither a regrettable necessity in a regrettable world, nor a temporary expedient that we can look forward to abandoning. It is a central and permanent feature of a just, liberal order.

NOTES

1. John Rawls, *Political Liberalism* (New York: Columbia University Press, 1993), 8.
2. Rawls, *Political Liberalism*, 10.
3. Rawls, *Political Liberalism*, 4, 47.
4. Rawls, *Political Liberalism*, 122–23, 157, 194–95.
5. Thomas Nagel, *Equality and Partiality* (Oxford: Oxford University Press, 1991); Charles Larmore, *Patterns of Moral Complexity* (Cambridge: Cambridge University Press, 1987) and *The Morals of Modernity* (Cambridge: Cambridge University Press, 1996); Brian Barry, *Justice as Impartiality* (Oxford: Clarendon Press, 1995). Barry and Larmore make scant use of the language of toleration but it is clear that they, no less than Rawls and Nagel, conceive mutual toleration as a central feature of a liberal society. All four thinkers provide reasons why people, who have different and conflicting conceptions of the good, should refrain from using political power to suppress or disadvantage conceptions with which they disagree—reasons that do not require them to forfeit their belief that those conceptions are wrong. It is not only the proponents of neutralism that associate toleration with political neutrality. Michael Sandel criticizes neutralism because it fails to deliver a better quality of respect for diverse forms of life than mere toleration: *Democracy's Discontent: America in Search of a Public Philosophy* (Cambridge, MA: Belknap, 1996), 107. Kok-Chor Tan and Will Kymlicka both criticize Rawls for giving an unduly fundamental role to the value of toleration in his political liberalism: Tan, *Toleration, Diversity and Global Justice* (Pennsylvania: Pennsylvania University Press, 2000); Kymlicka, *Multicultural Citizenship* (Oxford: Clarendon Press, 1995), 152–63.
6. Saladin Meckled-Garcia, 'Toleration and Neutrality: Incompatible Ideals?', in D. Castiglione and C. McKinnon, eds., *Toleration, Neutrality and Democracy*

(Dordrecht: Kluwer, 2003), 77–96. The current chapter originally appeared in the same edited volume as Meckled-Garcia's and was written in response to his essay.

7. Glen Newey observes, 'Toleration demands that the policy-makers have a particular motive, namely disapproval of the practice that they tolerate. But to the extent that they are thus motivated, the policymakers contravene neutrality'; *Virtue, Reason and Toleration* (Edinburgh: Edinburgh University Press, 1999), 124. Similarly, John Horton remarks, 'if we take neutrality toward competing conceptions of the good as central to liberalism, then it might reasonably be asked whether liberalism is properly described as *tolerant* even toward those conceptions it permits? Here the thought is not the familiar one that complete neutrality, however it is interpreted, is either incoherent or impossible, but simply that because liberalism professes to be neutral toward a range of conceptions of the good—that it has no objection to them—it cannot therefore be tolerant of them'; 'Toleration as a Virtue', in David Heyd, ed., *Toleration: An Elusive Virtue* (Princeton, NJ: Princeton University Press, 1996), 28–43, at 36.

8. Thus Newey, in denying the possibility of a 'neutralist justification of toleration', is looking at things the wrong way round; *Virtue, Reason and Toleration*, 130.

9. Meckled-Garcia, 'Toleration and Neutrality', 79–80.

10. Meckled-Garcia, 'Toleration and Neutrality', 81.

11. Meckled-Garcia, 'Toleration and Neutrality', 85–87.

12. Meckled-Garcia, 'Toleration and Neutrality', 85.

13. Joseph Raz, *Practical Reason and Norms* (London: Hutchinson, 1975).

14. Cf. Raz: 'a reason is a reason even if outweighed by other conflicting reasons'; *Practical Reason and Norms*, 25.

15. Raz, *Practical Reason and Norms*, 39.

16. Raz, *The Authority of Law* (Oxford: Clarendon Press, 1979), 17.

17. For discussions of positive second order reasons, see Raz, *The Authority of Law*, 16–17, and *The Morality of Freedom* (Oxford: Clarendon Press, 1986), 32–35.

18. Raz, *Practical Reason and Norms*, 47–106.

19. Raz, *Practical Reason and Norms*, 41–5, 74–75; 'Promises and Obligations', in P. M. S. Hacker and J. Raz, eds., *Law, Morality and Society* (Oxford: Oxford University Press, 1977), 210–28, at 220–23; *The Authority of Law*, 14–16, 21–25; *Morality of Freedom*, 41–42, 47–48, 58–62.

20. Raz, *The Authority of Law*, 18; Raz, *Morality of Freedom*, 37, 42.

21. Raz, *Practical Reason and Norms*, 40, 46–7.

22. Raz, *Morality of Freedom*, 402.

23. Meckled-Garcia, 'Toleration and Neutrality', 80.

24. Cf. Peter Jones, *Rights* (Basingstoke: Macmillan, 1994), 54–55.

25. Raz, *Practical Reason and Norms*, 39.

26. Raz, *Practical Reason and Norms*, 62.

27. Rawls, *Political Liberalism*, xviii.

28. Rawls, *Political Liberalism*, xviii, xxv–xxviii, 4, 10, 36, 133, 303.

29. Rawls, *Political Liberalism*, xxii–xxvi.

30. Rawls, *Political Liberalism*, xxvi.

31. Rawls, *Political Liberalism*, 12–14.

32. Rawls, *Political Liberalism*, xviii–xxi, 94–95, 127.

33. Rawls requires this only with qualification. The limits imposed by public reason apply to 'constitutional essentials' and 'questions of basic justice' rather than to less fundamental political questions, though Rawls thinks it highly desirable that even those less fundamental political questions should be settled by public reason insofar as that is possible (*Political Liberalism*, 214, 215, 230). Rawls also modifies the exclusionary character of public reason by 'allowing citizens, in certain situations, to present what they regard as the basis of political values rooted in their comprehensive doctrine, provided they do this in ways that strengthen the ideal of public reason itself' (*Political Liberalism*, 247).

34. Subject again to the qualifications described in note 33.

35. Rawls, *Political Liberalism*, 138; see also pp. 146, 155–57, 218–19, 241.

36. Rawls, *Political Liberalism*, 139.

37. Analogously, suppose that I promise to tolerate your objectionable conduct. That promise provides me with an exclusionary reason, but that is still a reason for my *tolerating* your objectionable conduct.

38. Rawls, *Political Liberalism*, 160, 246.

39. John Gray, *Enlightenment's Wake* (London: Routledge, 1995), 19.

40. Gray, *Enlightenment's Wake*, 19–20. See also Meckled-Garcia, 'Toleration and Neutrality', 84–85, 87.

41. Meckled-Garcia, 'Toleration and Neutrality', 90–95.

42. Rawls, *Political Liberalism*, 59.

43. Rawls, *Political Liberalism*, xvi.

44. Rawls, *The Law of Peoples* (Cambridge, MA: Harvard University Press, 1999), 87.

45. John Rawls, *Justice as Fairness: A Restatement* (Cambridge, MA: Belknap, 2001), 191.

46. John Rawls, 'The Idea of Public Reason Revisited', in his *Collected Papers*, Samuel Freeman, ed. (Cambridge, MA: Harvard University Press, 1999), 573–615, at 608–09.

47. Rawls, *Political Liberalism*, 54.

48. Rawls, *Political Liberalism*, 60–62.

49. Rawls, *Political Liberalism*, 58.

50. Rawls, *Political Liberalism*, 37.

51. Rawls, *Political Liberalism*, xvi; see also pp. xvii–ix, xxiv–v, 4, 36–37, 55–58.

52. Rawls, *Political Liberalism*, 36.

Chapter 3

Legalizing Toleration

A Reply to Balint[1]

Imagine a society the great majority of whose members are strongly committed to religious toleration. They have read Locke, Bayle, Voltaire, and other canonical proponents of toleration. They have also noticed the bloodshed and suffering caused by religious intolerance both in the past and in their own age. In light of their reading and experience, they are fully committed to religious toleration: they believe that all citizens should enjoy toleration in religious matters.[2] Their society is democratic so that, unlike their forbears who had to plead the case for toleration with monarchs or oligarchs, they can fashion their community as they see fit. How then should they act on their shared commitment to toleration?

The obvious answer is by framing laws and designing institutions that secure religious toleration for the members of their society. We can therefore suppose that they will enact laws that secure for citizens the right to pursue their own religion in their own way and that simultaneously impose upon each citizen the duty to allow others to pursue their own religion in their own way. They may go further and entrench the freedoms demanded by toleration in a constitutional bill of rights, perhaps modelled on the ECHR, particularly article 9. They will also ensure that their public institutions are even-handed with respect to people as religious believers, including as 'unbelievers', so that no citizen's opportunity to participate in public life is prejudiced by his religious convictions (unless a citizen's religious convictions themselves forbid that participation). As well as having read the classics of toleration, they may have read John Rawls's *Political Liberalism* (1993), in which case they may resolve that no use should be made of political power, of any kind, purposely to promote or to disadvantage a particular faith or variant of faith or lack of faith.

What adjective should we use to describe the political community that these individuals create? The obvious answer is 'tolerant', and their community is tolerant not primarily because of the attitudes of its population but because toleration is instantiated in, and secured by, the society's laws and institutions. We might contrast this society with a second that models intolerance. The intolerant society permits the preaching and practice of only a single variant of a single faith and forbids any manifestation of any other religious belief. It might also burden 'heretics' and 'infidels' with penal taxes, exclude them from public office, and brand them publicly as degenerate. Or it might simply expel or execute them.

But consider now a third society. Its members are hesitant about the merits of toleration. They fear the suffering that might accompany state-sponsored intolerance but they also fear for the survival of their own faith if other faiths were to be tolerated. Because of their ambivalence, they refrain from putting in place any of the laws and institutional arrangements that characterise the first society. Citizens remain free to tolerate or not to tolerate the religious lives of their fellows as they see fit. The society's population is divided between two faiths. Some in each faith group behave tolerantly towards members of the other. But many in each group do not; they violently attack members of the other group, desecrate their places of worship, use terror tactics to deter them from assembling for collective acts of worship, and discriminate against them at every opportunity.

Given my descriptions of these three societies, it seems just obvious that the first society is more tolerant than the second, while the third falls somewhere in between the two. Yet, as Peter Balint (2012) points out, if we adhere to the academic orthodoxy on toleration, that ranking would seem to be mistaken. The first society will have little claim to be more tolerant than the second, let alone the third. According to orthodoxy, toleration has two necessary or 'possibility' conditions. First, toleration entails disapproval or dislike; in the absence of some sort of negative appraisal, the tolerator has no occasion to tolerate the tolerated. That is how toleration differs from endorsement, acceptance, or indifference. Secondly, a person tolerates only if he or she has the power to do otherwise. If A disapproves of B's conduct but is powerless to affect it, A can neither tolerate nor not tolerate B's conduct. Toleration is an option for A only if intolerance is too.

Now consider how the first society performs in relation to these possibility conditions. That society, on my account, is tolerant in virtue of the laws and institutional arrangements it possesses. Yet laws and institutional arrangements cannot themselves disapprove or dislike. Their authors can disapprove or dislike but that suggests it is those authors who will be tolerant (or intolerant) rather than the rules and arrangements they establish. A similar objection can be mobilized in relation to power as a possibility condition of toleration.

Laws and institutions (institutions considered as inanimate structures without reference to those who staff them) cannot wield power. They can be the instruments only of somebody's power and it is that somebody, rather than the laws or institutional structures themselves, who will be the source of toleration or intolerance.

The power condition is at odds with my portrait of the tolerant society in another, potentially more damaging, way. That society has rules and arrangements that deprive its citizens of the option of intolerance; citizens are not allowed to interfere with or impede the religious freedom of their fellows. That prohibition, in removing from citizens the freedom to interfere in one another's religious lives, may seem to remove from them the power that is a possibility condition of toleration. If we deprive people of the possibility of behaving intolerantly, we also deprive them of the possibility of behaving tolerantly. So, rather than incarnating toleration, the first society would seem to have eliminated it.

The first society might still claim to be less intolerant than the second ('intolerant') society but, as Balint points out, not being intolerant is not always the same as being tolerant. However, judged according to the orthodoxy, the first society will be less tolerant than the third. In the third society, citizens remain legally free to impede one another's religious activity and, for that reason, toleration remains an option for them: they can choose to refrain from using their power to impede or persecute those whose faith or denomination they reject. If some citizens opt to be tolerant, that will render their society more tolerant than the first society, even if the citizens who tolerate are only a small minority of the society. The third society is therefore more tolerant than the first, and the first is no more tolerant than the second.

That conclusion is plainly fatuous and it is no less fatuous for the simple logic with which the orthodox conception of toleration delivers it. No one outside the academy is likely to recognize the third society as more tolerant than the first, or the first as no more tolerant than the second. Even if we were to suppose that every last person in the third society opted to behave tolerantly, the first society would still outperform the third on the score of toleration since it guarantees toleration for its citizens, while the third leaves each individual's toleration entirely at the mercy of others. The toleration secured by the first society is therefore superior to that available in the third precisely in the way that freedom conceived as nondomination is superior to freedom conceived as mere *de facto* noninterference (Pettit 1997).

How, then, can we avoid the absurdity of accounting the third society more tolerant than the first? The answer is by recognizing that toleration can be approached from more than one perspective. As well as conceiving it from the perspective of tolerator or tolerated, we can conceive it from a third-party perspective. We do so when we think about the sort of toleration that ought to obtain amongst the members of a society. Consider the position of the citizens of the first society when they are on the point of constructing rules and arrangements for their society. They take a view on the toleration citizens should extend to one another and they enact laws accordingly. If they believe citizens should enjoy a generous measure of toleration, they will establish an arrangement that requires citizens to extend that toleration to one another. However, in establishing that arrangement, they will not themselves engage in toleration. They are not tolerating anyone or anything; they are simply deciding upon and establishing rules that instantiate the demands of toleration. Once those rules are in place, their society will be tolerant not because it, as a society, extends toleration to someone or something but in virtue of the mutual toleration it secures for its members. Moreover, the toleration it secures will be 'horizontal' toleration amongst its citizens rather than 'vertical' toleration between ruler and subjects.

Although I associate this third-party perspective particularly with liberal democracy, it is a perspective that could have been assumed by a post-Reformation monarch and its third-party nature is perhaps more readily apparent in that case. If a monarch were 'an enlightened prince' of the sort contemplated by Kant (1991, 58), he would regard the religious lives of his subjects as none of his business and allow them complete freedom in matters of religion. Having decided upon his own position, he might then direct his attention to his religiously divided subjects, determine that they should be tolerant of one another, and legislate accordingly. In subjecting his population to a regime of mutual toleration, he would occupy the role of neither tolerator nor tolerated; rather he would stand in a third-party relation to his subjects and the toleration he secured would be, as before, horizontal toleration amongst his subjects rather than vertical toleration extended by himself to them.

Unlike the 'enlightened prince' who stands outside the tolerant regime he creates for his subjects, the citizens of the first society will be subject to the rules of toleration they themselves create. As agents they will be obliged to comply with those rules and as patients they will benefit from the compliance of others. But we should not confuse their two roles: deciding upon the rules of the game is not the same as playing the game. In the latter role, citizens will be both tolerators and tolerated. In the former, they will not; rather they will stand in a third-party relation to their particular selves as prospective participants in the game they create.

That is not to say that anyone who legislates in relation to toleration must, or will, do so from a third-party perspective. Post-Reformation monarchs typically legislated on religious matters from a first person perspective: they decided whom, if anyone, they would or would not tolerate and legislated accordingly. A democratic majority might similarly determine whom it will and will not tolerate and legislate accordingly. In both of these cases, 'political toleration' assumes a vertical form and conforms to a traditional tolerator-tolerated model.

I do not claim therefore that, in a democratic context, toleration must be provided for in a third-party way. I do claim, however, that a third-party approach is more consistent with the ideas of democratic equality and liberal democracy. Balint is right to point out that even liberal democracy can engage in ruler–subject toleration; it can do so when it confronts illiberal groups, such as the white supremacists instanced by Balint. But, if we insist that political toleration can take only a ruler–subject form, we shall join Glen Newey (1999) and David Heyd (2008) in driving toleration to the margins of liberal democracy rather than locating toleration at its centre.

If we think about toleration in a third-party way, do negative appraisal and power lapse as possibility conditions of toleration? Both remain preconditions of toleration but not quite in the way they do for tolerator and tolerated. A regime of toleration will be necessary and possible only for a population characterised by some form of disagreement, disapproval or dislike. If that negative appraisal were to disappear, so would the need for toleration. Similarly, a regime of toleration would be unnecessary if, in its absence, a population were somehow powerless to be intolerant of one another. But while negative appraisal and power (not) to tolerate remain possibility conditions of (necessary 'circumstances' for) toleration, they are not features of a regime of toleration itself or of citizens as sponsors of that regime. Balint's supposition that we must be able to find 'sites' of disapproval and forbearance somewhere within the regime itself, or amongst its sponsors, is therefore misplaced.

My original claim (chapter 1) was that a liberal democratic regime of toleration provides for toleration not by enabling people to engage in acts of toleration but by holding intolerance at bay. My second claim was that, in so doing, the regime secures what matters about toleration, which is that people should not suffer intolerance rather than that they should engage in wilful acts of toleration. We could hold, contrary to that claim, that the value of toleration lies in its enabling tolerators to display the virtue of toleration, just as we might hold that the value of poverty relief lies in its enabling the rich to display the virtue of benevolence. But neither option has much plausibility or appeal.

I now want to add a further claim: there is no compelling reason why, in describing a liberal democratic regime of toleration, we should abjure the language of 'toleration' and speak only of the 'absence of intolerance'. We can reasonably speak of people, under a regime of toleration, being legally required to behave tolerantly towards their fellows, where 'legally required' means that they have a legal obligation so to behave and 'behave tolerantly' describes their refraining from preventing acts of others that they find objectionable but that others are legally entitled to perform. If toleration entails forbearance and if forbearance remains 'forbearance' when it is legally required, why should toleration not also remain 'toleration' when it is legally required? Law does not render people incapable of doing what it prohibits; rather it requires them not to do what they remain capable of doing.[3]

Why, finally, should we persist with the language of toleration in describing liberal democratic arrangements? Why not abandon it and make do with the language of freedom? Two considerations argue against that proposal. First, toleration relates to a wider range of issues than is normally captured by the language of freedom; it relates, for example, to issues concerning the use of public resources and to the prohibition of direct and indirect discrimination. Secondly, the political ideal of toleration arose in response to circumstances of plurality and disagreement, circumstances that also shaped liberal democratic thinking. It would be perverse to veto any mention of toleration in describing political arrangements that have been inspired by that idea and that have sought to realise it more fully than any political alternative.

ACKNOWLEDGEMENT

I am grateful to Peter Balint for his comments on an earlier draft of this chapter.

NOTES

1. This essay was prompted by Peter Balint's critical comment (2012) on the article reprinted as chapter 1 in this volume.
2. For the sake of simplicity, I focus on the case of religious toleration, but the argument I make in this chapter is intended to apply to toleration generally.
3. I suspect our thinking on this issue will be affected by our thinking on another: the morality appropriate to toleration. If, like Newey (1999) and Benbaji and Heyd (2001), we think that toleration must be supererogatory, it will follow that toleration cannot be morally, let alone legally, required. But if we think (as I do) that people can be duty-bound to tolerate, we are more likely to accept that a duty to tolerate might be legal as well as moral.

REFERENCES

Balint, Peter. (2012). 'Not Yet Making Sense of Political Toleration'. *Res Publica* 18:259–64.
Benbaji, Hagit, and David Heyd. (2001). 'The Charitable Perspective: Forgiveness and Toleration as Supererogatory'. *Canadian Journal of Philosophy* 31:567–86.

Heyd, David. (2008). 'Is Toleration a Political Virtue?'. In *Toleration and Its Limits* (Nomos XLVIII), ed. Melissa Williams and Jeremy Waldron, 171–94. New York: New York University Press.

Kant, Immanuel. (1991). *Political Writings*, ed. Hans Reiss. Cambridge: Cambridge University Press.

Newey, Glen. (1999). *Virtue, Reason and Toleration*. Edinburgh: Edinburgh University Press.

Pettit, Philip. (1997). *Republicanism: A Theory of Freedom and Government*. Oxford: Clarendon Press.

Rawls, John. (1993). *Political Liberalism*. New York: Columbia University Press.

Chapter 4

Toleration, Religion, and Accommodation

Historically the idea of toleration has been most associated with religious belief and practice. Even nowadays we are inclined to think of religious toleration as the paradigm case of toleration. Why should that be? The obvious answer is that religious disagreements have been so prominent in human history—particularly in modern European history—and have fuelled such bitter and bloody conflicts that toleration has been especially necessary to deal with them. If there is to be peace without repression among the adherents of different religious beliefs, 'live and let live' is the only feasible option. But there is also a less contingent reason. To hold a particular religious belief is necessarily to dissent from and to reject other religious beliefs. To be a Muslim is to dissent from Christianity and to be a Christian is to reject Islam, just as to be a Protestant is to dissent from Catholicism and to be a Sunni is to reject Shi'ism; while to be an atheist is to reject all of these faiths and all of their variants. So different religious beliefs are not merely different; they are also conflicting. To embrace a particular religious belief is necessarily to reject others and that is why religious difference provides a paradigmatic site for toleration. Disapproval or rejection is a necessary feature of the circumstances of toleration and it is also a necessary feature of religious difference.

In saying that different religious beliefs conflict, I do not mean to say that their adherents must come to blows, even though they frequently have. I mean only that those adherents are putting forward rival sets of belief and, to that extent, they must disagree with one another. If they hold, nevertheless, that they should refrain from coercing or persecuting or disadvantaging those whom they reckon propagate and pursue mistaken beliefs, they are committed to toleration; and, if all parties to the dispute take that view, they will engage in mutual toleration. They may very well find reasons within their own faiths for desisting from intolerance but, even if they do, those will still be reasons for toleration.

Some people are uncomfortable with these obvious truths and insist that we should *celebrate* rather merely tolerate our differences. In the case of religious differences, however, it is very hard to make sense of that injunction. If I am a Muslim, how can I celebrate the fact that others refuse to recognize Muhammad as God's prophet, fail to accept that the Koran is the word of God, and pursue un-Islamic forms of life? If I am a Christian, how can I celebrate others' failure to recognize that Jesus Christ was the Son of God, that faith in him is the path to salvation, and that the worship of other gods or no god is deeply mistaken? To assimilate differences in religious belief to the kind of differences we *can* celebrate—differences in, for example, dress or music or literature or diet—is not to take them seriously.

RELIGIOUS TOLERATION: UNNECESSARY AND MORIBUND?

All that said, we might still question how much religious toleration matters nowadays. In the European world, people seem now to care less about religion than they did in the past and, the less they care, the less religious toleration matters. Moreover, even if we cannot yet do without religious toleration altogether, that sort of toleration might be thought dead as an issue. The battle for religious toleration was fought and won long ago and preaching the virtues of religious toleration is now a pointless exercise in preaching to the converted. In this chapter I challenge those dismissals of religious toleration. I shall say a little about why we still need religious toleration, but I shall devote most of the chapter to challenging the claim that religious toleration is now a dead issue. I shall do so primarily by arguing that issues of accommodation, which have become highly contentious in many European societies, are issues of toleration. Those issues have risen to prominence partly, though not wholly, as a consequence of the transformation of societies like Britain, France, Germany, Italy, and the Netherlands, from largely mono-faith (if multidenominational) societies to multifaith societies. But first a few words on why we still have, and still need, religious toleration.

Because religious toleration is such a widely accepted ideal in liberal democratic societies, it is easy to overlook its existence. Indeed, perversely, its widespread acceptance is sometimes mistaken for its nonexistence. Commentators sometimes suppose that toleration is toleration only if it hurts. If it comes easy, there is not much that is tolerant about it. There may be some merit in that view if we conceive toleration as a psychological phenomenon. The more people undergo inner torment and have to struggle to make themselves endure the conduct of others, to which they deeply object, the more toleration they actually display; and, if we think toleration is virtuous, the more virtuous they will be. By contrast, the nonchalant and the laid-back, to whom toleration comes easy, may be thought to display little of it and perhaps for that reason to be less worthy of congratulation.

However, logically, there is nothing to commend the view that toleration has to be painful to be real. Suppose I object to x, but I am so persuaded of the merits of toleration in cases like x, that I tolerate x painlessly and without hesitation. It would be perverse to hold that, because I am so convinced of the case for toleration, I do not really tolerate x. A tolerant society does not cease to be a tolerant just because its population is wholly sold on the merits of toleration. Of course, we must distinguish toleration from mere indifference and, insofar as the current age lives more comfortably with religious diversity than previous ages, that condition may owe more to indifference than to toleration (Williams 1996). That claim is not wholly mistaken, but it is very far from being wholly true. There are large swathes of people in European societies who are strongly committed to religious beliefs of various sorts; there are also large numbers of people who are deeply hostile either to religious belief in general or to particular faiths. Insofar as those people do not follow their historical predecessors and resort to political power to promote their own beliefs and to suppress the objectionable beliefs of others, why is that? The answer is not that they hold their beliefs any less fervently; it is that they are more persuaded of the rightness of mutual toleration. So, even if the battle for religious toleration has been fought and won, it is a simple error to suppose that religious toleration is no longer a feature, and no longer need be a feature, of contemporary European societies. But has the battle for religious toleration been fought and won? If we cast our eyes beyond Europe, it clearly has not. Think, for example, of conflicts between Sunnis and Shi'as in different parts of the Muslim world, or of the attacks suffered by the Ahmadi sect in Pakistan, or of conflicts between Christians and Muslims in Nigeria, Sudan, and, more recently, Egypt. Postwar Europe has also seen bitter and bloody conflicts between religiously divided populations in areas such as Northern Ireland and Bosnia. These may seem exceptional cases and, even though they have been associated with differences in religious identity, we may doubt how far the conflict has really been about religion. But we can still turn to cases like the Rushdie Affair, or the Danish cartoons, or the issues raised by niqabs and burkas, or conflicts over the merits of Sharia courts and legal pluralism, to show that issues concerning religious toleration are far from moribund. However, what is at stake in that last set of issues is not so much whether there should be religious toleration but what sort of religious toleration there should be. That is also true of the issues surrounding accommodation.

By religious accommodation I understand an arrangement that is designed to ease the lot of the accommodated and, without which, they would find themselves disadvantaged compared with others. As Martha Nussbaum (2008, 21) says, accommodation aims to give religious people a 'break' by, for example, exempting them from general rules that would otherwise compel them to betray their beliefs or to bear a burden not borne by others. However, I do not mean 'accommodation' to encompass just any adjustment a society makes in response to changes in the religious make-up of its population. If, for example, the religious make-up of chaplaincies in hospitals or prisons is adjusted to match changes in the religious make-up of a population, there is no reason to describe that as 'accommodation'. I limit the idea of accommodation to cases in which an adjustment is made to provide for the particular demands of a particular faith, such as a particular dress code or dietary requirement. Accommodation, as I shall use the term, is therefore difference-sensitive rather than difference-blind. This idea of accommodation is particularly associated with multiculturalism; indeed, it is often now treated as definitive of multiculturalism. I shall explain later why I choose to examine it with respect to religion in particular rather than culture in general. I shall draw my examples from Britain, simply because that is the case I know best, but the issues they exemplify are common to other European societies (Doe 2011), and to many non-European societies, that have multifaith populations. First, however, I need to explain the kind of toleration of which accommodation is a part.

TOLERATION AND LIBERAL DEMOCRACY

How are we to understand a tolerant political regime under modern liberal democratic circumstances? In simple analyses of toleration, we frequently use a model of person-to-person toleration. Person A objects to the conduct of person B, is able to prevent B's conduct if he she so chooses, but allows B to continue with that conduct. In that case, A tolerates B's conduct. If we turn to the types of regime that were prevalent in post-Reformation Europe, we can model their toleration or intolerance on the simple person-to-person case. An early modern monarch who was a Catholic, but who had Protestants among his subjects, could tolerate those subjects by, for example, allowing them to engage in Protestant forms of worship. Alternatively, the monarch could opt not to tolerate them by suppressing their forms of worship. We can tell the same story about a Protestant monarch and Catholic subjects. In both cases, it is clear who was doing the tolerating (or not) and who and what was being tolerated (or not).

Now fast forward to our own age. Where do we find religious toleration in contemporary liberal democratic regimes? We might try to find the answer by searching for an equivalent to the early modern monarch. But there are two problems with that strategy. First, liberal democratic regimes, at least ideally conceived, do not commit themselves to a particular religious faith or to a particular variant of a religious faith. On the contrary, we would think it quite improper for a liberal democracy to privilege, patronize, or promote any religious faith. But if a regime remains neutral on matters of religious faith, it will neither approve nor disapprove of any and so will be incapable of the toleration or intolerance that was open to an early modern monarch.

Second, it is not at all clear who or what we should conceive as the equivalent of the early modern monarch. Assuming that the democracy we are contemplating is an indirect democracy, the most obvious candidate might seem to be its elected government. But a democratic government (again in idea) stands in a quite different relation to its population than did an early modern monarch. An elected government is supposed to be the servant rather than the master of its population and it has no business either tolerating or not tolerating the population that it serves. Perhaps, then, it is the democratic majority that equates with the monarch and the minority with his subjects so that the 'monarchical' majority tolerates (or not) a 'subject' minority. However, that simple model of superordinate and subordinate fits ill with the equality that we associate with liberal democracy, especially with the equal status of citizens. It also misrepresents the reality of many modern democratic societies in which there is no simple majority that tolerates an identifiable minority.

It would seem, then, that if we are to make sense of toleration as a characteristic of a liberal democratic regime, we should turn away from the model provided by post-Reformation monarchies. It could be, of course, that toleration is a quality we cannot ascribe to contemporary democratic regimes. As a political ideal it may belong to a predemocratic age; liberal democratic arrangements, rather than instantiating toleration, may have superseded it (Heyd 2008; Newey 1999). Yet, tossing the idea of toleration aside in that manner also seems odd, since we typically conceive *liberal* democracy as in part driven by, and as realizing, an ideal of toleration.

The solution to these puzzles lies, I suggest, in conceiving a liberal democratic order as one that is committed to an ideal of toleration and that seeks to uphold that ideal. It is an order that secures freedom of religion for its citizens by not allowing them to use political power either to privilege their own faith or to suppress the faiths of others. The Christian is precluded from not tolerating the Muslim, and the Muslim is precluded from not tolerating the Christian; similarly the Sikh is not free to be intolerant of the Christian or the

Muslim, and neither of them is free to be intolerant of the Sikh. Thus, subject to a qualification I shall make in due course, the religious toleration secured by a liberal democratic regime is not one in which the regime itself does the tolerating. Rather, the toleration it secures is the toleration it requires of its citizens in relation to one another; it is 'horizontal' toleration among citizens, rather than 'vertical' toleration of subjects by government. It is toleration among people of equal status rather than the toleration of subordinates by a superordinate.[1]

The most obvious way in which a liberal democratic society can secure that tolerant order is by establishing rights to religious freedom for all of its members and by imposing upon them corresponding duties to respect the rights of others. It might do that by entrenching religious freedom in its constitution, through a bill of rights for example, so that citizens enjoy rights in the form of constitutional immunities. Or it might secure those rights through ordinary legislation. Or its commitment to mutual toleration may be deeply ingrained in its political culture, so that its citizens enjoy secure rights of religious freedom *de facto* even if not *de jure*.

One feature of this way of understanding political toleration is that it is an arrangement that *requires* people to be tolerant of one another, most obviously by subjecting them to a legal obligation that prohibits intolerance. But is 'required' behaviour of that sort consistent with the idea of toleration? If A is legally prohibited from violating B's religious freedom, does not that simply preempt A's toleration? A's being *able* to prevent B's conduct, if A so chooses, is normally regarded as a necessary condition of A's being capable of tolerating B; if A is deprived of that ability, A is in no position either to tolerate or not tolerate B. Thus, if a society establishes a legal arrangement that secures A's and B's religious freedom by prohibiting their being intolerant of one another, that arrangement might seem to displace, rather than to realize, toleration.

However, that chain of thinking relies on the person-to-person model of toleration, whereas my concern is with toleration as a feature of a political and legal system. If a society is committed to an ideal of toleration and seeks to organize itself in a way that realizes that ideal, how can it to do so except by upholding and limiting its citizens' freedom in relation to one another? It will not establish an order that leaves citizens free to tolerate one another, or not, as they so choose. Rather it will secure its citizens' freedom so that they are unprevented from doing those things that they ought to be unprevented from doing; it will secure toleration by holding possible or potential intolerance at bay. Thus a tolerant political order will be distinguished not by its allowing citizens to tolerate or not tolerate one another as they choose, but by the complex of freedoms and unfreedoms it secures for its citizens (see further, chapter 3).

We should note, however, that it is not the case that such an order must deprive individual citizens of the possibility of acting on their own commitment to toleration. On the contrary, A's treatment of B can still be motivated by A's own beliefs about how he or she should treat B. The existence of a law requiring A not to infringe B's freedom does not mean that A's conduct must be motivated (only) by that legal obligation, just as the existence of a law prohibiting murder or assault does not render us incapable of refraining from murder or assault for any reason other than our being subject to that legal obligation. The political liberalism of John Rawls (1993) provides a clear example of this sort of tolerant political order. It aims to provide a conception of justice for a society whose members possess different and conflicting comprehensive doctrines, including different and conflicting religious doctrines. Of the two principles of justice that Rawls constructs for this diverse society, it is the first that most obviously relates to religious toleration since it includes the right to religious freedom. But in fact both principles are relevant in that both embody the notion that a just, liberal society would not use political power of *any* sort either to promote or to disadvantage any reasonable comprehensive doctrine or its associated conception of the good. The 'neutrality' of Rawls's just society is a consequence of its thoroughgoing commitment to toleration (on which see chapter 2). The feature of Rawls's just and tolerant society to which I want to draw attention is that it is not a society that leaves its citizens free to tolerate one another in the political domain as they so choose. On the contrary, the society's basic structure is one whose laws and institutional design secure toleration by depriving citizens of the freedom to be intolerant of one another. Certainly good Rawlsian citizens will embrace the principles of justice and will, therefore, endorse the justice of their society's arrangements, including the justice of mutual toleration, but the society's commitment to toleration lies chiefly in the character and make-up of its basic structure rather than in the attitudes of its citizens.

TOLERATION AND ACCOMMODATION

How then does this relate to the issue of accommodation? Rawls's conception of a just society is often described as 'difference blind'. It is blind to difference because it establishes the rules and arrangements of a just society without reference to the specific demands of any particular comprehensive doctrine or conception of the good. By contrast, the idea of accommodation is associated with 'difference sensitivity'—with the need to take account of, and to adjust a society's arrangements to, the different demands of different religions and cultures. The move from difference-blindness to difference sensitivity is frequently associated with the rejection of neutrality. In fact, there is no reason why it should be, since the complaint that difference blindness fails to be genuinely neutral can be accompanied by the claim that genuine neutrality, genuine even-handedness, requires difference sensitivity, though that is not an issue that I shall pursue here.

While I do not intend to tie my argument on the relation between toleration and accommodation to Rawls's theory of justice, it is an argument that is broadly consistent with his theory. The kind of accommodation that is relevant to the polyethnic and multifaith character of Britain and other European societies, and that has been pursued in those societies, tends to be of two sorts. It consists either in refinements to what Rawls calls the 'basic structure' of those societies, or in adjustments to public policies pursued within that basic structure.

TOLERATION AND THE ECHR, ARTICLE 9

Consider the decisions made by the courts when they deal with cases relating to Article 9 of the European Convention on Human Rights (ECHR). The first clause of Article 9 gives everyone 'the right to freedom of thought, conscience and religion', including the freedom 'either alone or in community with others and in public or private, to *manifest* his religion or belief, in worship, teaching, practice and observance' (my emphasis). Its second clause, however, subjects the freedom to manifest one's religion or belief 'to such limitations as are prescribed by law and are necessary in a democratic society in the interests of public safety, for the protection of public order, health or morals, or the protection of the rights and freedoms of others'. Cases concerning Article 9 that come before the courts are typically cases in which a person claims that his right to manifest his religion in particular circumstances has been interfered with, while others either resist that claim of interference or argue that it is justified by the limitations listed in the Article's second clause.

The ECHR was drafted and ratified long before the issue of multifaith or multicultural accommodation arose to prominence. Even so, the issues that courts face in relation to Article 9 are frequently issues of accommodation. They raise the question of whether someone has the right to manifest his particular religion in particular circumstances and, in resolving that question, courts take account of the specific demands of a person's faith as well as of the specific features of the circumstances in which that person wishes to manifest his or her faith. They are cases, that is, in which the issue is whether and how far a person's wish to manifest his or her religion should be accommodated by others. Thus, in Britain, such cases have concerned the right of a Christian employee to be exempt from his employer's practice of requiring Sunday working[2]; the right of a Muslim teacher to attend Friday prayers, even though his doing so entailed his being absent from school during teaching hours[3]; the right of a Muslim schoolgirl to attend school wearing a jilbab, rather than the shalwar kameez provided by the school's uniform[4]; the right of a Christian schoolgirl to wear a 'purity' ring contrary to her school's no jewellery policy[5]; and the right of a Hindu on his death to be cremated by open pyre rather than by the enclosed form of cremation currently provided in Britain.[6]

These cases exemplify what I mean by 'refining' the basic structure. They take the right of freedom of religion (which, as a general right, is not in dispute) and consider how far that right should entitle the bearers of a specific religious belief to have that belief accommodated by others, in public or private capacities, so that they can manifest their religion (which, as a specific right, is in dispute). These are issues of religious toleration in that they concern the scope of freedom that a society should secure for its religious adherents, within which they can manifest their beliefs. Indeed, the toleration required in cases of accommodation is typically more demanding than in the 'standard case'. In the standard case, toleration requires no more of people than that they abstain from persecuting others for their religious beliefs or from preventing others' pursuit of their beliefs. In the case of accommodation, toleration typically requires people to make a sacrifice or bear a cost or endure an inconvenience for the sake of beliefs they do no share, and that can be significantly more demanding than the standard case. That is why this form of toleration remains controversial even in societies that claim to be wholly committed to religious toleration.

Another area of law that can be seen as refining the basic structure as it relates to religious freedom is the law on religious discrimination. In Britain, discrimination law often secures a greater measure of accommodation for the religious than human rights law. It has, for example, required a greater measure of accommodation from employers, in respect of their employees' beliefs, than has human rights law (Ahdar and Leigh 2005, 165–68; Vickers 2008, 86–94). But, before turning to that case, I want to consider a different sort of religious accommodation—accommodation through exemption.

TOLERATION AND EXEMPTION

Accommodation through exemption has attracted a great deal of attention, perhaps because exemptions are more conspicuous forms of accommodation than those provided by human rights law or discrimination law. In Britain, three cases of exemption are particularly well known: the exemption of turban-wearing Sikhs from the requirement to wear a crash helmet if they ride a motorcycle; the exemption of Sikhs from law that prohibits the carrying of knives in public, so that they can carry the kirpan as their faith requires; and the exemption of Jews and Muslims from animal welfare legislation requiring the stunning of animals before slaughter, without which Jews and Muslims would be unable to slaughter animals according to the rites of their religion.

These exemptions do not comport wholly with the model of political toleration that I sketched earlier, in that they are not cases in which the state acts as a third party that lays down rules requiring its citizens to be tolerant of one another. Rather, in these cases the state secures toleration by itself granting the exemption. In relation to Rawls's theory, they are most appropriately seen as cases that arise *within* the basic structure. That is why they typically have an *ad hoc* character. In each case, a particular public policy has been adopted that comes up against a particular demand of a faith and, in each case, adherents of that faith receive an exemption so that they will not be 'burdened' by the policy in ways that others are not.

What justifies our conceiving these exemptions as exercises in toleration? The reasons that justify the policies from which religious groups are exempt are reasons that apply to the exempted groups no less than to other members of the population. Public efforts to prevent head-injuries, reduce knife crime, and avoid unnecessary animal suffering are as relevant to and for Sikhs, Jews, and Muslims as they are for other citizens of the UK. That need not always be true of a public policy that makes an exception. Suppose, for example, that a government commits itself to a campaign of mass vaccination but that it can readily identify members of the population who possess a natural immunity to the disease it is combating. In that case, the government has reason to except those with a natural immunity from its campaign since that exception will in no way conflict with the campaign's purpose: vaccinating people who are already immune would be entirely pointless. In that sort of case, there are no conflicting considerations and nothing that requires toleration. But that is not true of the religious exemptions I have cited. Motorcycling Sikhs, for example, are exempted from wearing crash helmets not because turbans provide the same degree of protection from injury as crash helmets but in spite of the fact that they do not. Similarly, Muslims and Jews are exempted from animal welfare legislation not because concerns for animal welfare do not arise when animals are ritually slaughtered, but in spite the fact that they do. The reasons driving the public policy apply to all but, in the case of Sikhs, Jews, and Muslims, reasons grounded in respect for their beliefs are allowed to override the reasons for the public policy. That is why they constitute 'exemptions' rather than mere 'exceptions'. These exemptions might also seem to have the classic structure of a tolerated condition. The authors of the public policy have reason to object to anyone's not complying with the policy but, out of deference to the beliefs of Sikhs, Jews, and Muslims, they refrain from making those groups comply with the policy.[7]

There is, however, reason to question whether exemptions exhibit that 'classic' tolerant structure. It is clear enough who and what are being tolerated, but who is doing the tolerating? I previously spoke of the 'authors' of the policy from which the religious groups are exempt, but those who first devise the policy are not the only or the most significant party. No less relevant is the government that adopts the policy and the legislature that approves it and turns it into law. But the laws that instantiate the policy and that exempt religious groups from it will remain on the statute books and govern people's conduct long after those who were involved in their drafting and enactment have disappeared from the scene. Once again, the problem of identifying a tolerator arises from use of the person-to-person model of toleration. Rather than viewing exemptions according to that model, we would do better to see them as representing a society's public stance on what should and should not be tolerated. Toleration is a feature of the exemptions themselves rather than an expression of any particular person's or party's toleration. Because the religious groups involved are minorities, it is tempting to say that the exemptions constitute toleration of minorities by the majority. But that is likely to misstate the facts (e.g., how many members of the majority are even aware of the exemptions, and how and when have they bestowed that toleration?) and there is no reason why Sikhs, Jews, and Muslims should not endorse the society's general policy alongside their own exemption. For example, turban-wearing Sikhs can be expected to endorse their own exemption from crash helmet legislation, but they can also endorse the law that requires non-Sikhs to wear crash helmets: they can recognize that, since non-Sikhs do not possess the reason that Sikhs possess for not wearing crash helmets, the balance of considerations applying to non-Sikhs justifies the compulsory wearing of helmets. Similarly, Jews and Muslims can accept that, in the absence of reasons provided by their own faiths, the public policy that requires animals to be stunned before slaughter is entirely justified. Insofar as a population adopts that 'public' perspective, the toleration it secures through exemption fits ill with the imagery of 'vertical' toleration, even though the locus of this form of accommodation is the state rather than civil society.

TOLERATION AND INDIRECT
RELIGIOUS DISCRIMINATION

In Britain the most comprehensive provision for religious accommodation is now legislation governing indirect religious discrimination. British law prohibits both direct and indirect religious discrimination in employment and in the provision of goods and services.[8] If we take the case of employment, an employer discriminates *directly* against an employee if the employer treats that employee less favourably than the employer treats, or would treat, others because of the employee's religion or belief; if, for example, the employer refuses to employ or to promote a Muslim because that person is a Muslim. An employer discriminates *indirectly* against an employee if that employer has a provision, criterion, or practice (PCP) that the employer applies to an actual or potential employee, which disadvantages the employee by comparison with other employees because of the employee's religion or belief. However, an employer is not guilty of indirect discrimination if that employer can show that the application of his PCP is a 'proportionate means of achieving a legitimate aim'. If, for example, a security company required its officers not to leave their place of work during each working day of the working week, that PCP would, prima facie, discriminate indirectly against a Muslim employee who wished to be absent from his place of work during lunchtimes on Fridays so that he could attend a local mosque for Friday prayers. If, however, the security company had a contractual obligation to its client to provide day-long security and would suffer financial penalty if it did not honour that obligation, a tribunal or court might deem the company's PCP requiring the employee to remain on-site a 'proportionate means of achieving a legitimate aim', in which case the company would be not guilty of indirect discrimination.[9]

We might be reluctant to treat the prohibition of *direct* religious discrimination as a requirement of toleration, perhaps because direct religious discrimination seems so obviously wrong, as does direct discrimination on grounds of race, gender, or sexual orientation. But we should remember that the standard case of religious toleration requires people only to refrain from persecuting others because of their religion or from actively impeding the practice of their religion. Prohibiting direct religious discrimination does not seem very far removed from that standard case. However, I shall not press that point since my concern is with toleration and accommodation, and merely refraining from direct discrimination does not entail 'accommodation', as I use that term.

Proscribing *indirect* religious discrimination, by contrast, does entail requiring a form of accommodation. That accommodation differs from the accommodation secured by exemptions in that in discrimination law it is not the state, or the public qua public, that does the accommodating. Rather, the state requires members of civil society—employers and providers of goods and services—to do the accommodating. The relevant accommodation is therefore more straightforwardly 'horizontal' than in the case of exemptions, although civil society includes the government in its role as employer and provider of goods and services. To simplify matters here, I shall focus on the case of employment. The law on indirect religious discrimination requires an employer to accommodate the demands of an employee's religious faith insofar as doing so is consistent with using proportionate means to pursue a legitimate aim. This may involve the employer in a degree of genuine inconvenience and require subordinating his or her own preferred way of running the organization to the demands of an employee's faith. To that extent, it imposes an obligation of toleration upon the employer.

The kind of accommodation that this obligation can entail is well illustrated by the case of *Noah v. Desrosiers.*[10] Sarah Desrosiers ran a small hairdressing salon in London. She described the kind of hairstyling the salon offered as 'funky, spunky and urban'. Bushra Noah was a Muslim and Desrosiers was aware of that when she invited her to attend an interview for a position in the salon. However, during the course of the interview, Desrosiers discovered that Noah would refuse to remove her headscarf, which covered her hair entirely, while she worked in the salon. Desrosiers required her staff to make their own hair visible to customers so that customers could see the sort of styling the salon offered (a practice that is apparently common in hairdressing salons in Britain). For that reason, she did not offer the position to Noah. Noah then registered a complaint of direct and indirect discrimination against the Desrosiers. An Employment Tribunal found Desrosiers not guilty of direct discrimination but guilty of indirect discrimination. In particular, the Tribunal held that Desrosiers's applying to Noah her PCP requiring staff to make their own hair visible to customers did not constitute 'a proportionate means of achieving a legitimate aim'. Thus, in this case, Desrosiers was required to tolerate the demands of Noah's religious faith as Noah herself interpreted them, and the demands of a faith that Desrosiers did not share, to the extent of having to sacrifice her own (not unreasonable) preference about how she should run her salon.

In the eyes of the Employment Tribunal, Desrosiers's application of her PCP to Noah failed to pass the test set by the proportionality criterion. The natural way of understanding 'proportionate' here is with reference to the employer's aim: given the employer's aim and supposing it to be legitimate, what sort of means is proportionate to that aim? In other words, it will be the end that justifies, or fails to justify, the means. Understood in that way, the proportionality criterion sets a simple threshold test: up to that threshold the employer is obliged to accommodate the demands of his employee's faith, but, once the threshold is reached, she is freed from that obligation, even if her failure to accommodate affects the religious employee more adversely than the employer herself. However, tribunals and courts in Britain have often interpreted the proportionality test more expansively: to be proportionate the means must take account of the extent of the PCP's impact upon religious employees, or potential employees, as well of its relation to the employer's aim.[11] That interpretation sets a test that potentially enlarges the domain in which an employer is required to accommodate.

British law allows employers to take account of a 'protected characteristic', including religion or belief, if it is a genuine occupational requirement.
Both 'organized religions' (e.g., churches and mosques) and organizations
with an 'ethos based on religion' (e.g., religious charities and faith schools)
are entitled to discriminate, directly as well as indirectly, on grounds of
religion in employment, provided the religious requirement they apply is an
occupational requirement and a proportionate means of achieving a legitimate
aim (Equality Act 2010, schedule 9, paras. 2 and 3). So, for example, there is
no problem in a church's discriminating on religious grounds in its appointment of a priest or in a mosque's doing so in its appointment of an imam,
although there may well be a problem if either takes account of an applicant's
faith when it appoints a gardener or a cleaner or an accountant.

In addition, 'organized religions' (but not organizations merely with an
'ethos based on religion') have a limited right to discriminate on grounds
of gender, sexual orientation, and marital status.[12] That right clearly ranks
as an 'exemption'. How should we understand it in relation to toleration?
If we take the Catholic Church as our example, from its perspective taking
account of gender, sexual orientation, and marital status in making ecclesiastical appointments may be no different from taking account of a candidate's
faith. It is simply a matter of complying with the doctrines and traditions of
the Catholic Church; gender, for example, is a relevant job qualification for
a Catholic priest, just as plumbing skills are for a prospective plumber and
medical qualifications are for a prospective doctor. But how should these
exemptions be understood from the perspective of public policy? They
might be understood in precisely the same way as they are by the Catholic
Church. Discrimination on grounds of gender, sexual orientation, or marital
status, which would ordinarily be wrong, is rendered right—or at least not
wrong—when it is engaged in for religious reasons. In that case, exempting
the Catholic Church would be like exempting the naturally immune from a
public vaccination campaign; there would be nothing for public policy to tolerate. However, the character of recent British public policy on these forms
of discrimination indicates otherwise. The exemption enjoyed by the Catholic
Church (and other organized religions) is more analogous to exemptions that
allow biking Sikhs not to wear crash helmets and Jews and Muslims not to
stun animals before slaughter. Public policy in Britain now embodies a clear
commitment to the wrongness of discrimination on grounds of gender, sexual
orientation, or marital status. It also embodies a more general commitment
to the equal status of men and women and of heterosexuals and homosexuals. It is committed to giving gays and lesbians equal public recognition,
where 'recognition' means accepting their identity as normal, legitimate,
and unexceptionable. It is similarly committed to rejecting and opposing
treatment of homosexuals that implies that their homosexuality marks them

out as perverse, inferior, or unfortunate. But, where religious beliefs sanction discrimination on grounds of gender or sexual orientation, public policy allows its own commitment to nondiscrimination and equal recognition to be overridden by deference to the beliefs of organized religions. In other words, for public policy the exemptions it grants to organized religions in relation to gender and sexual orientation are exercises in toleration.[13]

That is also indicated by the way in which public policy has tightly limited the religiously inspired discrimination that it is willing to tolerate. Organized religions are not at liberty to discriminate on grounds of sex and sexual orientation in employment merely as they see fit. Discrimination is permitted only if it is needed 'to comply with the doctrines of the religion' or to avoid conflict with 'the strongly held religious convictions of a significant number of the religion's followers' (Equality Act 2010, schedule 9, para. 2). The exemptions are 'intended to cover a very narrow range of employment: ministers of religion and a small number of lay posts, including those that exist to promote and represent religion' (Equality Act 2010: Explanatory Notes, para. 799). The discriminatory requirement must also be 'crucial to the post and not merely one of several important factors' (ibid., para. 800).[14]

The limited extent to which public policy is willing to tolerate religiously inspired discrimination is also indicated by the way in which judicial decisions have prioritized the claims of sexual orientation over those of individual religious believers. Among several cases in which the claims of individual religious belief and sexual orientation have clashed, those of Lillian Ladele and Gary McFarlane are particularly instructive.

Lillian Ladele had worked for the London Borough of Islington since 1992 and became a registrar of births, deaths, and marriages in 2002. The Civil Partnerships Act came into force in 2005, enabling gays and lesbians to enter into legally recognized partnerships. Ladele asked not to be required to officiate at civil-partnership ceremonies, since she believed that actively participating in enabling same-sex unions was contrary to her Christian faith. The Registrar's Office at which she worked stated candidly that it would have no problem in fully employing Ladele in other duties; moreover, other registrar's offices were known to have accommodated requests like Ladele's. Even so, Ladele lost her job because she was unwilling to officiate at civil-partnership ceremonies. She took her case to an Employment Tribunal, claiming direct and indirect discrimination and harassment. The Tribunal found in her favour on all counts.[15] The case then went to an Employment Appeal Tribunal, which overturned the previous ruling and held that the Council was entitled to require all of its registrars to participate in the full range of its services.[16] The Court of Appeal upheld that decision.[17]

Gary McFarlane worked for the relationship counselling service, Relate. Like Ladele, he was a committed Christian and, because of his Christian beliefs, he was unwilling to provide sex therapy for gay and lesbian couples. Relate found his unwillingness contrary to its Equal Opportunities and Professional Ethics policies and dismissed him from his post. McFarlane claimed he had suffered direct and indirect discrimination and unfair dismissal, but the tribunals that heard his case rejected his claim and the Court of Appeal dismissed his application for permission to appeal against their decision.[18]

I cite these cases to illustrate the issues of toleration they present. Of course, a court or tribunal is not itself engaged in decisions about the rights and wrongs of toleration and accommodation. Its task is only to determine what the law requires in cases that come before it, although what the law requires in this area is often far from straightforward. But the existence of these sorts of case obliges legislators, and ultimately the citizens on whose behalf they act, to confront issues that are essentially about how much, and what sort of, toleration people should be able to demand of one another.

The Ladele and McFarlane cases are interestingly complicated in relation to toleration. Was the issue here not one of toleration *simpliciter*, but rather one of whose intolerance should prevail? We might think that the employers' negative response to Ladele's and McFarlane's requests was no more than intolerance of intolerance. Glen Newey (1999) has argued that demands that are ostensibly demands for toleration are typically demands by competing parties for intolerance of the other. Is that true of these cases?

Ladele's and McFarlane's disapproval of same-sex relationships might attract the description 'intolerant', but disapproval is a normal feature of toleration. Toleration consists in not preventing what we disapprove of or dislike. In orthodox usage, if we take no exception to the conduct that we refrain from preventing, our nonprevention does not constitute toleration. But Ladele and McFarlane did not merely disapprove; they acted on the principles and beliefs that underlay their disapproval. Should that earn them the description 'intolerant'? We would not normally describe someone as intolerant merely in virtue of their refraining from doing what they believe to be wrong. For example, we would not normally describe as 'intolerant' a vegetarian's refraining from eating meat, or a Muslim's insisting on attending Friday prayers, or a Catholic doctor's refusal to perform an abortion, or a conscientious objector's refusal to fight in a war, even though others may wish those individuals to behave differently. If we are intolerant merely in virtue of not behaving as others wish us to, toleration turns into nonsense. The Christian would be intolerant for not complying with the Muslim's wish that the Christian should convert to Islam, and the Muslim would be intolerant for not complying with the Christian's wish that the Muslim should convert to Christianity (see further, chapter 1).

There is, however, a further consideration. Had Ladele's and McFarlane's request for exemptions been granted, that might have adversely affected the opportunities of others. In fact, in the case of Ladele, sufficient registrars were available to take her place in officiating at civil-partnership ceremonies and she could have been fully employed on other tasks of her post. McFarlane too claimed that it was entirely practicable for Relate to exempt him from counselling same-sex couples.[19] However, had enough registrars and enough counsellors requested and received the exemptions that Ladele and McFarlane sought, the opportunities of same-sex couples to enter into civil partnerships and to receive sex therapy might have been seriously diminished. It would be odd if we accounted people's conduct tolerant or intolerant according to the contingencies of circumstance, so that they were 'intolerant' if circumstances were such that, in remaining faithful to their convictions, people just happened to diminish the options available to others, and they were 'not intolerant' if circumstances conspired to preclude any adverse effect for others. It is intentions rather than consequences that mark people out as tolerant or intolerant. Someone who intends to impede another's conduct behaves intolerantly even if that person fails in his or her aim; and someone who unintentionally impedes another's conduct is not intolerant in spite of the impediment he or she actually causes.

Another consideration is that Ladele and McFarlane occupied professional roles. Normally we would think that the demands of toleration are satisfied by restraint rather than positive assistance—it is enough that we refrain from preventing what we object to; we need not positively promote it. But if employees occupy a role in which they are tasked with providing a service for others and if they withhold that service, their act of withholding can reasonably count as intolerance.

However, Ladele and McFarlane might have met these points by protesting that they sought exemption only insofar as that was consistent with their organization's continuing to provide a full service to all of its clients, including same-sex couples. If their exemption would really have impeded the delivery of services, they would have recognized the unreasonableness of that state of affairs and have been willing to resign from their posts. If that was their position, so that they did not seek to prevent the activities from which they wished to be exempt, their requests for exemption would not qualify as intolerant. A gay man and a lesbian work colleague did claim to have been 'victimized' and 'discriminated against' by Ladele and those two individuals played a leading role in securing her dismissal; but their complaint seems to have been only that Ladele's unwillingness to officiate at civil partnerships constituted an 'act of homophobia'.[20]

If Ladele and McFarlane were not themselves being intolerant, what could justify the law's intolerance of their belief-based wishes? It is here that the claims of toleration come up against those of recognition. In *Ladele* the Employment Appeal Tribunal and the Court of Appeal treated as irrelevant the fact that Ladele's wish could be accommodated without impairing the service the Council provided for civil partnerships. Ladele was requesting an exemption for a discriminatory reason and her request was contrary to Islington's Dignity for All policy; that sufficed to make the Council's treatment of Ladele proportionate.[21] Similarly McFarlane lost his case because his request to be exempt from giving sex therapy to same-sex couples amounted to discrimination against gays and lesbians, which was in direct conflict with Relate's equal opportunities policy. In *Ladele*, there was also argument, endorsed by the Court of Appeal, that the Council was legally obliged *not* to accommodate Ladele's wish.[22] The sum of all this is that the exemptions requested by Ladele and McFarlane were found intolerable not—or not only—because they were liable to reduce the opportunities actually open to gay men and lesbians. They were intolerable because they were an affront to gay men and lesbians; they were at odds with the equal status and the equal respect to which gays were entitled. It is in that sense that public policy prioritized the claims of the gay community to recognition over those of religious adherents to toleration.

But, if that is the legal position with respect to religious individuals, why is it not also the position with respect to organized religions? Why should public policy tolerate the wishes of some, but not of others, to discriminate against gays for religious reasons? The answer would appear to lie in a balancing of competing considerations—a balance of a sort that we frequently confront when we have to set the boundary that divides the tolerable from the intolerable. There are many forms of employment in which those who have religious objections to homosexual conduct need encounter no conflict between their religious convictions and their legal obligation not to discriminate on grounds of sexual orientation. Many such employment options were open to Ladele and McFarlane, so that not permitting them to discriminate in their roles as, respectively, registrar and counsellor did not compel them to compromise their religious convictions. Similarly, religious organizations that do not have clear doctrinal obligations to discriminate on grounds of gender or sexual orientation are not compelled to betray their beliefs by being prevented from practising those forms of discrimination. By contrast, if the doctrine of an organized religion requires it not to have female or sexually active homosexual priests or imams, a law requiring it not to discriminate on grounds of sex and sexual orientation in appointing priests and imams would prevent it from complying with its own doctrine. That would be a serious infringement of its religious freedom and would almost certainly contravene Article 9 of the ECHR. So, although there is an element of compromise in the way British public policy has dealt with the conflicting claims of religious belief and sexual orientation, there is a rationale for the particular compromise that it has adopted. That is not to say that the compromise upon which it has settled is uncontroversially 'right'. For example, discrimination law does not condone gender or racial disadvantage in employment on the ground that the employees who are the victims of that disadvantage have many other jobs open to them in which they would suffer no such disadvantage. Ladele and McFarlane might therefore ask why, when they suffer disadvantage because of their religious beliefs, it should fall to them to avoid that disadvantage by finding another job.

CONCLUSION

I conclude, then, that issues of religious accommodation present us with issues of toleration and issues that we cannot plausibly pronounce 'dead'. People's reluctance to conceive issues as issues of toleration often stems from their belief that toleration must entail an unequal relationship between tolerator and tolerated and that toleration itself must be a form of condescension, a matter of grace and favour (e.g., Addis 1996; Brown 2006; Phillips 1999). I cannot refute that belief here, so I simply observe that both of its elements are false. Toleration can be mutual and equal, and it can be grounded in deontological reasons such as respect for persons. Indeed, as Rawls argues, it can be a matter of right and a requirement of justice.

Would it be more appropriate in contemporary circumstances to characterize the issues I have examined here as issues of 'cultural' rather than religious difference? Most of the cases I have considered could be characterized as issues of cultural accommodation,[23] but polyethnic societies do not typically treat all aspects of culture as having the same claim to accommodation. In the cases I have considered, the conduct that has been eligible for accommodation is rule-governed conduct rather than merely habitual conduct; it is conduct that people understand themselves to be obligated to engage in or to refrain from. The degree to which the accommodation of a group's culture in European societies turns out to be accommodation of its religion is striking and is, I believe, no accident, since it is people's believing themselves to be normatively not at liberty to behave or not to behave in certain ways that is so often crucial to the case for accommodation (Jones 2015b). I see no good reason, therefore, to pretend that the differences that have been my concern are other than religious differences, particularly since the religious do not see themselves in other terms.

At the same time, my argument about the relationship between toleration and accommodation does not apply only to religious belief. It applies equally to cases in which the different and conflicting beliefs are moral but nonreligious in character.[24] It is worth recalling in this connection that Article 9 of the ECHR accords people freedom of thought and conscience as well as religion, and that British discrimination law applies to 'belief' as well as to religion, although what sort of nonreligious belief counts as 'belief' for purposes of discrimination law the courts have still largely to settle.[25]

Just as I have not substituted the language of culture for that of religious belief, so I have not couched my argument in the language of 'identity'. 'Identity' is too undiscriminating a notion. It cannot begin to explain why polyethnic or multifaith societies do, or why they should, accommodate some practices and not others. And there is another way in which the notion of (mere) identity seems inadequate for the issue of religious accommodation. On many occasions, religion does serve merely as a marker of identity in the same way as does race or ethnicity or sexuality or occupation or class. Indeed, bloody conflicts in religiously divided societies often seem to owe more to differences in identity than to differences of belief. Moreover, where religion is a mere marker of identity, where it is only 'skin deep', toleration can seem as inappropriate as it is in cases of racial difference. But, in cases of religious accommodation, belief matters. In all three of the forms of accommodation I have considered—exemptions, Article 9 of the ECHR, and the law on indirect religious discrimination—people's *believing* that certain forms of conduct are required of them is crucial to the existence, and to the case for, accommodation. If the relevant population did not hold different and conflicting beliefs, the need for accommodation would not arise, and it is because these accommodations cater for different and conflicting beliefs that they present us with *bona fide* issues of toleration.[26]

NOTES

1. I set out and defend this view of liberal democratic toleration at greater length in chapter 1.

2. *Copsey v. WWB Devon Clays Ltd*, [2004] UKEAT/0438/03/SM; [2005] EWCA Civ 932. The Court of Appeal's judgment in this case is particularly interesting in relation to accommodation. While all three judges found against Copsey (the employee), they expressed different views on the degree of accommodation Article 9 requires of employers.

3. *Ahmad v Inner London Education Authority*, Employment Appeal Tribunal: [1976] ICR 461; Court of Appeal: [1978] 1 QB 36; [1977] 3 WLR 396. I examine this case in Jones (1994).

4. *Begum v Denbigh High School*, [2004] EWHC 1389 (Admin); [2005] EWCA Civ 199; [2006] UKHL 15. A subsequent and similar case concerned the right of a twelve-year-old Muslim schoolgirl to wear a niqab contrary to her school's uniform policy: *X (by her father and litigation friend) v. The Headteachers and Governors of Y School*, [2007] EWHC 298 (Admin).

5. *R (Playfoot) (A Minor) v. Governing Body of Millais School*, [2007] EWHC 1698 (Admin).

6. *Davender Kumar Ghai v. Newcastle City Council* [2009] EWHC 978 (Admin); [2010] EWCA Civ 59.

7. The case of Sikhs' exemption from the law prohibiting the carrying of knives in public is not so clear. The toleration required in this case might be thought all the greater, since the potential consequences for others (being stabbed and possibly killed) are so much more severe. On the other hand, the aim of the law is to prevent knifings and therefore to prevent those people carrying knives who intend to use them, or who are liable to use them, to harm others. People who carry knives for innocent reasons are not the law's target; the legislation that exempts people who carry knives for religious reasons also exempts those who do so for reasons related to their work, and those for whom knives are part of their national dress (e.g., Scotsmen wearing Highland dress, which includes a dirk inserted into a sock). So the general spirit of the law is that people should not carry knives in public unless they have good reason to do so. Read in that way, the 'exemption' enjoyed by Sikhs is more like an exemption enjoyed by the naturally immune from compulsory vaccination and makes no call upon toleration.

8. In Britain, legislation governing religious discrimination in relation to employment was introduced in the Employment Equality (Religion or Belief) Regulations 2003, in response to an EU Directive establishing a general framework for equal treatment in employment and occupation (Council Directive 2000/78/EC). Legislation prohibiting religious discrimination in the provision of goods and services was included in the Equality Act 2006. Both sorts of regulation were incorporated in the Equality Act 2010, which harmonized the law governing discrimination in relation to a number of 'protected characteristics' including disability, race, gender, and sexual orientation, as well as religion or belief.

9. This example is based on *Cherfi v. G4S Security Services Ltd* [2011] UKEAT/0379/10/DM, in which the Muslim employee's claim of indirect discrimination was dismissed. Two other important features of that case were that a prayer room was available to the employee at his place of work, and the company offered him the option (which he declined) of working on Saturdays or Sundays instead of Fridays.

10. My account of this case is based on details given in *Noah v. Desrosiers* [2008], (unreported) judgment of the Employment Tribunal, case number 2201867/2007. I examine the general issues raised by the case in Jones (2015a).

11. For example, ibid., para. 160: 'the function of the legislation, in its application to indirect discrimination, is to outlaw particular means of pursuing what may be found, in principle, to be entirely legitimate aims, *because of their disproportionately discriminatory impact*' (my emphasis). In addition, Lucy Vickers (2010, 289, 295–96) has suggested that the number of individuals affected by a requirement might be taken into account in assessing proportionality, as might the issue of whether a belief is, or is not, core to the believer's faith, although courts have not been consistent on that issue.

12. In addition, 'organizations relating to religion or belief' are permitted to restrict their memberships and those to whom they provide goods and services on grounds

of sexual orientation as well as religion, provided such restrictions are necessary to comply with the organization's doctrines or to avoid conflict with the strongly held convictions of a significant number of the religion's or belief's followers (Equality Act 2010, schedule 23, para. 2).

13. Anna Elisabetta Galeotti (2002) has argued that recognition can be itself a form of toleration. However, if by 'toleration' we mean enduring what we view negatively (the sense in which I use the term in this article), recent British public policy in relation to homosexuality has been committed to combating the negativity that toleration presupposes, so that the recognition it directs towards the gay population has been quite different from toleration. Indeed, one might say that public policy has sought to substitute recognition for toleration. For more general reservations about the possibility of combining recognition with toleration, see chapter 7.

14. For analysis and comment on the law now relating to who may and who may not discriminate on grounds of religion, including in respect of gender and sexual orientation, see Sandberg (2011a, 117–28), and Sandberg (2011b, 173–80).

15. *Lillian Ladele v. London Borough of Islington* [2008], (unreported) judgment of the Employment Tribunal, case number 2203694/2007.

16. *Ladele v. London Borough of Islington*, [2008] UKEAT/0453/08/RN.

17. *Ladele v. London Borough of Islington*, [2009] EWCA Civ 1357. For discussion of *Ladele*, see Vickers (2010).

18. *Gary McFarlane v. Relate Avon Ltd*, [2009] UKEAT 0106/09/DA; [2010] EWCA Civ 880. The facts and the legal considerations relating to *Ladele* and *McFarlane* were complicated and I use the cases here only to highlight the issues of toleration they raise; I do not pretend to give a full and fair account of all the factors that bore on them.

19. Relate disputed McFarlane's claim that it was practicable to exempt him from same-sex therapy, although the organization's main claim was that his exemption would be unacceptable in principle rather than merely inconvenient in practice. [2009] UKEAT 0106/09/3011, paras. 25, 26, 29.

20. *Ladele* [2009] EWCA Civ 1357, para. 40. In fact Ladele's objection was not directed only at homosexual relations. She held it a sin for sexual relations to take place outside marriage; [2008] UKEAT/0453/08/RN, para. 3. Two fellow employees of Ladele also objected to officiating at civil partnerships. One accepted the offer of different employment by the Council. The other, a Muslim, left the Council's service. [2009] UKEAT/ 0453/08/RN, para. 6.

21. [2008] UKEAT/0453/08/RN, paras. 95–117; [2009] EWCA Civ 1357, paras. 43–53.

22. [2008] UKEAT/0453/08/RN paras. 102–7; [2009] EWCA Civ 1357, paras. 62–75.

23. It might then become relevant that both Ladele and McFarlane are members of the British Afro-Caribbean community and that their evangelical Christianity has strong roots in that community.

24. I believe it, for example, to be consistent with the claims of 'self-legislation' (as opposed to 'divine legislation') that Emanuela Ceva examines in Ceva (2010).

25. One case in which this issue has arisen is *Grainger PLC and others v. Nicholson*, [2009] UKEAT/0219/07/ZT. In that case, the judge ruled that a belief

in man-made climate change, and the moral imperatives arising from that belief, did qualify as a 'philosophical belief' for purposes of the 2003 Religion or Belief Employment Regulations.

26. This chapter draws on a paper presented to a conference held in July 2010 at the University of Copenhagen on 'Toleration, Respect and Space—Concepts, Conceptions and Applications', which formed part of the RESPECT Research programme, and on another paper presented in May 2011 to a conference on Toleration organized by the Political Theory Group of the Irish Political Studies Association. I am grateful to the participants in both events for their comments on those papers. Special thanks to Ian Carter, Emanuela Ceva, Elisabetta Galeotti, Iseult Honohan, Sune Laegaard, Andrew Shorten, and to the *European Journal of Philosophy*'s referees.

REFERENCES

Addis, A. (1996), 'On Human Diversity and the Limits of Toleration'. In I. Shapiro and W. Kymlicka, eds., *Ethnicity and Group Rights*, 112–53. New York: New York University Press.

Ahdar, R., and Leigh, I. (2005). *Religious Freedom in the Liberal State*. Oxford: Oxford University Press.

Brown, W. (2006). *Regulating Aversion: Tolerance in the Age of Identity and Empire*. Princeton, NJ: Princeton University Press.

Ceva, E. (2010). 'Self-Legislation, Respect and the Reconciliation of Minority Claims'. *Journal of Applied Philosophy* 28:14–28.

Doe, N. (2011). *Law and Religion in Europe: A Comparative Introduction*. Oxford: Oxford University Press.

Galeotti, A. E. (2002). *Toleration as Recognition*. Cambridge: Cambridge University Press.

Heyd, D. (2008). 'Is Toleration a Political Virtue?'. In M. Williams and J. Waldron, eds., *Toleration and its Limits, Nomos XLVIII*, 171–94. New York: New York University Press.

Jones, P. (1994). 'Bearing the Consequences of Belief', *Journal of Political Philosophy* 2:24–43.

——— (2015a). 'Belief, Autonomy and Responsibility: The Case of Indirect Religious Discrimination'. In G. B. Levey, ed., *Authenticity, Autonomy and Multiculturalism*, 66–85. London: Routledge.

——— (2015b). 'Liberty, Equality, and Accommodation'. In T. Modood and V. Uberoi, eds., *Multiculturalism Rethought: Interpretations, Dilemmas and New Directions*, 126–56. Edinburgh: Edinburgh University Press.

Newey, G. (1999). *Virtue, Reason and Toleration: The Place of Toleration in Ethical and Political Philosophy*. Edinburgh: Edinburgh University Press.

Nussbaum, M. C. (2008), *Liberty of Conscience: In Defense of America's Tradition of Religious Equality*. New York: Basic Books.

Phillips, A. (1999). 'The Politicisation of Difference: Does This Make for a More Intolerant Society?'. In J. Horton and S. Mendus, eds., *Toleration, Identity and Difference*, 126–45. Basingstoke: Macmillan.

Rawls, J. (1993). *Political Liberalism*. New York: Columbia University Press.

Sandberg, R. (2011a). *Law and Religion*. Cambridge: Cambridge University Press.

———— (2011b). 'The Right to Discriminate'. *Ecclesiastical Law Journal* 13:157–81.

Vickers, L. (2008). *Religious Freedom, Religious Discrimination and the Workplace*. Oxford: Hart.

———— (2010). 'Religious Discrimination in the Workplace: An Emerging Hierarchy?'. *Ecclesiastical Law Journal* 12:280–303.

Williams, B. (1996). 'Toleration: An Impossible Virtue?'. In D. Heyd, ed., *Toleration: An Elusive Virtue*, 18–27. Princeton, NJ: Princeton University Press.

Chapter 5

Beliefs and Identities

In this chapter I examine the relationship between beliefs and identities. More particularly, I examine how interpreting beliefs as expressions of identity affects the status of beliefs, the conduct of democratic politics, and the standing of freedom of belief and freedom of expression. The relationship between beliefs and identities is a complex one.

Beliefs do not contribute uniformly to people's identities and some of their beliefs may contribute little or nothing to their sense of who they are. Their beliefs about the depth of the earth's crust or about how best to fillet a trout are unlikely to shape people's identities—at least not in our world. Other beliefs may assume great importance for people's self-conceptions. The most prominent candidates are religious, moral, and political beliefs. Beliefs about the past, particularly a past that people understand as 'their' past, may also be significant for their identities. So too may be their beliefs about the nonhuman world and about how we relate, or should relate, to it. It is not easy to state simply what it is that makes some beliefs more significant for identities than others, but clearly one factor is the impact that beliefs have upon the lives of their holders. Beliefs, such as religious and moral beliefs, which give shape and direction to people's lives, will generally have more significance for their identities than beliefs which are merely 'academic' in that they have no impact upon how people live or upon how they relate to others. Another factor which has significance for the impact of beliefs on identity is the social context in which they occur. The very notion of identity is a social one and it is social in at least two ways. First, our identity is a matter of how we stand in relation to others—of how we see ourselves in relation to others and how we are seen by them. Second, what has significance for our identity is usually socially defined. For example, in contemporary Western societies hair colour has no significance for people's identities, but skin colour might. But those

93

different significances are not fixed features of the world and it is possible to imagine a world in which they were reversed. Thus, what has significance for people's identities—including which, if any, of their beliefs—may vary from one society to another and, within the same society, from one time to another. The very significance of 'identity' is itself contingent upon social circumstances. People will be more conscious of, and more concerned about, their identities if they are aware of and have contact with others who seem significantly different from themselves than if they appear to be members of a largely undifferentiated population.

That relates to a third factor affecting a belief's significance for identity: group membership. A belief may be held by an individual qua individual with no sense of its being a belief shared with others. It may also be that belief contributes significantly to an individual's self-conception entirely as an individual. But the kind of belief that is significant for a person's identity is much more likely to be one which is shared with others and its greater significance is to be explained partly by its being shared with others. Identity is commonly a matter of belonging, of being defined by one's membership of a group or community. For that reason, a belief-based identity is likely to be much more imposing where it assumes a group form.

One prominent way in which beliefs take this group form is when they are constituents of cultures. 'Culture' is a generous term—perhaps too generous, for it is typically used to encompass a great variety of phenomena which are of very diverse character. Much of what is included in cultures, such as diet, dress, or music, may have no epistemic content. But cultures also typically include beliefs. Indeed, a set of beliefs, rather than merely being included in a culture, may stand at its centre and provide it with the coherence that cultures are commonly supposed to possess, so that even matters such as diet, dress, and music may be informed by beliefs.

Beliefs, then, like gender or race or language or sexuality, can contribute significantly to people's identities. However, beliefs have dimensions which those other sources of identity do not. Beliefs are capable of being true or false, right or wrong, well-informed or ill-informed, whereas none of these descriptions applies to race or gender or language. People can also change their beliefs whereas they can do nothing to change their ethnic origins and can change their gender or race only by going to extraordinary lengths. For those reasons, belief-based identities give rise to issues which do not normally arise in relation to other forms of identity, and it is those issues that I shall examine in this chapter.

In particular, I want to consider something that I shall call 'the identity argument'. That argument holds that we should recognize that certain of people's beliefs are central to their identities and that, accordingly, we should approach those beliefs primarily or exclusively as expressions of identity. We should value and respect people's identities which, in turn, requires that we should not impugn or seek to undermine those identities. Thus, in so far as people's identities are based on their beliefs, we should refrain from treating those beliefs in ways which disrespect or threaten the identities of their holders.[1]

I shall also include within this identity argument a commitment to treating people's different identities with equal respect. By that I mean only a commitment to respecting no identity less than any other. If the notion of equal respect seems too aggressively Kantian, we might substitute a commitment to showing equal care and concern in the way that we respond to people's identities. That commitment is likely to be limited in some way. Given the vast range of identities that people do, and might, present, it would be hard to take seriously an unqualified assertion that we should accord equal and indiscriminate respect to all identities. At the very least, we have a problem with people whose self-conception involves their being superior to others; we cannot simultaneously insist on the equal status of all identities and acknowledge the superiority of some identities over others. Identity politics does not therefore provide an easy escape for those fleeing from universalism to particularism. I shall not grapple with the question of how we should discriminate between acceptable and unacceptable identities here; in what follows, I shall simply suppose that the particular beliefs and identities that we confront fall within the limits of the 'acceptable' however that might be defined.

Some of what I say will be no more than an attempt to work through the implications of the identity argument as it applies to beliefs. But I do not pretend to present an entirely detached analysis of this question, since my interest in it arises largely from my worries about the implications of the identity argument for beliefs. I shall use religious beliefs as my primary examples since it is those beliefs that people seem to fasten on most readily as expressions of identity. However, as I have already indicated, religious belief is only one of many sorts of belief which may claim significance for a person's identity and what I say is intended to apply to any kind of belief which is thought relevant for a person's or a group's identity.

FROM BELIEFS TO IDENTITIES OR FROM IDENTITIES TO BELIEFS?

For the most part, I shall suppose that the linkage between beliefs and identities runs from beliefs to identities. However, I must start by noticing the possibility that the relationship might run in the opposite direction: that it may not be people's beliefs that give rise to their identities but rather their identities that lead them to hold particular beliefs. Social psychologists have long observed the 'expressive' function that beliefs and opinions might serve. People are sometimes induced to adopt a belief or opinion because that belief or opinion is linked to their self-conception or to an identity which they wish to possess. They might, for example, embrace a belief or espouse an opinion because they conceive it as appropriate to people who are 'enlightened' or 'radical' or 'solid' or 'sensible' or 'patriotic'.[2]

The psychological processes at work here may run more or less deeply. At the most superficial level, the adoption of opinions because of their association with a favoured identity may be little more than disingenuous posturing. People sometimes seem to choose their opinions as they choose their clothes—merely as ways of presenting themselves to others.

At the other extreme, preoccupation with an identity may be enough to cause someone to be genuinely committed to a belief, even though the origins of that commitment lie in their preoccupation with the identity rather than in the perceived intrinsic merit of the belief they adopt.

I concede that the mechanisms at work here may not be easily separable into cause and effect. For example, someone's commitment to an identity may stem from their commitment to certain fundamental beliefs or values so that, when they endorse a particular belief because of its association with an identity, ultimately that endorsement can be linked back to the fundamental beliefs which underlie the identity. That, for example, may often be true of the dynamics of political belief and political identity. Relying on an identity may then be an economical strategy for settling upon the 'right' opinion. On the other hand, people can also be observed favouring an identity for social reasons such as peer group pressure, so that beliefs adopted for reasons of identity cannot always claim a foundation that is ultimately epistemic.

Where the relationship between identities and beliefs runs from identities to beliefs, it would seem a relationship which we should discourage rather than one to which we should pander. Surely we want people to hold beliefs because they possess genuine convictions about their content and not because they wish to project a favoured identity or a fashionable image of themselves. When, for example, we confront questions of public policy, such as which measures will most successfully reduce crime or secure world peace or conserve the natural environment, we want people to address seriously the issues involved in those questions. We do not want public decision making to be used merely as an occasion for projecting an image or displaying an identity. We do not want that because, at best, it would be a form of self-deception and, at worst, a form of pretence. We want questions of public policy to be confronted and to be answered as questions of public policy and not as if they were merely opportunities for people to fashion themselves in the eyes of others.

I take it that, generally, when people take seriously the link between beliefs and identities, they suppose that it is beliefs that inform identities rather than identities which manipulate beliefs. In what follows, I shall assume that the beliefs with which we are concerned are deep and genuine and that they constitute the parents rather than the children of identities.

BELIEFS, EMBEDDEDNESS, AND CHOICE

In recent political philosophy, much attention has been paid to the nature of the self and its relation to its ends. Critics of liberalism have complained that philosophers, such as Rawls, conceive the self as separable from its ends in ways that are quite implausible.[3] Individuals' selves, contend the critics, cannot be so devoid of content, nor should we suppose that selves can choose their own make-up; individuals' identities are given rather than chosen. Much of this criticism of liberal thinking is misplaced,[4] but the general question of how far people have control over their own make-up may seem central to the issues with which I am concerned here. How we should respond to belief-based identities may seem to turn on whether those identities are chosen or unchosen features of their possessors.

How far people have, or can have, an active role in relation to their identities is a complicated matter. In so far as it is an empirical matter (and it does not always seem to be that), the answer is likely to vary for different people, for different circumstances and for different elements of identity. The idea of the entirely self-made person has to be a fiction if only because there must be a prior un-self-made self that creates the self-made self, and it is hard to see how that self-made self could owe nothing to the un-self-made self that generated it. There are also features of an individual's identity, such as gender and ethnicity, that are by their very nature given rather than adopted.

Beliefs are more complicated. They do not have a straightforwardly 'given' character—we do not emerge from the womb with beliefs—but the language of choice is still questionable when it is used of beliefs.

For one thing, people often absorb beliefs from the social and cultural context in which they develop in a manner which confounds claims that they have, in any real sense, chosen those beliefs. For another, people cannot simply choose what to believe in the way that they might choose what to do with their money or choose what to do with their spare time. They cannot choose what to believe because they can believe only what appears to them to be the case. Thus, even when beliefs are arrived at consciously and reflectively, it misrepresents that process to describe it as an individual's 'choosing' what to believe.[5]

On the other hand, to deny that beliefs are chosen is not to claim that people can have no active role in the formation of their beliefs. People can and do reflect critically on their beliefs, they can pursue lines of inquiry, investigate this or that aspect of their current beliefs, forsake or modify old beliefs, take up new beliefs, and so on. Beliefs cannot therefore be regarded as fixed features of people which have been irremediably planted in their heads by circumstances. That is why it can make sense to hold people responsible for what they believe, even though it would make no sense to hold them similarly responsible for their gender or their ethnic origins.

Beliefs may then be more malleable features of people's identities than other features of their make-up. Even so, it might be thought that, as soon as we begin to use the language of identity, that gives greater and possibly exclusive significance to those beliefs which are given and fixed features of persons. The language of identity, it might be supposed, points us towards ideas of the embedded self, associated with communitarians such as Sandel and MacIntyre, and away from beliefs which are the products of people's conscious reflection. However, I can see no good reason why the concerns expressed in the identity argument must be associated with communitarian ideas of the embedded self. Beliefs which people acquire or revise during adulthood may be no less important for their identities merely because those beliefs have not been permanent parts of their make-up.[6] Is there any reason to think that Christianity or Islam must be less crucial to the identity of a person merely because that person is a convert to, rather than someone born within, that faith? Even if we were to allow that people's beliefs could be chosen, so that at least part of their identity could also be chosen, it would not follow that those chosen identities should command less by way of concern and respect from us. If we should respect people's choices—particularly choices that are fundamental to their ways of life—it is arguable that people's identities are no less morally significant or worthy of respect for being chosen. It is even arguable that features of persons that are the offspring of their considered judgements are, for that reason, all the more deserving of respect.

Thus, the issue of how far people's beliefs, and therefore their belief-related identities, can be said to be given is not as crucial to the identity argument as it might seem at first sight. However, if I am mistaken in holding this, the implications for the identity argument are far from simple for, as I have already observed, people stand to their beliefs in a variety of relations depending upon their circumstance and upon features of their personal make-up, so that the appropriate response to belief-related identities will be not be open to simple generalization.

THE VALUE OF IDENTITY

If people's beliefs do shape their identities, why should that matter? How is that morally significant? Two basic forms of answer follow the familiar distinction between the right and the good.

In a Kantian spirit we might hold that, if people's beliefs are constituents of their very selves, respecting them as persons must entail respecting the beliefs that are intrinsic to their identities. We cannot simultaneously respect a person but have no respect for that person's beliefs for there can be no gap between a person and what that person believes. Thus, the general injunction 'respect persons' must entail the more specific injunction 'respect their beliefs'.[7] Although I have formulated this argument in the language of persons, this Kantian mode of thinking can be applied equally to groups and to group-beliefs.

Alternatively, we might focus not on the deontological demands of personhood but upon the demands of personal well-being. Having a secure sense of identity and receiving the respect of others for that identity is often reckoned essential to people's self-esteem and their general psychological well-being. No one can flourish if their society regards their identity with derision and contempt. Thus, if people's beliefs are essential to their identity, respecting their beliefs can be deemed essential to maintaining and promoting their well-being.[8]

I shall not attempt to choose between these two forms of argument, partly because that choice turns upon more fundamental issues concerning the relative standings of these two sorts of ethic. But either would seem to provide strong reason for showing concern and respect for the beliefs of others.

Before proceeding, however, we should notice that each form of argument might be turned around and used to opposite effect. For example, if we have to treat beliefs as integral to persons, perhaps that means that the Kantian conception of the person should lose its immunity. If persons cannot be conceived independently of their beliefs, the standing of individuals might then have to be geared to the standing of their beliefs. If we rightly regard some beliefs as ridiculous, contemptible, or evil, perhaps we also rightly regard their holders as ridiculous, contemptible, or evil. If we cannot separate the sin from the sinner, perhaps in hating the sin we must also hate the sinner. A strong identification of persons with beliefs need not therefore be benign in its implications—as the history of persecution illustrates only too well.

Similarly, although, other things being equal, it is better that people's well-being should be promoted rather than frustrated, things may be regarded as far from equal if their well-being relies upon the maintenance of beliefs that are false or pernicious. People may be thought to have no right to have their well-being promoted in so far as that requires us to collude in the maintenance of false or pernicious beliefs. Alternatively, it might be argued that a genuine state of well-being cannot rest upon beliefs which are evil or erroneous; people cannot really flourish on the basis of unsatisfactory identities. So, if we have an obligation to promote people's well-being and if we confront someone with false beliefs, we must begin by transforming their beliefs and so transforming their identity.

Thus, the integration of beliefs into identities does not necessarily mean that people's beliefs find an inviolable sanctuary within their identities. It might mean, on the contrary, that their identities acquire all the vulnerabilities of their beliefs, although I shall not pursue that possibility any further in this chapter.

BELIEFS AND THE POLITICS OF IDENTITY

If we conceive diverse beliefs as so many diverse identities, how should a society respond to that diversity? If we work from the assumption that those different identities should be recognized rather than ignored or suppressed, we seem to have two options.

One might be described as the private option. As far as possible, beliefs of the relevant sort should be placed outside the domain of public decision. Provision should be made for individuals or groups to live according to their own beliefs and that should be achieved by treating the subject matter of their beliefs as something to be dealt with privately by each of them. 'Private' is a word with a variety of nuances. The strategy described here would be 'private' only in that the relevant matters would not be subjects of public decision. The strategy does not require that statements of belief, and the forms of life based upon them, must be kept from the ears and eyes of those who do not share them. This privatizing strategy is therefore quite compatible with individuals' manifesting their beliefs in public. The beliefs are treated as private only in that they are excluded from the arena of public decision. The other strategy may be described as the public option. Beliefs should be expressed in and decided on in the arena of public decision making. People should state their own beliefs and argue about the merits of others' beliefs in the public forum and ultimately decisions should be taken which constitute public judgements upon those matters of belief.

The private strategy might be described as the 'liberal' option and the public strategy as the 'democratic' option and I shall use those terms in that way. I readily concede that these crude usages do not do justice to the complex meanings of 'liberal' and 'democratic' but they will suffice for my purposes.

Many recent writers have urged a shift from liberal to more democratic ways of dealing with plurality.[9] Rather than coping with diversity by removing it from the public domain so that each group can follow its own path, the prescription has been that diversity should manifest itself in the public sphere and be dealt with there. One reason for this shift has been a growing scepticism about the possibility of lighting on a principle setting the terms of a public/private division which will be equally acceptable to all groups of believers or which can properly claim to be neutral amongst all beliefs. Perhaps, therefore, rather than providing for conflicting beliefs by keeping them out of the democratic process, the conflicting demands of those beliefs should be negotiated within that process. Another reason has been the sense that shuffling certain beliefs into the private sphere devalues and discriminates against them. Excluding some matters of belief from the public arena is sometimes thought to endow them with a second-class status (even though the opposite might also be inferred from that exclusion).

But how will things appear if we treat beliefs as expressions of identity? In spite of the trend of current thinking, that conception of beliefs seems, in the first instance, to call for a liberal rather than a democratic response. It does so in two ways.

First, in so far as beliefs enter the public arena and become subject to public decision, people's identities will be subject to public endorsement or public rejection. This public discrimination between identities, in which some groups find their beliefs formally approved while others find their beliefs formally repudiated in public decision making, is hardly consonant with the principle of respecting identities equally. The best way of avoiding this public approval or public repudiation of people's identities would seem to consist in keeping their beliefs out of the public arena to the maximum possible extent.

Secondly, if the relevant beliefs are merely different manifestations of identity, it is hard to see how they can provide a foundation for authentically 'public' decision making. Expressions of belief will be merely so many declarations of identity which hold no promise of providing a common foundation for public discussion. If people are going to address issues and reach decisions in a genuinely public manner, they must possess something in common as a public. Clearly, that 'something in common' cannot be found in people's distinct identities—except in so far as their identities happen to overlap.

So the optimal strategy (if it is an eligible strategy) for safeguarding the integrity of each group's identity would seem to lie in ring-fencing the area of life to which their beliefs relate so that, within that area, each group can conduct its own life in its own way. This privatizing strategy does not have to be an individualist strategy. Certainly, within liberal thinking the privatizing of beliefs has commonly been achieved by way of individual rights. On the relevant matters, each individual has been accorded a right to act as his or her beliefs require. Institutionally, those rights have typically been conceived as immunities. They remove authority over the relevant areas of life from the public domain so that individuals are free to determine those matters for themselves rather than be subject to the power of others. However, that is not the only way in which beliefs may be privatized.

An alternative strategy is to provide for the sort of arrangement that Lijphart calls 'segmental autonomy'.[10] That is, decision making relevant to beliefs may be devolved upon groups of believers, so that each group acquires the authority to decide matters for its own members. That strategy differs from the individual rights strategy in that individuals remain subject to authority in matters of belief—albeit the authority of their group rather than the authority of the state. Nevertheless, segmental autonomy remains a fully privatizing strategy in the sense that I have identified.

However, the liberal strategy is unlikely to provide a comprehensive solution. Short of total separatism, in which different groups cease to be members of the same society, it will not be possible to maintain a public/private distinction all of the time. Religious beliefs are, perhaps, the beliefs most commonly consigned to a private sphere, but that is often a matter of convenience rather than something appropriate to the very nature of those beliefs. Certain matters which cannot escape public decision will impinge upon people's religious identities and there are many religious faiths which are intrinsically public in orientation. If we shift from religious to political beliefs, which need have no less significance for people's identities, those beliefs are by their very nature public in character.[11]

But even when beliefs enter the public arena, the identity view implies that we should conceive those beliefs as so many interests which are private to their holders.[12] That is not to say that the relevant beliefs will themselves articulate wants which are selfish to the group that expresses them. On the contrary, that is just what beliefs typically do not do. In themselves, Christian or Muslim or Hindu beliefs are not a set of demands for private satisfaction. Rather, they express a view of what is true of the world and of how human life ought to be conducted. Those beliefs will generate wants—wants that life should be organized and conducted as the beliefs prescribe. But those wants would not be conceived as wants for goods which are good only for the believers. Granted the truth of Christianity, the Christian life is the life that is right and good for everybody; granted the truth of Islam, the life prescribed in the Koran is the life that is right and good for everyone; and so on. Taken at face value, then, the claims that these beliefs express do not constitute so many private wants demanding satisfaction or so many special interests calling for promotion.

But if we regard beliefs merely as expressions of identity, we translate them into so many private interests. Different and rival beliefs are conceived not as different and competing conceptions of a common good or a single truth but as indicators of a range of separate and private goods. What are offered by believers as agent-neutral reasons for doing this or that are reinterpreted by identity theorists as agent-relative reasons to be dealt with accordingly.

This does not follow from the mere fact that people enter the public arena with diverse beliefs. People can approach a decision from different points of view derived from different preoccupations, different experiences, different knowledge, and different judgements.

Nevertheless, these different perspectives can be pooled in the public discussion of a matter so that each person can take them fully into account in reaching an ultimate judgement about what the public decision should be. To adapt Aristotle's famous analogy, if everyone makes diverse contributions to a feast, the feast will be a far better feast than if everyone makes the same contribution. Public discussion directed towards the reaching of a public judgement does not therefore have to start out from a like-minded public.

But different identities do not constitute so many different perspectives on an issue which can be incorporated in a shared view of how that issue should be resolved. They stand simply as so many identities calling for recognition. So, on the identity view, when beliefs do find their way into the public arena, they do so as private interests needing to be brokered.

How then should a demos respond to the different demands of different identities? Suppose, for example, that a demos confronts the issue of the proper content of school education. Suppose, too, that issue is controversial because different religious groups hold different and conflicting views on it and because each group regards its favoured type of education as crucial to the maintenance and the continued expression of its identity. How should the demos proceed?

There are two possibilities. First, the demos might provide for each group to have its own schools and then allow each group to decide for itself what is to be taught in its schools. In that case, the demos will have opted for what I previously described as a private or liberal solution, and that solution would be no less 'private' in character for having been arrived at through a public decision-making process.

Alternatively, the demos might decide that the proper content of school education is a public question which ought to receive a public answer and so, instead of passing the decision on to others, itself decree what the content of education is to be. But how, in circumstances of diversity, could that be consistent with respecting identities? Imposing a uniform syllabus on different groups would inevitably thwart the identities of some of them. It might be possible to avoid merely subordinating one identity to another by securing a compromise in which no identity would be fully recognized but in which each would receive a degree of what it demands. But a coherent compromise on issues of this sort is not always available. Moreover, whereas we might think that ordinarily interests can be—and perhaps have to be—compromised or subordinated one to another, identities seem much less amenable to that sort of treatment.

Thus, democracy does not provide a ready solution to the problem of reconciling diverse identities. A demos may opt for a liberal solution but it cannot then escape the limits of that solution. Or it may respond to the conflicting demands of different identities by making fully public judgements, but in that case it cannot avoid compromising the identities of different groups of believers. It is not easy, therefore, to see how the democratic ideal can be satisfactorily reworked to accommodate the demands of identity politics.

IDENTITIES AND LIBERTIES

What does the primacy of identity imply for freedom of belief and freedom of expression? The identity argument would seem to constitute no threat to freedom of belief, if by that we understand merely the freedom of people to hold and to live according to their existing beliefs. In a context of diversity, it may not be easy to sort out just what constitute fair and workable social arrangements enabling people to live according to their beliefs. Given the conflicting demands of different beliefs, it may be impossible to provide fully for every belief-based form of life. But, given that beliefs are crucial to identities and given that all identities are to be accorded equal respect, there is a clear imperative in the identity argument to provide people with the maximum possible freedom to hold and to live according to their beliefs.

The implications of the identity argument for freedom of expression are much less straightforward. If people's beliefs are crucial to their identities, so that questioning and criticizing their beliefs entails questioning and criticizing their identities, the demand that we respect and protect their identities implies that freedom of expression must be curtailed accordingly. Attacking a belief entails assaulting a person and such assaults should be proscribed. Undermining a belief involves eroding an identity and that erosion must be checked. Thus, in effect, the identity argument passes to each group of believers a right of veto over those expressions which are reckoned to assault or threaten its identity.

In this context, the identity argument seems to demand more by way of respect than is normally implied in the idea of 'respect for persons'. If a belief is built into who a person is, it becomes more difficult to accept that respect demands only that we recognize a person's right to hold and to espouse that belief and that we are still permitted publicly to execrate the belief. Clearly, the demands of respect cannot go all the way to requiring each of us to make a positive appraisal of everyone else's beliefs.[13] That would be absurd, since other people's beliefs may be incompatible both with one another and with our own belief. Indeed, one of the problems that arises here is whether the demands implicit in the identity argument make sense. However, in so far as they do, they seem to require a 'hands off' approach to one another's beliefs; we can hold and follow our own beliefs but, as far as possible, we should steer clear of the beliefs of others.

Against this, it might be said that the identity argument cannot have such restrictive implications for freedom of expression since each expression is itself but the expression of an identity. To limit freedom of expression would therefore be to limit people's opportunity for disclosing and affirming their identities. The identity argument might therefore be said to provide an argument for, rather than an argument against, freedom of expression.[14]

There is clearly some force in this counter-argument, but the identity argument is not quite as even-handed as it suggests. If my beliefs are essential to my identity, they will not be essential in equal degree and some may not be essential at all. If I am a Christian, it will be my Christian beliefs that will be essential to my identity. In addition to these Christian beliefs, logically, I must also have beliefs about the mistaken nature of Islam and Taoism. But, empirically, I may know little or nothing about those other faiths. Even if I do know something about them, my conception of Islam and Taoism is most unlikely to stand at the centre of my identity and to have the same significance for me as my Christian beliefs. Similarly, if I am a Muslim, my Islamic beliefs will be central to my identity in a way that my associated beliefs about the limited truth of Judaism or the erroneous character of Hinduism will not. For that reason, the identity argument gives greater significance to people's positive beliefs (what it is that they themselves believe in) than to their negative beliefs (their beliefs about the different and conflicting beliefs of others). So, in a contest between positive believers and their negative opponents, the identity argument will privilege believers over doubters.

This distinction between positive and negative beliefs may sometimes be difficult to sustain. A positive belief is by implication critical of other positive beliefs with which it conflicts. A clash of identities may therefore be difficult to avoid. As I have already indicated, if it is pushed too hard, the claim that each group is both entitled to express its own beliefs and forbidden to impugn the beliefs of others will collapse into incoherence.[15] In addition, it may be that some people's identities derive from negative beliefs; who they are is defined by what they are against. For example, members of the British National Secular Society may find their identity primarily in their militant rejection of religious faith. But, even allowing for these difficulties, the general thrust of the identity argument is to encourage each group of believers to stay within its own domain and to refrain from intruding into the territories of others so that, as far as possible, the integrity of each group's identity remains undisturbed.

Here again, then, we see the privatizing impetus of the identity argument. It encourages us to regard a body of belief as a domain over which its adherents have something akin to a right of ownership. The beliefs of a group are peculiarly 'theirs' in that they have been absorbed into that group's identity. We can also see here the splitting apart of the logic of belief and the logic of identity. The identity argument pushes us towards treating the beliefs of a group as properly the business of no one but that group. Yet it is usually in the nature of beliefs, including religious beliefs, that they make general claims about the world and about proper human conduct so that believers cannot regard the content of their beliefs as properly of concern to no one but themselves.

The appropriative character of the identity argument is reinforced by the way in which it renders the public discussion of beliefs a curiously point-less activity. I have already noticed this in relation to democracy, but it also applies more generally. In discussion, people normally exchange thoughts and information in ways which imply some shared concern or purpose. People talk with one another rather than simply at one another. But if beliefs simply manifest identities, authentic discussion of this sort will be foreclosed. People will simply indicate 'who they are' and 'where they are coming from'. The different participants will inform each other about their different identi-ties and, in that way, but only in that way, enlighten one another. Through the expression of their identities different groups of believers may gain an understanding of what each believes and therefore of what is crucial to the identity of each. This may enable them to work towards an agreement on how all of their different identities might be accommodated within their single society. But this way of regarding beliefs rules out any aspiration to evolve a shared view of the world and what we should do in it. Freedom of expression will cease to be the instrument of a shared endeavour to discover the truth of things and will be reduced, at best, to a form of social therapy.[16]

Moreover, if the point of free expression becomes that of securing peace-ful coexistence amongst rival groups of believers, a lively exchange of views of the sort typically associated with the ideal of free expression may not be the best mechanism for achieving that outcome.[17] Here, however, something must be conceded to the identity argument. If beliefs are translated into iden-tities, groups with rival beliefs cease to be rivals and become merely groups marked by difference.

To that extent, the redescription of beliefs as identities should remove a source of conflict. Unhappily, the logic of that redescription is not always reproduced in people's conduct. Sometimes the legacy of conflicting beliefs is conflicting identities and, sadly, differences of identity seem capable of fuelling hatred and violence long after the substantive differences of belief from which they derived have lost their potency as sources of social conflict.

I began this section by commenting that the identity argument seemed to provide a secure underpinning for freedom of belief but even that freedom may not remain wholly unimpaired by the identity argument—if, that is, we allow that people are capable of taking an active role in determining beliefs. If people are capable of appraising, forming, and revising beliefs, that capacity will be frustrated to the extent that people are denied the material and the ethos essential to its exercise. If established beliefs are surrounded by protective measures designed to shore up the identities of their holders, a population will be deprived of circumstances which encourage and facilitate the appraisal of beliefs. The demands of the identity argument are therefore at odds with conditions conducive to individuals' arriving at beliefs consciously and reflectively. That is to make no more than the obvious point that arrangements designed to protect people's identities will be conservative in their aim and impact.[18]

Up to now I have tried to work out the implications of the identity argument taken in isolation. It is quite possible, of course, that someone who accepts the identity argument might also recognize other considerations which bear upon freedom of expression and which weigh in the opposite direction. Thus, how far we should be governed by the identity argument may depend not only upon its intrinsic merits but also upon how its demands fare when they are weighed against the competing demands of other arguments. I shall not attempt any general audit of arguments for and against freedom of expression here. But I want to conclude by saying something on two matters relating to free expression, one particular, the other general.

The more particular issue concerns the distinction between serious criticism and scurrilous attack. That distinction was central to the controversy over Salman Rushdie's *Satanic Verses* and it is likely to figure prominently in other arguments concerning beliefs, particularly religious beliefs, and the limits of free expression. Does the identity argument underwrite that distinction; does it provide reason for finding the serious criticism of beliefs more acceptable than mocking and scurrilous attacks? Clearly the answer depends upon how we interpret the demands of identity. If we limit those demands to the manner in which we engage with an identity, that would seem to favour serious criticism over scurrilous attack. Serious criticism seems altogether more consistent in spirit than mocking derision with recognizing the centrality of a belief to a person's or a group's identity and acknowledging the respect with which that belief ought to be treated.

If, on the other hand, the demands of identity include the demand that we should not set about undermining people's identities, the privileged position of serious criticism becomes much less secure. Serious criticism is likely to be far more corrosive of people's beliefs, and therefore of their identities, than mocking and disrespectful attacks. Serious criticism gives people reason to doubt their beliefs and so to forsake that source of their identity. Scurrilous attack is less likely to induce doubt than to provoke indignation amongst those whom it assails and may do more to reinforce than to diminish a group's sense of identity.[19]

So, if there is significance in the distinction between serious criticism and scurrilous attack, that may be explained not by serious criticism's being licensed by the identity argument but by the different merits of the two activities. What is special about serious criticism may be simply its own seriousness of purpose. The seriousness of that purpose may be sufficient to trump the competing claims of identity, whereas there may be little or nothing to justify our giving that sort of priority to scurrilous attack.

TAKING BELIEFS SERIOUSLY

The more general observation I want to make underlies everything that I have said up to now and concerns what it is to hold a belief and how that relates to possessing an identity. I want to suggest that there is a tension—perhaps even an antinomy—between actually holding a belief and treating that belief as the expression of an identity.

To hold a belief is to hold that something is the case. It is not to declare 'this is who I am'. We may, of course, think, in a general way, that it is a good thing for a person to have some definable identity. More specifically, we may wish people to continue with their current beliefs in order to maintain their existing identities; or we may wish that they would adopt new beliefs so that they would acquire new and more desirable identities. Even then, it seems slightly odd to value a belief-based identity independently of any estimate of the belief upon which it is based, although perhaps we might intelligibly wish that people would believe in something—just anything—so that their lives will have meaning and their selves will have substance. But none of these concerns for identity can be offered as reasons for believing something to be the case because none is a reason for believing something to be the case. I cannot believe that Christ was the Son of God or that Muhammad was God's Prophet because that belief maintains my identity as a Christian or a Muslim, since the belief's impact upon my identity has nothing to do with whether Christ was indeed the Son of God or whether Muhammad was indeed God's Prophet. An identity may be a byproduct of a belief, but that is all it can be. Consciously holding a belief in order to acquire or to maintain an identity belongs to Elster's family of self-defeating strategies.[20] A genuinely belief-based identity is an outcome that can be achieved only as a consequence of doing something for reasons other than producing that outcome.

Logically, then, I cannot believe that something is so because of its supposed consequences for my identity.[21] To that extent, it runs counter to the very nature of believing to give primacy to its consequences for one's identity rather than to the content of what it is that one believes. But, more than that, I cannot hold that what matters about my belief is its impact upon my identity. That is, my commitment to what I believe cannot be primarily a commitment to an identity; it must be a commitment to the truth or the rightness of what I believe. I may welcome and cherish the impact that a belief has upon my life but, again, that impact can only be a consequence of my believing what I do. If I become convinced that a belief is false, that belief cannot be rescued by its cherished consequences.

There is one further way in which giving primacy to identity is problematic in relation to one's own beliefs. The identity argument assumes primacy most readily when we cast doubt upon the epistemological standing of beliefs. If we regard certain beliefs (such as religious beliefs) as having no epistemic status, if we regard them merely as epiphenomena of social circumstances, if we treat them as incapable or unworthy of any kind of serious intellectual consideration, we can see them as little other than characteristics of their holders. And, if we go on to attribute significance to them, we can find that significance only in their being characteristics of their holders. Thus, the identity argument is likely to appeal most readily to the sceptic and the relativist since, from where they stand, the value of beliefs, if they have value, can be found in little else. But, clearly, that is not a way in which people can regard their own beliefs and not a foundation upon which they can give primacy to identity in valuing their beliefs. Nor can they be happy to find their beliefs defended in that way by others. Beleaguered believers should therefore beware of identity theorists bearing gifts for those gifts may have a concealed price.

There is, then, a tension between taking beliefs seriously as beliefs and treating them as expressions of identity.[22] Taking beliefs seriously entails understanding them as claims about the world; treating them as expressions of identity transforms them into mere characteristics of persons. Thus the identity argument has, or should have, least appeal for those who take beliefs qua beliefs most seriously, and most appeal for those who take beliefs qua beliefs least seriously.

If we return to the more specific matter of freedom of expression, none of this, of course, argues for free expression. But what it does imply is that those who hold beliefs, and who take their beliefs seriously, should approach the issue of freedom of expression as an issue to be argued out in terms of beliefs rather than identities.

CONCLUSION

In questioning the identity argument, I have not meant to dismiss the significance of identity for human beings either as individuals or as members of groups. Nor do I deny the empirical significance that beliefs can have for people's identities. What I have tried to show is some of the oddities involved in treating beliefs merely or primarily as expressions of identity. When we come across someone saying 'I believe that Christ is the Son of God' or 'I believe that Muhammad was God's Prophet' and then adding 'what is centrally important about this belief is that it is a manifestation of my authentic self' or 'what really matters about this belief is that it expresses the identity of my group', something has gone awry.

My sympathies are on the side of responding to beliefs as beliefs rather than as identities, but my purpose has not been to argue that case. Rather, it has been to point out the difficulties in trying to have it both ways. But do we have a choice? If beliefs are indissolubly joined to identities, perhaps we have simply to live with a tension that we can do nothing to remove. However, there is surely some room for manoeuvre. The spirit in which we hold and evaluate beliefs is not entirely beyond our control; in some measure at least, we can decide whether we approach matters of belief in the spirit of belief or in the spirit of identity.[23]

NOTES

1. For an example of this sort of approach, see Susan Mendus, 'The Tigers of Wrath and the Horses of Instruction', in John Horton, ed., *Liberalism, Multiculturalism and Toleration* (Basingstoke: Macmillan, 1993), 193–206. I am indebted to Susan Mendus's original and searching article on the issues raised by the Rushdie affair for stimulating the arguments I develop in this chapter.

2. See, for example, M. Brewster Smith, Jerome S. Bruner, and Robert W. White, *Opinions and Personality* (New York: John Wiley, 1964); Daniel Katz, 'The Functional Approach to the Study of Attitudes', in Fred I. Greenstein and Michael Lerner, eds., *A Sourcebook for the Study of Personality and Politics* (Chicago: Markham Publishing Company, 1971). Analogously, it seems that people sometimes adopt opinions because those opinions are endorsed by the political party with which they identify, rather than support a political party because it espouses opinions of which they independently approve. See Hugh Berrington, 'British Public Opinion and Nuclear Weapons', in Catherine Morse and Colin Fraser, eds., *Public Opinion and Nuclear Weapons* (London: Macmillan, 1989).

3. See Michael Sandel, *Liberalism and the Limits of Justice* (Cambridge: Cambridge University Press, 1982); and Charles Taylor, 'Atomism', in *Philosophical Papers, volume 2* (Cambridge: Cambridge University Press, 1985).

4. See Simon Caney, 'Liberalism and Communitarianism: A Misconceived Debate', *Political Studies* 40 (1992): 273–89.

5. I give a fuller justification of these claims about the relationship between choice and belief in 'Bearing the Consequences of Belief', *Journal of Political*

Philosophy 2 (1994): 24–43. I am commenting here upon the logic of belief. I do not deny that, psychologically, people are capable of coming to hold a belief because they want it to be true; when that happens, they might be said, colloquially, to 'choose' what to believe. It is also possible for someone intentionally to place himself in a position which he reckons will lead him to believe something that he does not currently believe. For example, an agnostic might join a religious community in the expectation that living in that community will eventually induce in him the confident belief in God that he currently lacks. Prima facie, there is something odd about consciously inducing oneself to believe something that one now regards as false, but someone might adopt that tactic because he reckons the new belief will make his life happier or more bearable. However, even in this rather unusual sort of case it still requires more than an act of choice to bring about the belief.

6. Sandel seems to think otherwise. See *Liberalism and the Limits of Justice*, 62, 179.

7. Cf. 'beliefs of this sort [moral and religious beliefs] define what we are, in the sense of specifying where we belong. If they are undermined or despised, we ourselves are also undermined and despised'; Mendus, 'Tigers of Wrath', 204.

8. See Axel Honneth, *The Struggle for Recognition* (Oxford: Polity Press, 1995), 92–139; Charles Taylor, 'The Politics of Recognition', in Amy Gutmann, ed., *Multiculturalism: Examining the Politics of Recognition* (Princeton, NJ: Princeton University Press, 1994), 25–26.

9. See, for example, Richard Bellamy, *Liberalism and Modern Society* (Oxford, Polity Press, 1992), 252–61; Iris Marion Young, *Justice and the Politics of Difference* (Princeton, NJ: Princeton University Press, 1990), 96–121, 156–91.

10. Arend Lijphart, *Democracy in Plural Societies* (New Haven, CT: Yale University Press, 1977), 41–44.

11. Although even different political beliefs, in some measure and for some issues, might be dealt with by way of a privatizing strategy. Segmental autonomy might be used to establish a sort of politically based federalism so that, for certain issues, different political groups would form a number of separate subpolities. We could, of course, go all the way to total separation so that different political groups became wholly separate publics; separatism is merely the most extreme version of the private solution. See Robert Nozick's idea of Utopia in Anarchy, *State and Utopia* (Oxford: Basil Blackwell, 1974), 297–334.

12. By 'private to their holders' I mean only that the interest is conceived as an interest of each holder. I do not mean to imply that the demands of identity can always be fully satisfied by measures confined to the belief-holder's 'private sphere'.

13. See Stephen Darwall, 'Two Kinds of Respect', *Ethics* 88 (1977/1978): 36–49.

14. See Mendus, 'The Tigers of Wrath', 205; and Joseph Raz, *Ethics in the Public Domain* (Oxford: Clarendon Press, 1994), 146–69.

15. See Peter Jones, 'Respecting Beliefs and Rebuking Rushdie', *British Journal of Political Science* 20 (1990): 415–37.

16. See Gutmann, *Multiculturalism*, 1994, 24: 'Multicultural societies and communities that stand for the freedom and equality of all people rest upon mutual respect for reasonable intellectual, political, and cultural differences. Mutual respect requires

a widespread willingness and ability to articulate our disagreements, to defend them before people with whom we disagree, to discern the difference between respectable and disrespectable disagreement, and to be open to changing our own minds when faced with well-reasoned criticism'. That is the sort of vision with which I believe the identity argument to be at odds.

17. See Lijphart, *Democracy in Plural Societies*, 87–99.

18. See Michael Oakeshott, *Rationalism in Politics* (London: Methuen, 1962), 170–71.

19. I accept that this can vary with circumstances. Derision and mockery may provoke a strong and determined reaction among a group of believers. But ridicule may also cause people to become shamefaced and less confident about their beliefs.

20. Jon Elster, *Sour Grapes* (Cambridge: Cambridge University Press, 1983), 43–108.

21. Again, I use the word 'logically' advisedly. I do not deny that, psychologically, a wish may be father to a thought.

22. Even Rorty's ironist would not claim to be able to yoke these together. It seems she might play along with other people's beliefs—or rather with their illusions about their beliefs—but only out of her desire not to humiliate. She seems to be someone who has a split-level understanding of her own beliefs so that she can take them both seriously and not seriously, but that trick seems possible only because, in my terms, she might be more properly described as possessing commitments rather than beliefs. See Richard Rorty, *Contingency, Irony and Solidarity* (Cambridge: Cambridge University Press, 1989). For what seems to be an attempt to resist the kind of argument I develop here, see Charles Taylor, *The Ethics of Authenticity* (Cambridge, MA: Harvard University Press, 1992), especially chapter 8.

23. An early draft of this chapter was presented to the Workshop on 'Citizenship and Plurality' organized by Anne Phillips for the Joint Session of the ECPR held in Leiden in April 1993. I am grateful to the participants in the workshop for many helpful comments. I have also benefited from discussions with several of my colleagues at Newcastle, particularly Mark Bevir, Kay Black, David George, and Martin Harrop. I am especially indebted to Simon Caney and John Horton for their careful scrutiny of my argument and for their many helpful comments and criticisms.

Chapter 6

Toleration, the Rushdie Affair, and the Perils of Identity

Toleration can be demanded by both the proponents and the opponents of belief. For a belief's proponents, the demand concerns their freedom to hold, to express, and to act upon the belief. For a belief's opponents, it concerns their freedom to dissent from and to criticize the belief. In deciding upon how we should respond to those demands, something turns upon our conception of the nature and significance of the belief that is at issue. By this I do not mean only that we must take account of whether the relevant belief is a religious or moral or political or scientific belief, although, certainly, different arguments may be relevant to, and different arrangements appropriate for, different sorts of belief. Rather, I mean that something depends upon our interpretation of what is going on when people hold beliefs. For example, in arguing for toleration, Locke for the most part approached beliefs as impersonal claims about what is true, whereas Rawls and many modern liberals treat beliefs as convictions which figure in the personal interests of their holders. These different approaches to belief yield different, if usually complementary, approaches to questions of toleration.

In this chapter I examine how the issue of toleration is affected by a particular way of regarding beliefs: the conception of beliefs as expressions of identity. On this view, beliefs matter because they are defining features of the people who hold them. Of course, beliefs are not the only sources of people's identities and not all beliefs have a defining quality for their holders. But some beliefs can be significant both for the way in which people see themselves and for the way in which they are seen by others. For example, religious beliefs, particularly in the context of multifaith societies, can be potent sources of individual or group identities.

If we hold that beliefs and their associated forms of life are significant primarily as expressions of identity, how should that affect our response to

113

those beliefs? For those who are anxious to promote the cause of toleration the representation of beliefs as identities may seem a shrewd move. Historically, one of the most common justifications given for not tolerating beliefs and for not permitting practices has been that the beliefs are false and the practices wrong. But 'false' and 'wrong' are terms which do not fit easily into the vocabulary of identity. People are simply who they are; it seems misplaced rather than just improper to assess whether people's identities are true or false or right or wrong. Consequently, if we interpret the possession of a belief as the possession of an identity, we seem able to bypass a major argument for intolerance.

Despite this apparently liberal effect of the appeal to identity, I shall argue that freedom of thought and freedom of expression are seriously threatened by the redescription of beliefs as identities. The claims of identity are most obviously hazardous for the opponents of belief since those claims can be used severely to curtail the freedom to question and to criticize the beliefs of others. But the proponents of belief also have reason to be wary of a redescription of beliefs as identities since that can undermine the case for taking their beliefs seriously as *beliefs*.

I shall consider these issues in the context of the Rushdie Affair since that affair brought questions of toleration, belief, and identity into sharp focus. In examining the general issues emanating from the affair, I shall concentrate on Rushdie as offender rather than as victim; that is, I shall consider what it is that Rushdie might have done wrong rather than how he himself has been wronged. Eventually, I want to focus upon objections brought against Rushdie in the name of identity, but I begin by saying a little about other sorts of objection to indicate their separateness from claims whose ultimate appeal lies with the notion of identity.

Three preliminary points might help to avoid misunderstanding. First, in considering how Rushdie's 'wrong' might be understood, I am not taking for granted that he committed some sort of wrong in writing *The Satanic Verses*. My remarks will be more conditional in character: if Rushdie was guilty of a wrong, what sort of wrong might that have been?

Secondly, even if Rushdie is reckoned to have been guilty of something, the question of what, if anything, ought to be done about that still remains to be settled. Clearly, it does not follow that Khomeini's *fatwa* is vindicated. Nor does it follow that *The Satanic Verses* ought to be banned or that laws should be enacted proscribing any similar literary adventure. We may even fight shy of curtailing our conception of the nonlegal rights of authors; we can criticize the use that people make of their rights without implying that they have no right to do what we criticize.[1]

Thirdly, 'wrong' here obviously has to mean morally wrong rather than merely 'mistaken' or 'incorrect'. For example, some of Rushdie's critics have complained that (what they take to be) his suggestions about the origins of Islam are unsupported by historical evidence. Given Rushdie's intentions in the novel, those complaints are really beside the point but, even if they were not, it is not Rushdie's academic competence nor even his qualities as a novelist that have been on trial in the Rushdie Affair.

What, then, might Rushdie have done wrong? The most direct and straightforward objection to *The Satanic Verses* comes from within Islam. Rushdie treated Muhammad and other Islamic holy figures in a manner which Islam forbids. Islam is not a monolithic religion and the Muslim response to *The Satanic Verses* has not been unanimous. I am not competent to enter into debates about what Islam requires, forbids, or permits and, anyway, differences amongst Muslims have focused less upon the nature of Rushdie's wrong than upon what should be done to remedy or to punish his wrong. *That* he transgressed the rules of Islam few Muslims seem to doubt.

For the Islamic believer, this sort of objection is likely to provide by far the most powerful indictment of Rushdie. The wronging of God or his Prophet must be far more serious than any offence Rushdie might have committed against ordinary mortals. But, equally, that sort of objection cannot weigh with non-Muslims. If Muhammad was not God's Prophet, if the Koran is not the word of God, if there is no God, objections made avowedly and solely in the name of Islam have no force. Islam, even more than Christianity, is a religion for which 'revealed knowledge' is absolutely fundamental and it is in the nature of claims based upon revelation, that they divide people in the sharpest possible way. For those for whom an allegedly divine revelation is indeed the revealed word of God, nothing can be more true or compelling. Muslims have been particularly sensitive to the way Rushdie seemed to challenge the authenticity of the Koran.[2] But for those for whom a 'divine revelation' is really nothing of the kind, demands based upon revelation derive from nothing better than a delusion.

Consequently, if Rushdie's words are to be recognizable as a wrong by non-Muslims, they cannot be wrong only in a way that presupposes the truth of Islam. Rushdie has to be guilty of a wrong that is other than a purely Islamic wrong. What sort of wrong might that be?

A variety of related, yet significantly different, answers have been offered. One is that Rushdie wrote 'offensively', that he wrote without due regard for Muslim sensibilities. Complaints about 'offensiveness' are often ambiguous. People will sometimes describe behaviour as 'offensive' when what they really mean to protest about is the intrinsic wrongfulness of the behaviour itself rather than its disagreeable impact upon themselves. In any event, these two are not easily separated; for the most part, Muslim offence at the content of *The Satanic Verses* stemmed from, and depended upon, beliefs about the religious wrongfulness of what Rushdie had written. Even so, if we identify the wrong unequivocally as one of offensiveness, the essence of the wrong becomes the mental distress that people are caused to suffer rather than the moral or religious wrongfulness of the offending act itself. What is bad is that people are caused to undergo a disagreeable experience; they are made to suffer 'mental pain' or 'injured feelings'.

Given this focus upon the painfulness of the experience, 'offence' perhaps defines the wrong too narrowly. The implication is that causing any 'hurtful' reaction in people is, prima facie, bad and ought to be avoided, even when that hurt is unaccompanied by the indignation and censure that we normally associate with offence.

If offence should count at all, it has a strong claim to count in the context of religious faith. Given the central place of the sacred in religions such as Judaism, Christianity, and Islam, their adherents are peculiarly susceptible to offence. On the other hand, offence is such a common experience and one which is so easily aroused that too generous a concern for its avoidance would radically impair freedom of discussion and inquiry. As Rushdie himself wrote, with only mild hyperbole, 'What is freedom of expression? Without the freedom to offend, it ceases to exist'.[3]

Another accusation that has frequently been levelled at Rushdie is that he wrote in a way that failed to respect the beliefs of Muslims. The underlying notion here is that everybody is entitled to a minimum of respect from their fellows which, in turn, requires that we behave in ways that respect people's most cherished beliefs. Like arguments based upon offence, this claim does not presuppose the truth of the beliefs at issue for, ultimately, what we are required to respect is not disembodied beliefs but the people who hold them. Unlike protests against offence, however, the appeal here is not to the undesirability of an unpleasant experience, but to the moral status of persons and to conduct which is consonant with that status. The principle of 'respecting persons', including respecting them as individuals who hold beliefs, is now widely shared; indeed, it has become fundamental to liberal political culture. The main question that *The Satanic Verses* poses for that principle is just how much it demands from us. Is the principle satisfied if we merely allow people the usual freedom to hold and to live according to their own beliefs? Or does it require more than that? Does it also limit what we may write or say about the beliefs of others in a way that significantly curtails our freedom of expression?[4]

A third and, again, very common charge brought against Rushdie was that of libel: his words were wrong because they were defamatory.[5] However, that is a charge that non-Muslims cannot easily concede. Who is it that Rushdie is alleged to have defamed? The answer most frequently given is Muhammad along with his wives and companions. But, if we are to extend the idea of defamation from the living to the dead, how far should we go? Should the reputation of every past person be of equal concern? Should the reputations of Alexander the Great or Marcus Aurelius or Martin Luther be safeguarded along with those of Muhammad and his associates? Presumably not. Presumably, what makes Muhammad special is the belief that he was God's Prophet. But that takes us back inside the circle of Islam. For Muslims, Muhammad's status as God's Prophet provides the best of reasons for his being spoken of only in the most respectful terms; for non-Muslims it provides no reason at all.

However, Rushdie's defamation may be conceived in other terms. Perhaps, it is the besmirching of Muslims themselves to which we should take exception, rather than the denigration of central figures of their faith. We can recognize that a group of believers has been mistreated and we can condemn their mistreatment, even though we do not share their beliefs. This interpretation of Rushdie's 'libel' need not, therefore, be confined to Muslims. Yet it is a charge that is hard to find convincing. The link between Rushdie's treatment of Islam and any consequent aspersions he might have cast upon the good character of Muslims is altogether too tentative and too indirect to amount to anything approaching the ordinary legal offence of defamation. If Muslims present themselves, rather than Muhammad, as the victims of Rushdie's words, their allegations of defamation are likely to be disguised forms of other complaints, such as the unwarranted offence caused to their sensibilities or the disrespectful treatment of their beliefs.[6]

These complaints do not, however, exhaust the field. Accusations of libel begin to approach a much broader charge: that *The Satanic Verses* constitutes an assault upon the Muslim identity. That charge represents a further distinct objection and it is that objection that I shall consider in the remainder of this essay.

In distinguishing complaints focused upon identity from the other complaints I have described, I do not mean to suggest that they are at odds with, or that their use must exclude, those other complaints. On the contrary, all of these objections can be, and have been, used alongside one another. In addition, Rushdie has often been indicted in terms which straddle, or which relate ambiguously, to these different objections. For example, Rushdie has frequently been accused of 'insulting' Muslims and their faith, and that complaint is clearly one that might figure in all of the objections I have distinguished. Even so, the appeal to identity constitutes a separate objection and one with its own logic.

If we approach the Rushdie Affair as an issue about identity, we may seem to shift the dispute onto a territory of Rushdie's own choosing.[7] Identity is a category of which he makes frequent use and which is at the centre of the issues and experiences explored in *The Satanic Verses*. It also figures most commonly in the vocabulary of those, like Rushdie, who work with a postmodern conception of the world. It is much less congruent with the world of faith and belief which is sometimes characterized (tendentiously) as 'premodern'. That is one reason why invocations of identity are more commonly found amongst those who speak on behalf of Muslims than amongst Muslims themselves. As I shall explain in a moment, Muslims (or any other set of believers) have reason to be chary of the language of identity.

If Rushdie is so apprised of the significance of identity, how can that idea be used to condemn his work? The objection runs as follows. People are constituted by their identities. If we try to think of an individual person as somehow having a being which is independent of, and phenomenologically prior to, all of the particular characteristics that make that person the distinct human being that he or she is, we make a mistake. People are simply all of those things that give them their particular identities either as individuals or as members of groups. We cannot therefore respect them as persons yet not respect their specific identities.

The features that contribute towards people's identities are many and various—they are likely to include their gender, race, ethnicity, nationality, language, occupation, and so on. There can be no definitive list of sources of identity since identity is socially defined and will differ in different social contexts. Indeed, the very significance of identity is itself contingent upon social circumstances. In the world that Rushdie portrays in *The Satanic Verses*, where people move amongst and interact with others who are significantly different from themselves, people will be much more sensitized to identity than if they encounter only their own kind. It is no accident that identity has become a preoccupation in modern plural societies in a way that it was not in traditional homogeneous societies.

Given this understanding of identity and, in particular, given the idea that people are constituted by their identities, it is no great step to assert that their identities must be valued and respected. The thought here is often essentially Kantian in character—all persons deserve respect simply as human persons and, since 'persons' cannot be divorced from their specific identities, respecting them as persons entails respecting their identities. If 'persons' sounds too individualistic, the same thought can be expressed in terms of groups or communities or cultures. Alternatively, the thought may be less deontological in character. It may be simply that, as far as possible, human beings should flourish and live well and that they can do neither of those things if their identities are despised and derided. Either way, the clear implication is that we that we should refrain from acting in ways which assault or impugn or undermine people's identities.

Among the factors which significantly inform identity in our world is belief. That is not uniformly true of belief. Some of people's beliefs may be utterly insignificant for their identities; for example, their beliefs about the existence of black holes or the causes of dandruff. Others may be highly significant and amongst those are their religious beliefs. Indeed, the contribution of religious belief to identity is potentially very great, since religions typically provide their adherents with a comprehensive conception of existence, of their own place in it, and of the way in which they should conduct their lives. For many Muslims living in the West, the Rushdie Affair provided an opportunity to reassert the significance of their faith for their lives and to protest against the dismissive way in which their beliefs have often been treated by their would-be patrons in the majority society. Their religion, they have insisted, is much more important to their self-conception than the merely racial or ethnic identities that others have ascribed to them.[8]

Of course, if people's identities are as shifting and as mixed, as crisis-ridden and as uncertain, as those of Rushdie's characters, Gibreel Farishta and Saladin Chamcha, they will be too unstable and ill-defined to have this significance. It has sometimes been suggested that the intemperate reaction of Muslims to *The Satanic Verses* is symptomatic of just this sort of insecurity about their identity as Muslims. But the evidence does not bear that out. Certainly, the hostile reactions of Muslims to Rushdie have often been accompanied by a more general fear and resentment of the pretensions of Western culture and the ambitions of Western political power. But feeling that one's identity is being challenged or threatened is very different from being unsure, or feeling uncomfortable, about that identity.

In so far as people's identities are informed by their beliefs, including their religious beliefs, we cannot separate our treatment of their beliefs from our treatment of their identities. If we threaten their beliefs, we threaten their identities. If we treat their beliefs with contempt or derision, we treat their very selves with contempt and derision. That, it has been alleged, is what Rushdie did and that is why he is to be condemned.[9]

What estimate are we to make of this argument? Its restrictive potential is, I want to suggest, far greater than its sponsors seem to appreciate. But I want first to indicate why this way of reading the Rushdie Affair is problematic not only for Rushdie but also for his Muslim critics.

Those who take their beliefs seriously as beliefs must be uncomfortable to find those beliefs regarded merely as expressions of identity. To hold a belief that such and such is the case is to make an impersonal claim about the world; it is not, *qua* believer, to manifest a merely personal characteristic analogous to one's gender or sexuality. But, if beliefs are treated as no more than individual or group identities, they are no longer taken seriously as beliefs.

That is, they cease to be regarded as embodying propositional claims which merit serious consideration by others as affirmations of what is right or true; instead, they come to be regarded merely as features of persons to be acknowledged, but also to be responded to, merely as features of persons.

Equally, the translation of beliefs into identities shifts the significance of belief from what it is that is believed to the persona of the believer. That may be acceptable to those who seek merely to strike attitudes, but it cannot be welcomed by the genuine believer. Consider the case of Islam. If I adhere devoutly to the Islamic faith, I believe that Muhammad was God's Prophet and that the Koran is the word of God. But, if my Islamic faith is merely a constituent of my identity, it is no longer God and Muhammad who are significant; it is me. My beliefs become merely a manifestation of myself. Yet it is obviously deeply unsatisfactory for me to assert my belief that Muhammad was God's Prophet and then to go to claim that what is centrally important about that belief is that it is an expression of my authentic self. That narcissistic self-concern, so far from being a proper representation of my faith, is utterly at odds with it. It misrepresents my own conception of what is important in my belief.

The same sort of antinomy arises if believers switch into the language of 'culture'. A conception of humanity as bearers of cultures is one that comes heavily freighted with relativism. A culture is usually understood as a view of the world fashioned, if not consciously, by the community to whom it belongs. So, if we substitute the language of culture for the language of belief, there is a strong suggestion that those beliefs are merely the creations of the group that holds them. If, in addition, those different cultures are attributed with an equal status, all beliefs are given equal standing and are to be regarded as equally true or, more honestly, as equally false. And, anyway, if beliefs are understood merely as expressions of cultural identity, their truth ceases to matter. Strictly, that can be denied. Logically, it is possible to conceive the world in terms of cultures and also to hold that one of those cultures is uniquely 'true' or 'right'. But the nuances of the term 'culture', and the kind of vision with which it is usually associated, imply the opposite.

So, while there is good reason why those who do not hold Muslim (or Christian or Jewish or other) beliefs should be ready to recast those beliefs as expressions of identity, there is even better reason why people should refrain from conceiving and presenting their own beliefs in that way.

There is another reason why believers should be wary of endorsing the translation of their beliefs into identities. I previously explained how a Kantian train of thought might be used to join persons to identities and identities to beliefs so that the respect due to persons might also be claimed for their beliefs. But the integration of beliefs into identities might be used to opposite effect. If persons cannot be attributed with identities independently of their beliefs, their standing as persons may come to depend upon the standing of their beliefs. If a group's beliefs are reckoned to be odious or evil or absurd, perhaps the group itself should be reckoned odious or evil or absurd. If we cannot distinguish the sin from the sinner, perhaps, in hating the sin, we must also hate the sinner. Thus, a strong identification of persons with beliefs, rather than augmenting the status of beliefs, may diminish the status of persons.

Similarly, although, other things being equal, it is better that people's well-being should be promoted rather than frustrated, things may be regarded as very far from equal if their well-being relies upon the maintenance of beliefs which are false or pernicious. People may be thought to have no right to have their well-being promoted in so far as that requires us to collude in the maintenance of false or pernicious beliefs. Alternatively, it might be claimed that a genuine state of well-being cannot rest upon beliefs which are evil or erroneous; people cannot really flourish on the basis of unsatisfactory identities. If we have an obligation to promote people's well-being and if we confront someone with false beliefs, we must begin, it might be said, by transforming their beliefs and so transforming their identities.

I do not claim that the integration of beliefs into identities must have these unfortunate implications. I suggest only that the integration of beliefs into people's identities does not necessarily mean that their beliefs find an inviolable sanctuary within their identities. It might mean, on the contrary, that their identities acquire all the vulnerabilities of their beliefs. The history of persecution, religious and political, indicates that that is not an entirely fanciful danger.

If the appeal to identity is fraught with dangers for those who felt most immediately involved in Rushdie's 'wrong', it is potentially no less hazardous for those who seek to defend Rushdie's rights as an author.

As I have already indicated, the incorporation of belief into identity removes any space between what a person believes and who that person is. That is inescapably problematic for freedom of expression, including the freedom of novelists to explore themes of belief and commitment. If people's beliefs are essential to their identities, questioning and criticizing their beliefs entails questioning and criticizing their identities. An attack upon a belief becomes an assault upon the person or the group who holds the belief—and people ought not to be assaulted. Undermining a belief entails eroding an identity—and we cannot simultaneously respect and destroy an identity. Thus, the redescription of beliefs as identities yields a world which is far from hospitable to freedom of inquiry and freedom of expression.

The demands of identity are not uncomplicatedly prohibitive. Surely, it might be argued, people must have freedom to express their identities. If people are denied that freedom, won't they be denied the freedom to articulate and to affirm their identities? Do not authors have identities? Will not the censorship of their writings be simultaneously the suppression of their identities? A concern for identity might therefore seem to argue as much for, as against, freedom of expression.[10]

But the demands of identity are not quite so indeterminate. In so far as beliefs inform identity, it will be what people themselves believe, rather than what they do not believe, that will determine their identities. Thus, for Muslims, it will be their Muslim beliefs; for Christians, it will be their Christian beliefs; for Hindus, it will be their Hindu beliefs, and so on. It is true that each of these systems of belief implies a total or a partial rejection of the others. For example, if Islam is true, Christianity can be, at best, only partially true and Hinduism must be false. To that extent, the affirmation of one belief (and identity) may seem to be, inevitably, the repudiation of another belief (and identity). But what is centrally important to the Islamic identity is the belief that Muhammad was God's Prophet and that the life prescribed in the Koran is the life prescribed by God. What is centrally important to the Christian identity is the belief that Christ was the Son of God and that salvation is to be achieved through Christ. Logically, these positive beliefs may entail correspondingly negative beliefs about the conflicting faiths of others, but, psychologically and sociologically, it is likely to be people's positive beliefs, rather than their nonacceptance of the beliefs of others, that are crucial to their identities.

Thus, if we interpret beliefs as identities, we shall place a much higher premium upon respecting and preserving people's beliefs than upon exposing those beliefs to criticism and challenge. Since identities must be respected, each belief-based identity must, as far as possible, remain undisturbed.

So the general thrust of the appeal to identity is to encourage each group of believers to stay within its own domain of belief and to steer clear of the beliefs of others, so that each group's identity remains unthreatened and undefiled. More especially, the celebration of belief-based identities implies a corresponding hostility to scepticism. Doubt and questioning and 'unbelief', of the sort that pervades *The Satanic Verses*, will appear as mere negations whose corrosive effects upon an identity cannot even be excused as the unavoidable consequences of an alternative identity.

Focusing upon identity also has a generally 'privatizing' impetus. If beliefs are absorbed into the identities of their holders, they are removed from the public domain and placed within the confines of their holders. Beliefs cease to be propositional claims, the truth or value of which is quite independent of whoever puts them forward. They become, instead, the private property of their holders which are to be neither tampered with nor encroached upon by outsiders.

Some of what Rushdie has said in his own defence may be read as a protest against this tendency to make some subjects the private possessions of particular groups. He has been keen to point out that Muhammad is a subject in history,[11] which is to say that Muhammad is 'out there', in the public domain, situated in human past, the legitimate object of anyone's attention.

Likewise, if the Koran is offered to the world as the word of God, how can it become the private property of one section of humanity? '[E]verything is worth discussing. There are no subjects which are off limits and that includes God, includes prophets'.[12]

Nor, in one respect, would Muslims themselves dissent from this. Certainly, they would not accept that the essentials of their faith are fair game for any sort of treatment. But they would accept that their faith is a 'public' faith—that it deserves the attention of all.[13] The Koran reveals the word of God to everyone for everyone. It does not proclaim a truth that is somehow true or relevant only for those who are already Muslims. For Muslims, the truth of Islam is not a postmodern 'truth'; it is the real truth. So it runs counter to the very nature of Islam, as a system of belief, to treat its content as the private or clandestine preserve of the Islamic Ummah.

But the logic of identity is not the same as the logic of belief. If the claims of Islam are translated out of the language of belief and into the language of identity, those claims come to be seen not as public pronouncements which are the legitimate concern of all, but as the private concerns of Muslims with which others should not interfere.

Indeed, if beliefs become nothing but identities, their examination becomes as otiose as it is improper. As I have already indicated, the reinterpretation of beliefs as identities entails that they are no longer to be responded to as claims about the world. Inquiring into the truth or rightness of beliefs becomes as pointless and as absurd as considering whether someone's ethnicity is 'true' or whether their gender is 'right'.

Identity may be invoked to exact a still higher price from an author. Rushdie found himself upbraided not only for having assaulted the Muslim identity but also for having committed 'treason'. One sort of treason of which he was accused was apostasy, the betrayal of Islam.[14] But he was also charged with another sort—'cultural treason', the betrayal of a cultural identity into which he was born and to which he owed a loyalty. Sometimes this charge was made explicitly, sometimes it was left implicit as, for example, in descriptions of Rushdie as a 'self-hater' or a 'brown sahib' or as 'Simon Rushton'.[15] Here, once more, we see the potential restrictiveness of identity. If writers are to be limited, not only by the identities of others, but also by their own 'given' identities, their scope for creativity, imagination, and criticism will be severely attenuated.

All that I have said so far may seem to have ignored one crucial matter. What most Muslims have objected to in *The Satanic Verses* is not that it is critical of Islam. After all, they have protested, there have been many sober and respectful critiques of Islam to which Muslims have raised no objection and there has also been a sceptical, questioning tradition within Islam itself. Rather, what they have taken exception to is the treatment of characters, sacred to their faith, in ways which they describe variously as filthy, obscene, profane, abusive, indecent, and insulting. Most Muslims understand themselves, therefore, to be challenging not the fundamental principle of free expression but only its abuse.

The distinction between criticism and abuse is both important and legitimate. It is also a distinction that is not easily rendered precise. It might seem to imply a concern for language rather than substance. But that is too simple. Muslims objected not only to Rushdie's obscene and deprecatory language but also to the substance of what he seemed to be suggesting about Muhammad's character and behaviour. Moreover, distinguishing manner from matter, attempting to proscribe form without proscribing substance, is much more difficult in a novel or a poem than in academic argument or factual inquiry. However, that there are difficulties in interpreting and applying the distinction between criticism and abuse does not entail that there is no distinction to be interpreted or applied. I shall not attempt to evaluate the distinction here.[16] Rather, I want to consider whether it is underwritten by the demands of identity.

Does concern and respect for a group's identity permit serious criticism of their beliefs but forbid mocking and scurrilous attacks? The answer is not altogether clear. If we limit those demands to the manner in which we engage with an identity, that would seem to favour serious criticism over scurrilous attack. Serious criticism seems altogether more consistent in spirit than mocking derision with recognizing the centrality of a belief to a person's or a group's identity and acknowledging the respect with which that belief ought, therefore, to be treated.

If, on the other hand, the demands of identity include the demand that we should not set about undermining people's identities, the privileged position of serious criticism is much less secure. Serious criticism is likely to be far more corrosive of people's beliefs, and therefore of their identities, than mocking and disrespectful attacks. Serious criticism gives people a reason to doubt the truth of what they believe and so to forsake that source of their identity. Scurrilous attack is less likely to induce doubt than to provoke indignation amongst those whom it assails and may do more to reinforce than to diminish a group's sense of identity. That is certainly how many Muslims have interpreted the effect of *The Satanic Verses* upon their own communities.

So, if there is significance in the distinction between serious criticism and scurrilous attack, that may be explained not by serious criticism's being licensed by the imperatives of identity but by the different merits of the two activities. What is special about serious criticism may be simply its own seriousness of purpose. Certainly, serious criticism can weaken and eventually destroy an identity; but the aims of serious criticism may be reckoned sufficiently important to take priority over the claims of identity—particularly for those of us who want take beliefs seriously as beliefs. By contrast, there may be little or nothing to justify scurrility or abuse or obscenity, and therefore little or no justification for permitting them to override the claims of identity.

We are driven, then, to what might seem a curious conclusion. In many Western minds, the Muslim reaction to *The Satanic Verses* represented a survival into the modern era of a premodern system of belief. It seemed redolent of pre-Enlightenment Christianity with its certainties of belief and its readiness to demand that life should be regimented according to those certainties. Rushdie's work, by contrast, belonged to the postmodern age, an era of fragmentation, 'hybridization', and uncertainty. Thus, some observers saw the Rushdie Affair as a clash not merely of cultures but also of ages: the clash of an old but surviving age of certainty, repression, and intolerance with a new and still evolving age of doubt, experiment, and emancipation.

That view is altogether too simple. I have explained why those who take their beliefs seriously should be unhappy to find their beliefs redefined as identities. They should be joined in their unhappiness by those who are worried about the freedom of authors. A world which dismisses belief but exalts identity is not necessarily one that is friendlier to literary freedom. Indeed, it may be less so. There are well-established reasons—established, amongst others, by John Milton and John Stuart Mill—why beliefs should always remain open to question and to critical inquiry.[17] But those reasons cut no ice if demands for censorship come not from 'true believers' but from the modern or postmodern aficionados of 'identity'.

Throughout the Rushdie Affair there have been complaints that the defenders of Rushdie have 'fetishized' freedom of expression. Certainly, the ideal of free expression has often been invoked in too simple-minded a way. But there has been little recognition of the dangers of 'fetishizing' identity. 'Language and the imagination', wrote Rushdie, 'cannot be imprisoned, or art will die, and with it, a little of what makes us human'.[18] Literary imprisonment can take many forms and one of those is the insistence that authors must write only within the confines of their 'given' identities and only in ways which do not trespass upon the identities of others. In such a world, little space will remain for 'voices talking about everything in every possible way'.[19]

NOTES

1. Cf. Jeremy Waldron, 'A Right to Do Wrong', *Ethics* 92 (1981): 21–39.
2. Cf. Shabbir Akhtar: 'Muslim sensibilities have been sharply provoked by Rushdie's allegations about the textual impurity of the Koran', *Be Careful with*

Muhammad! (London: Bellew Publishing, 1989), 22. See also Preston King, 'Rushdie and Revelation', in B. Parekh, ed., *Free Speech* (London: Commission for Racial Equality, 1990), 28–48; and Ziauddin Sardar and Merryl Wyn Davies, *Distorted Imagination: Lessons from the Rushdie Affair* (London: Grey Seal, 1990), 144–58, 161–62.

3. 'In Good Faith', *Imaginary Homelands* (London: Granta, 1991), 396. For a thorough investigation of the issues raised by offensiveness, see Joel Feinberg, *The Moral Limits of the Criminal Law*, vol. 2, *Offense to Others* (Oxford: Oxford University Press, 1985). I have examined these issues as they arise in relation to religious belief in 'Blasphemy, Offensiveness and Law', *British Journal of Political Science* 10 (1980): 129–48.

4. I try to answer these questions in 'Respecting Beliefs and Rebuking Rushdie', *British Journal of Political Science* 20 (1990): 415–37; reprinted in J. Horton, ed., *Liberalism, Multiculturalism and Toleration* (London: Macmillan, 1993), 114–38.

5. For examples of the charge of libel, see Mashuq Ibn Ally, 'Second Introductory Paper', *Law, Blasphemy and the Multi-Faith Society* (London: Commission for Racial Equality, 1990), 27–28; Akhtar, *Be Careful with Muhammad!*, 1–12; Peter Mullen, 'Satanic Asides', in D. Cohn-Sherbok, ed., *The Salman Rushdie Controversy in Interreligious Perspective* (Lampeter: The Edwin Mellen Press, 1990), 25–36.

6. In addition to these objections, Rushdie was accused of wrongs which were more contingently related to his words, such as fomenting public disorder, causing the deaths of demonstrators in India and Pakistan, and damaging race relations in Western societies. I pass over these.

7. The subject of identity has figured prominently in discussions of the Rushdie Affair. It is, for example, a conspicuous theme in two books on the affair which display very different sympathies: Malise Ruthven, *A Satanic Affair: Salman Rushdie and the Rage of Islam* (London: Chatto and Windus, 1990), and Sardar and Davies, *Distorted Imagination*.

8. See Tariq Modood, 'Muslims, Race and Equality in Britain: Some Post-Rushdie Affair Reflections', *Third Text* 11 (1990): 127–34; Akhtar, *Be Careful with Muhammad!*, 58, 122–23; Rana Kabbani, *Letter to Christendom* (London: Virago Press, 1989), 9 and passim; Muhammad Mashuq Ibn Ally, 'Stranger Exiled from Home', in Cohn-Sherbok, ed., *The Salman Rushdie Controversy in Interreligious Perspective*, 136–38.

9. A clear and considered statement of this position in relation to the Rushdie affair is given by Susan Mendus, 'The Tigers of Wrath and the Horses of Instruction', in Parekh, ed., *Free Speech*, 3–17; reprinted in Horton, ed., *Liberalism, Multiculturalism and Toleration*, 193–206. I am indebted to Mendus's original and searching article on the issues raised by the Rushdie Affair for stimulating my interest in the subject of this essay.

10. Cf. Mendus, 'The Tigers of Wrath and the Horses of Instruction', 16; and Joseph Raz, 'Free Expression and Personal Identification', *Oxford Journal of Legal Studies* 11 (1991): 303–24.

11. Rushdie, 'Is Nothing Sacred?', *Imaginary Homelands*, 424. More generally Rushdie commented (p. 416), 'the act of making sacred is in truth an event in history.

It is the product of many and complex pressures of the time in which the act occurs. And events in history must always be subject to questioning, deconstruction, even to declarations of their obsolescence'. See also the interviews in Lisa Appignanesi and Sara Maitland, eds., *The Rushdie File* (London: Fourth Estate, 1989), 28, 41.

12. Appignanesi and Maitland, eds., *The Rushdie File*, 41.

13. Cf. 'Islam is not the property of Muslims nor of anybody on this earth. It belongs to God and God can take care of Islam as He has done so for so many centuries'; Shoaib Qureshi and Javed Khan, *The Politics of Satanic Verses: Unmasking Western Attitudes* (Leicester: Muslim Community Studies Institute, 1989), 23.

14. For discussions of the charge of apostasy, see Akhtar, *Be Careful with Muhammad!*, 71–79 and Ally, 'Second Introductory Paper', 21–27.

15. The charge of 'cultural treason' is made by Ali A. Mazrui, 'The Satanic Verses or a Satanic Novel? Moral Dilemmas of the Rushdie Affair', in Parekh, ed., *Free Speech*, 80–81, 99–101; see also his remarks in Appignanesi and Maitland, eds., *The Rushdie File*, 221–23. For a reply to Mazrui's 'cultural tribalism', see Reza Afshari, 'Ali Mazrui or Salman Rushdie: *The Satanic Verses* and Islamist Politics', *Alternatives* 16 (1991): 107–14. For similar accusations, see Muhammad Manazir Ahsan and A. R. Kidwai, eds., *Sacrilege versus Civility* (Leicester: The Islamic Foundation, 1991), 98, 144, 232. For more moderately phrased suggestions of this sort, see Kabbani, *Letter to Christendom*, 65–68. For 'self-hate', 'brown sahib', and 'Simon Rushton', see Ahsan and Kidwai, eds., *Sacrilege versus Civility*, 65, 143, 176, 201, 203, 281–82, and Sardar and Wyn Davies, *Distorted Imagination*, 82, 140–41, 261, 270–71.

16. I say more about the problems involved in distinguishing serious criticism from scurrilous abuse in 'Blasphemy, Offensiveness and Law', 141–44, and 'Respecting Beliefs and Rebuking Rushdie', 430–35.

17. Two contributions to the debate on *The Satanic Verses*, written in the spirit of Milton's *Areopagitica* and Mill's *On Liberty*, are Jeremy Waldron, 'Too Important for Tact', *Times Literary Supplement*, 10–16 March 1989, pp. 248, 260, and Albert Weale, 'Freedom of Speech vs. Freedom of Religion?', in Parekh, ed., *Free Speech*, 49–58.

18. Rushdie, 'In Good Faith', *Imaginary Homelands*, 396.

19. Rushdie, 'Is Nothing Sacred?', *Imaginary Homelands*, 429.

Chapter 7

Toleration, Recognition, and Identity[*]

Toleration has a long history both as personal virtue and as a political ideal. But is it an ideal that has now run its course? Toleration is associated with disapproval: we tolerate only that to which we object. That negativity seems at odds with the mood of our times. The prevailing spirit, at least amongst the intelligentsia of the Western world, is one that views human diversity positively as something we should embrace and celebrate. Rather than regarding the differences that human beings exhibit as tiresome inconveniences that we should grudgingly accommodate, we should recognize the positive value of human diversity and the many ways in which it enriches our lives.

It is not only the negativity of toleration that suggests that its time may have passed. The way in which the make-up of human diversity is now conceived calls into question the appropriateness of toleration. The traditional subject matter of toleration is beliefs and values and the practices to which they give rise. But nowadays, the differences that human beings present are more commonly construed as differences in identity and culture. Indeed, the very word 'difference' has come to be associated with one particular form of difference: differences of identity. Whether toleration retains its relevance and value once we conceive the world as characterized by different identities rather than different beliefs and values is moot.

The demand that is most commonly associated with differences in identity is a demand for recognition rather than for toleration. 'Being recognized' seems to imply a form of positive endorsement that goes beyond being merely

[*] Earlier versions of this chapter were presented to seminars at LSE and at the Universities of Newcastle, Oxford, Pavia, and Stirling. I am grateful to participants in those seminars for making me think harder and particularly to Andrea Baumeister, Susan Mendus, Monica Mookherjee, and *The Journal of Political Philosophy*'s anonymous referees for their detailed comments.

tolerated and that is altogether more consonant with cherishing and celebrating diversity. Yet, in contemporary circumstances, demands for recognition are also not without difficulty. In so far as the members of a society possess different and conflicting beliefs and values, and in so far as those conflicting beliefs and values are caught up with differences in identity, the endorsement of identities implied by 'recognition' may not be easily secured. If people possess different and conflicting conceptions of what is right or good or commendable or acceptable that relate to the different identities they confront, those different and conflicting conceptions would seem, prima facie, to present obstacles to the mutual recognition for which theorists of identity so frequently call. They also signal that toleration is a far from redundant ideal. It may be therefore that, rather than treating toleration and recognition as alternatives, we need to find some way of bringing them together so that people can simultaneously tolerate and recognize. In this chapter I investigate whether it is possible to combine toleration with recognition and, if it is, what sort of recognition is possible in circumstances of toleration. I also examine whether the idea of toleration retains its appropriateness and appeal if it is translated from its traditional concern with beliefs, values, and practices to a world in which social diversity is configured as a diversity of identities.

I investigate these issues by examining an argument recently developed by Anna Elisabetta Galeotti.[1] In a stimulating and imaginative analysis, she presents a new understanding of toleration and one that, she believes, makes it a more serviceable ideal for contemporary liberal democratic societies. She is acutely aware of differences between the past social and cultural circumstances in which the traditional idea of toleration flourished and those that characterize contemporary Western societies. But she believes that these changed circumstances require us to revise, rather than to abandon, the ideal of toleration. Her proposal is that we should reconceptualize toleration as recognition.

GALEOTTI ON TOLERATION AS RECOGNITION

Galeotti focuses on what she describes as genuine, nontrivial issues of toleration. By 'genuine issues' she means issues that are genuinely controversial. In Western societies, many once-fevered issues of toleration are now largely moribund: for example, while issues may still arise at the edges of religious toleration, the battle for freedom of worship as a general right has been fought and won. But there are other issues of toleration that remain matters of real dissensus.

One example on which Galeotti focuses is *l'affaire du foulard*: the celebrated issue of whether French secularist policy on state education should be relaxed so that Muslim girls are permitted to wear headscarves while attending state schools. That affair is emblematic of a whole range of cases that have arisen in Western societies in which cultural minorities—typically recent migrant minorities—have encountered a clash between their beliefs and customs and the established rules and conventions of the wider society. The question then arises of how the clash should be resolved: should the existing social norms be revised to accommodate the minority or should they be maintained leaving the minority to adapt to them, or to suffer the consequences if it does not?

Another group on whom Galeotti focuses is homosexuals. In most Western societies, the debate about whether homosexual conduct should be criminalized is now largely over, but some matters concerning homosexuality have persisted. One is the question of whether there should be provision for same-sex marriage. Another has been the issue of whether the army in the United States and many European countries should continue with a policy of not recruiting gays.

Galeotti is clearly right to characterize these as matters of genuine controversy in contemporary Western societies.[2] She also insists that they are issues of toleration; but, as issues of toleration, they are significantly different from past issues and require a revised understanding of toleration which contrasts in a number of ways with the traditional conception.[3] For ease of expression, I shall label these contrasting conceptions of toleration 'old' and 'new'.

Old toleration was concerned with moral disagreement, initially religious disagreement but eventually disagreement of belief and value more generally. The beneficiaries of toleration were people conceived as individuals and what was tolerated—their beliefs and values—were self-chosen rather than ascriptive features of those individuals.[4] Toleration was extended to individuals by granting them rights to choose and by consigning matters such as religious belief and practice to a realm of private choice. Because old toleration took this form, it had an essentially negative character: it required the state or others merely to refrain from interfering in matters that were consigned to the individual's private domain. Galeotti often describes this traditional form of toleration as 'liberal', but that is potentially misleading since she considers the revised conception of toleration that she offers also as liberal and, indeed, as consistent with liberal neutrality.

New toleration must be directed at identities rather than beliefs and values. Identities (of the sort with which Galeotti is concerned) are necessarily group phenomena so that new toleration must be directed at groups rather than individuals. The features of these groups that require toleration are ascriptive; identities, unlike beliefs and values, are matters over which their bearers have no choice. New toleration must depart from the old model in form as well as focus. Tolerating identities is not primarily about extending the range of liberties available to people. Rather, it is about according recognition, and equal recognition, to the groups who bear those identities. Its primary concern is not to allow people to do something to which others might object but to accord respect and standing to their identities so that there is no bar to their full inclusion in society. Such recognition is necessarily public in character; it cannot be secured by a strategy of privatization. It also requires action rather than inaction and so has a positive character that contrasts with the negative policy of noninterference that characterized old toleration.

How then does Galeotti think we should give effect to toleration as recognition? I have said that toleration in this new form is not about extending people's freedoms, but that is true only with qualification. Take the headscarves case. If the French government were to adjust its rules so that Muslim girls were permitted to wear headscarves while attending state schools, those girls would then be free to do something that they were not previously free to do. Likewise, if the rules on army recruitment are changed so that self-declared homosexuals are free to join the army, or if provision is made for same-sex marriage, a new option becomes open to gays. The tolerant measures that Galeotti argues for would therefore extend the freedom of minorities.

However, what really matters about those measures for Galeotti is not the additional freedom they would give but the recognition they would bestow. Recognition is something that must be delivered symbolically. It must piggyback on measures that ostensibly have a more immediate and narrow purpose. If the French government were to modify its secularist policy to enable Muslim girls to wear headscarves while attending state schools, the real significance of that measure would lie not in the additional freedom gained by Muslim girls. It would lie in the recognition that the measure would accord, symbolically, to the entire Muslim community in France. Similarly, if policy is changed to allow openly gay people to join the army, the real value of that change lies not in the new career opportunity it opens up to gays. It lies in the public recognition that that reform accords to the gay identity. Galeotti is inclined to regard the freedoms at stake in these reforms as, in themselves, relatively minor. What gives these apparently minor reforms major significance is their symbolic potential as gestures of recognition.

TOLERATION AND NEGATIVE APPRAISAL

As I have explained, in developing this idea of toleration as recognition, Galeotti understands herself to be revising the traditional conception of toleration. But she does not cast aside every element of the traditional conception and one that she retains is the idea that toleration involves a negative appraisal of what is tolerated. Toleration is relevant only in contexts of disagreement, dislike, or disapproval, since we can tolerate only that to which we object.[5]

What then provides this negative element in the cases with which Galeotti is concerned? The answer lies in what she presumes to be the view of the majority. The majority dislikes or disapproves of the minorities in question. But more than mere dislike or disapproval is involved. Majorities have the power to define what counts as normal in a society and they define their own identity as normal and the different identities of minorities as abnormal or deviant or alien. Indeed, the majority treats minorities with contempt and despises and stigmatizes them in ways that are damaging to their self-respect and self-esteem and that effectively exclude them from full participation in the life of the society. The majority also resents the demands made by minorities conceiving these as threats to what is, for the majority, the established, normal, and proper arrangements of their society.[6]

So then, we have in modern Western societies minorities, such as Muslims and gays, who present distinct identities. Those identities are foci of dislike and disapproval by majorities who define these minority identities as abnormal or deviant. That, in turn, marginalizes and stigmatizes these minorities and damages their self-respect and self-esteem. This state of affairs calls for toleration, but not merely toleration that allows minorities the freedom to live as they see fit. Rather, it must be toleration that accords recognition to minorities so that they cease to suffer humiliating assaults upon their self-respect and self-esteem and are enabled to function as full members of the society to which they belong.

THE IDEA OF RECOGNITION

In examining Galeotti's idea of toleration as recognition, I want to begin by saying something about the idea of recognition itself. In one of its everyday senses, to recognize means to re-cognize, to discern someone or something with which we are already acquainted. So I might 'recognize' my neighbour in the supermarket, or the image of a celebrity in a cartoon, or a piece of music with which I am familiar. In another everyday sense, to recognize means to be aware of, to appreciate, to accept. Thus I might say that I 'recognize' that I will become a competent violinist only if I practise regularly, or that I have been treated fairly, or that I ought to devote more of my income to charities.

This second usage is closer to, but still falls short of, the recognition with which Galeotti is concerned. Recognition in a stronger sense requires acknowledgement rather than mere acceptance. Thus, recognizing a person's talents or their success entails openly acknowledging these in some way; for example, by rewarding them. Similarly, a society's public rules and arrangements may recognize a particular group by formally acknowledging its presence in the society, perhaps by making special provision for it. But acknowledgement is still insufficient to capture all that 'according recognition' implies. Acknowledgement can be evaluatively positive, but it can also be neutral or negative. I may recognize someone's talents but also their limitations; I may recognize their success but also their failure. A society may formally acknowledge the presence and identity of a group only so that it can demean and persecute the group—a fate that has befallen many groups, for example Jews, in many societies. Acknowledgement need not, then, entail a positive appraisal of who or what is acknowledged.

By contrast, those who call for 'recognition' in relation to identity and difference intend it to convey something affirmative.[7] To accord recognition is to accord some sort of positive value to whoever or whatever is recognized. Typically it entails an acceptance or an attribution of status or standing. In some cases, recognition seems to work simply by way of acknowledgement, as though the proper status of the recognized is in no way a product of the process of recognition itself but merely something discovered and acknowledged by the recognizer. In other cases, recognition has a more constitutive role, so that it is the process of recognition itself that bestows status: recognition confers rather than merely notices value. And sometimes recognition seems to hover uncertainly somewhere between these two poles of discovery and conferral.[8] Thus, when we recognize a group in this sense, we do more than merely acknowledge its presence and identity. We indicate our acceptance that, in some way, the group matters, that it properly counts for something. Hence, other things being equal, it is better to be recognized than to pass unrecognized, and to be deprived of recognition is to suffer a loss. In the same spirit, we might insist that an individual or a group deserves, or is worthy of, or is entitled to, recognition. It is the 'good' of recognition that explains why individuals and groups clamour for it and why it is typically characterized as an object of 'struggle'. When Galeotti urges us to tolerate by recognizing, she clearly means that we should recognize in this positive sense: majorities should tolerate minorities not merely by allowing them to live as they wish but also by extending to them the positive good of recognition.

However, the combination of toleration and recognition creates a puzzle. According recognition to a group entails ascribing it some sort of positive value. Yet we can tolerate only that to which we object. So how can we simultaneously tolerate and recognize? How is it possible to retain the disapproval that is essential to an act of toleration while according the approval that is embodied in an act of recognition? In short, how can there be 'toleration as recognition'?

POLITICAL RECOGNITION AND
MAJORITY DISAPPROVAL

In examining this puzzle, the first possibility I shall explore is whether we can intelligibly combine toleration with recognition by separating the locus of each. The idea here is that a society might be able both to tolerate and to recognize a group because its approval and disapproval emanate from different sources.

Considering this possibility will require a brief excursus on what we are to understand by 'political toleration' or a 'tolerant political order' in contemporary circumstances. Modern liberal-democratic states would typically be described as tolerant. Yet what justifies that description is not altogether straightforward. I shall use the standard case of religious toleration to indicate why.

In the past, political regimes have committed themselves to particular religious affiliations. So, for example, in previous centuries some European states were officially committed to Catholicism and others to forms of Protestantism. In those circumstances, it was easy to characterize political regimes as either religiously tolerant or intolerant. They were tolerant if they permitted, and intolerant if they did not permit, the practice of religions other than their officially approved religion. Because they disapproved of certain beliefs and practices (implicitly if not always explicitly), they were in a position either to tolerate or not to tolerate them.

Nowadays, we expect liberal-democratic states to be religiously neutral. I do not wish here to become entangled in large questions about the neutral state, nor to claim that every vestige of religious favouritism has been expunged from the public arrangements of contemporary liberal-democratic societies. I point only to the fact that, nowadays, we do not think it a proper task of a liberal-democratic state to embrace and patronize one particular religious affiliation as its officially approved faith and formally to disapprove of others.

But if a state remains neutral on matters of religious faith, how can it be religiously tolerant? If it neither approves nor disapproves, how can it be capable of toleration? Thus we might conclude that, in these circumstances, the idea of political toleration makes no sense.[9] Yet that would seem an odd conclusion, since we typically think of a society whose political and legal system adopts a 'hands-off' approach to religious diversity as the very model of a religiously tolerant society. So how can we make sense of a political order that is simultaneously neutral and tolerant?

I suggest in this way. We should understand a tolerant political order as one that vetoes the use of political power to prohibit beliefs or practices, even though some of its citizens may disapprove of those beliefs and practices. Its commitment to toleration is manifest not in its refraining from acting on its own disapproval, but in its establishing arrangements that prevent others from acting on theirs. Thus, for example, it will allow neither Protestants to use political power to suppress Catholicism, nor Catholics to use political power to suppress Protestantism. The political order is tolerant because it upholds an ideal of toleration rather than because it itself engages in toleration.[10]

Now let's return to Galeotti's idea of toleration as recognition. If we understand a tolerant political order in the way I propose, we can try to make sense of toleration as recognition by separating the source of disapproval from the source of approval. The majority disapproves, but the state recognizes: the state accords recognition to minorities in spite of their being disapproved of or disliked by the majority. Just as the society's tolerant public arrangements ensure that all are free to live as they wish, even though a majority may disapprove of the use that minorities make of that freedom, so its arrangements should accord recognition to minorities even though a majority may despise or disapprove of those minorities. The majority's dislike or disapproval is not an acceptable reason for a liberal state's withholding recognition from minorities.

Does this present us with a satisfactory way of combining recognition with toleration? The answer depends upon what sort of recognition we seek. If it requires only that a society adjust its arrangements to accommodate the wishes of a minority, it may be feasible. A revision of public policy in France to enable Muslim girls to wear headscarves while attending state schools will then, of itself, constitute recognition of Muslims; and a revision of public policy in Britain and the United States so that gays can join the army will, of itself, constitute recognition of gays. (It may, of course, prove impossible for a democratic state to institute these measures in the teeth of majority opposition, but I leave that problem to one side.)

But it would seem that, for Galeotti, recognition is not reducible to a mere institutional arrangement. It requires an attitude rather than merely an act. It consists in a society's according status, respect, legitimacy, to a group. It relates to the way in which the members of a society regard a minority rather than merely to how its political and legal system provides for that minority. It inheres not in a society's rules and institutions but in what those symbolize. Thus changes in public policy will accord recognition only if they symbolize a positive regard that the wider society (the majority) has for the minority.[11] So, in the kind of democratic society that is Galeotti's concern, it is not possible for recognition to be accorded independently of the attitude of the majority.

The psycho-social character of the recognition that Galeotti seeks is also implicit in the way she conceives its value. It matters not for its own sake but for its consequences. It matters because it will result in the members of a minority ceasing to feel marginalized and excluded, ceasing to confront obstacles to the development of their self-esteem and self-respect, and coming to see themselves through the eyes of others as full members of society, able and entitled to participate fully in a society that is equally theirs.[12] It would seem impossible to achieve those consequences through government-driven institutional changes that leave undisturbed the hostility of the majority and its refusal to accord recognition to the minority. Rather, the whole social context in which the minority conducts its life must change. It would seem then that, if we are to secure toleration as recognition, those who dislike and disapprove must also be those who recognize.

COMBINING RECOGNITION AND DISAPPROVAL

In fact, it is not difficult for people simultaneously to recognize and to disapprove. The simplest way in which they can achieve that combination of views is by recognizing someone under a description that is different from the description that incurs their disapproval. Before developing that thought further, I want to make three distinctions relating to recognition.

General versus Specific Recognition

We can distinguish between general and specific forms of recognition simply in virtue of the more or less inclusive character of the category that is recognized. Thus, according recognition to persons and to Muslims might be, respectively, examples of general and specific recognition. In recent political theory, the concept of recognition has frequently been taken up and deployed as if it were uniquely appropriate to particularity and in some way at odds with more general notions such as 'respect for persons'. In fact, there is no reason why recognition must be recognition only of particularity. The concept of recognition makes perfect sense when deployed in relation to inclusive categories such as personhood and citizenship. Indeed, historically, the demands of excluded and marginalized groups have frequently been demands for general forms of recognition—demands that they too should be recognized as persons, or as citizens, or as human beings fully possessed of the rights common to all human beings.

In this context, the terms 'general' and 'specific' are entirely relative. The category 'person' is more general than 'Muslim' but less general than 'sentient being'. The category 'Muslim' is more specific than 'religious believer' but less specific than 'Sunni' or 'Shi'a' or 'Sufi'. That is why the simple dichotomy between 'universal' and 'particular', commonly used in discussions of recognition, is misleading. Nevertheless, a distinction, albeit relative, between general and specific is useful in considering forms of recognition.

Subject and Identity Recognition

The distinction between subject and identity recognition describes two ways in which we might extend recognition to people. In subject-recognition, we extend recognition to individuals or groups by including them within a category that already enjoys recognition. Thus we might accord recognition to a set of individual subjects by recognizing them as persons. In doing so, we attribute to them the status of personhood and we accept that they are due the treatment and respect that befits persons. Here it is not the category 'person' that is being recognized; that already enjoys recognition. Rather it is individuals who are the candidates for recognition and who receive it in being recognized as persons. If 'personhood' were not already a recognized status, categorizing individuals as persons would not accord them recognition.

Recognition takes this form when we 'recognize as'. So we may accord recognition to people by recognizing them as citizens or as equals or as human beings with rights. Similarly, we may recognize a group as a nation or as a 'people' in international law and so ascribe to that group the status and the rights that go with being a nation or a people. As I have already observed, struggles for recognition have frequently been of this sort: the struggles of people not for recognition of their distinct identity but for their inclusion within an identity that already enjoys recognition.

In identity recognition, by contrast, what is at issue is the status of an identity itself. So if we insist that Muslims should be recognized *qua* Muslims, or gays *qua* gays, we are insisting that that identity should itself be a marker of status or standing or legitimacy or, in Axel Honneth's phrase, 'social validity'.[13] The issue is not who should be included within an already recognized identity; it is rather which identities or descriptions or categories should receive recognition. Most commonly when people call for the recognition of particularities, or what I have called 'specific' recognition, it is identity-recognition that they demand.

Before leaving this distinction, I want to dispose of what might seem a problematic feature of it. I have distinguished between two types of case: (i) cases in which the issue is whether particular individuals or groups should be included within an existing status category and so receive the recognition that goes with that inclusion (subject-recognition), and (ii) cases in which the issue is which categories should receive recognition (identity-recognition). However, in the first sort of case, the individuals who ask to be included within an already recognized identity are unlikely to be a nondescript set of disparate individuals who have merely been overlooked. They are more likely to be a group distinguished by a common identity whose exclusion is related to their identity. For example, the exclusion of women and Afro-Americans from the franchise was an exclusion from full citizenship of subjects with those specific identities, because they bore those identities. Hence their enfranchisement amounted to the inclusion of their identities within full citizenship. So does the distinction between recognizing subjects and recognizing identities stand up? It does since, when people with a given identity receive recognition by being included within a broader identity, the recognition they receive is not recognition of their specific identity but recognition as members of the more inclusive category. Thus, when women were enfranchized, for example, they were accorded recognition not specifically as women but as citizens and citizenship became a gender-independent identity.

Unmediated versus Mediated Recognition

The distinction between unmediated and mediated recognition describes two routes that recognition may take, one direct, the other indirect. Suppose we accord recognition to a particular religious group as that religious group (e.g., to Jews as Jews, to Catholics as Catholics, etc.). That would be an example of 'unmediated' recognition. The category that receives recognition is recognized as such; its recognition does not depend upon its falling within some other category that is a prior and independent object of recognition.

But suppose now that we do not accord the religious group that immediate form of recognition. Rather, we accord it recognition only because we recognize its members as 'persons' and only because, since they are persons, we accept that what matters to them should matter to us because it matters to them. That would be an example of 'mediated' recognition. The religious group as such is not accorded immediate recognition; rather its specific recognition by others depends, for those others, upon its first being recognized under a different, more general and logically prior, description. The inclusion of the subjects of the group within a more general identity provides the rationale for a subsequent and further act of recognition: recognition of the group's specific identity.

Thus the recognition of people under a general description may be a vehicle for their receipt of mediated recognition under a more specific description. But it does not have to be. For many purposes, it may be enough that we recognize individuals merely as persons, or groups as nations, for example; these categories need not have significance only as conduits for recognizing individuals or groups under further, more specific, descriptions. None of the three distinctions I have made maps wholly onto one of the other two.

With these distinctions in place, let us now return to the issue of how it might be possible to accord recognition to a group of whose identity we dis-approve. Suppose we are Christians or Jews or atheists and we take a negative view of Islam. How, even so, might we accord recognition to a group whose identity is provided by Islam? The most obvious answer is by a combination of general, subject, and mediated recognition. Since we take a negative view of Islam, we can hardly regard someone's Muslim identity as something that, in and of itself, commands our recognition. If we are to accord recognition to an Islamic identity, it must be by a more indirect route.

So, for example, our thinking might run as follows. Personhood is a general status that we recognize and we would certainly include Muslims within the category of persons, not *as* Muslims but simply as human individuals—and not in spite of, but simply independently of, their Muslim identity. But recog-nizing someone as a person entails respecting the way of life that that person embraces. Thus we may accord recognition to an Islamic identity because we recognize the significance that that identity has for those who embrace it. We do so because recognizing identities that matter to people is (arguably) part of what is entailed in recognizing them as persons. I have used 'person' here as the general category through which recognition of a particular identity is mediated, but a similar result might be achieved by way of other general categories of recognition.

It might be objected that this sort of mediated recognition of particularity is not really recognition at all. If we take this mediated route, we are not really according recognition to a specific religious or cultural or sexual identity. All we are doing is recognizing that we should give significance to what has significance for people themselves and that we should shape social, political, and legal arrangements accordingly. We are according recognition to the fact that someone embraces a specific identity rather than to the specific identity that they embrace. That may be true. But, if an identity is controversial, it is difficult to see how we can expect more by way of recognition from those who view it negatively.

Yet Galeotti, when she calls for toleration as recognition, seems to demand more than the kind of recognition I have just described. Much of what she says seems to call for the direct recognition of particular identities; in other words, she seems to call for specific and unmediated identity recognition. Like many critics of contemporary liberalism, she dismisses the adequacy of Rawlsian liberal neutralism (though not neutralism as such), inveighs against its difference blindness, and insists that it is people's *particular* identities that we should recognize. So, for example, she insists that recognition should be accorded 'not despite one's origin, culture, skin color, or sexual preference, but precisely because of such features'; that 'recognition works only if it is granted to particular identities . . . it must be granted to each difference separately'; and that, when we achieve toleration as recognition, 'the public presence of minority identities is publicly declared acceptable, not just the public presence of individuals members *as individuals*, but with their full-blown identities, customs and ways of life'.[14]

HONNETH AND TAYLOR ON RECOGNIZING PARTICULARITY

Galeotti is not alone in insisting upon the need for a society to accord unmediated recognition to its members' particularities. Specific unmediated recognition figures equally prominently in Axel Honneth's account of the recognition that people need. For Honneth, recognition of individuals as legal and moral persons, and consequently as beings who possess the rights and who are due the respect that goes with personhood, constitutes a crucial form of recognition. Modern systems of law deliver recognition, through these universal categories, equally to the members of a society or, through the idea of human rights, to humanity at large.[15] But for Honneth, as for Galeotti, this general form of recognition is not enough. People also need to be recognized in their particularity. Social respect needs to be accompanied by social esteem which is directed at 'the particular qualities that characterize people in their personal difference'[16]; 'to acquire an undistorted relation-to-self, human subjects always need . . . a form of social esteem that allows them to relate positively to their concrete traits and abilities'.[17] Although this form of recognition is directed at difference rather than commonality, Honneth accepts that it presupposes a common standard of appraisal or 'intersubjectively shared value-horizon'.[18] A society's shared value-horizon provides the foundation for its 'overarching system of esteem'.[19] But, given the diversity that characterizes modern societies, can we reasonably expect each society to possess the value consensus that is necessary if its members are to have a common basis for esteeming one another's particularity?

Honneth deals with this issue, in part, by noticing the 'pluralization of the socially defined value-horizon' under modern circumstances.[20] By that he means not that people possess different and conflicting values but rather that a society's value-horizon can embrace value-pluralism: it can accord value to many different social contributions and ways of life. But what if there is no such consensual value-pluralism?[21] What if, as in the circumstances of toleration, people possess different and conflicting value-horizons so that they hold different and conflicting views on the merits and demerits of one another differences? It is difficult to see how under those circumstances the particularized form of recognition that Honneth seeks can be possible. In other words, the circumstances of toleration seem to preclude the circumstances that, for Honneth, are essential for particularized recognition.[22]

Charles Taylor also notices that, for the politics of recognition, it is not enough that we recognize one another only under general descriptions such as 'person' or 'citizen'. We must also recognize the unique identity of each individual or group. According that identity-specific recognition entails 'recognizing the equal value of different ways of being. It is this acknowledgement of equal value that a politics of identity-recognition requires'.[23] Like Honneth, Taylor observes that this sort of recognition presupposes a shared horizon of value. If equal recognition of difference is to be genuine, 'we have to share . . . some standards of value on which the identities concerned check out as equal'. Without that, our assertion of the equal value of different identities will be 'empty and a sham'.[24]

In the context of cultural difference, Taylor insists that the politics of recognition demands 'that we all *recognize* the equal value of different cultures; that we not only let them survive, but acknowledge their *worth*'.[25] But is that a reasonable demand to make? As things stand, Taylor observes, we lack shared inter-cultural standards from which we can meaningfully assess different cultures and, in the absence of those standards and their careful application to each culture, an assertion that all cultures are of equal value can be no more than a pretence.[26]

Under current circumstances, we have at most, he argues, reason to operate with a *presumption* of the equal value of different cultures, where 'presumption' means that we have reason to adopt this proposition only as a working hypothesis.[27] That presumption will be vindicated only if and when we have developed the 'fusion of horizons' that will enable us to engage in genuine and meaningful appraisal of different cultures, and only if, judged from those fused horizons, all cultures do indeed prove to be of equal worth. Thus, as things stand, the politics of recognition must remain unsatisfied.

If we apply Taylor's remarks to cases in which groups take exception to one another's identities, that is, to cases in which toleration is at issue, it must be true that those groups lack the shared horizons from which they can accord equal worth to one another's identity. Indeed, those groups may have no aspiration to develop fused horizons and may regard any such aspiration as misplaced, deviant or evil. For Taylor as for Honneth therefore, differences that demand toleration would seem to be differences that preclude unmediated recognition.[28]

GALEOTTI ON RECOGNIZING DIFFERENCE

In one respect, Galeotti's demands may seem to fall short of the specific recognition that Honneth believes must accompany general recognition. Ultimately, her concern is with citizenship, though with citizenship understood in its broadest sense so that it includes genuinely equal opportunities to participate fully in the life of a society rather than the mere formal possession of legal and political rights. Thus, logically, her concerns would seem to be for what I have called subject-recognition rather than identity-recognition: the recognition that she seeks for minorities is recognition as citizens. Hence the emphasis that she places upon 'inclusion'. Yet she seems to think that that outcome can be achieved only by way of a significant measure of identity-recognition.[29] Only if Muslims secure recognition as Muslims, and gays as gays, will we surmount the obstacles to their full recognition as citizens. Thus, like Honneth, she still sees a need for unmediated specific recognition even though the nature and objects of that recognition are significantly different from the particularized recognition that Honneth identifies as a universal need.[30]

How substantial does that recognition need to be? What sort of positive evaluation does it require? Galeotti draws back from the strong form of evaluation that figures in Taylor's account of the politics of recognition: a recognition that requires 'acknowledging, or even endorsing, the intrinsic value of the difference in question'.[31] This strong form of recognition, she says, 'definitely ought not to be extended by democratic institutions to particular forms of life'.[32] She is clearly unhappy with the prospect of state officials' evaluating the content of differences and dispensing approval and disapproval to their bearers. Any such move would sacrifice the antiperfectionism and the impartiality amongst difference that remain essential features of her revised form of liberalism.[33]

Instead of a strong form of recognition that demands public recognition of the *intrinsic* value of differences, she claims to seek only a form of recognition that values differences *instrumentally*, that is, 'for the value they have for their bearers'.[34] The majority need acknowledge only that the differences of minorities have the same value for those minorities as putatively 'normal' characteristics and practices have for the majority. This more modest form of public recognition requires only 'the acceptance, and hence inclusion, of a different trait, behavior, practice, or identity in the range of the legitimate, viable, 'normal' options and alternatives of an open society'.[35]

However, this retreat from strong recognition does not free Galeotti's account of toleration as recognition from all difficulty. Recognizing differences as 'legitimate, viable, normal', if taken at face value, still seems to involve a public evaluation of those differences of a sort that she wants to avoid. It is also problematic if differences are genuinely objects of toleration; if, that is, people find themselves having to recognize as legitimate and normal forms of life that they believe actually to be illegitimate and properly assigned to the abnormal.[36]

Can we dilute the demands of recognition still further to avoid these difficulties? Perhaps we can by adopting Galeotti's suggestion that, rather than recognizing the intrinsic value of differences, we can limit ourselves to recognizing the value that they have for their bearers. That seems to imply something like the following. If you are a Muslim and I am not, the recognition I accord you as a Muslim should stem not from the value *I* give to Islam (which may be nil or negative), but from the value Islam has for *you*. So I accord recognition to your identity because that identity matters to you rather than to me. But that stance seems to rely upon precisely the kind of mediated recognition that I described earlier: because I recognize you as a person (independently of any particular identity you possess), I ascribe value to whatever identity you have—not because I value that identity in and of itself but because respecting you as a person requires that I respect the identity that you embrace. That form of recognition gives primacy to the general rather than the specific, to personhood rather than to difference, and its 'respect' for an identity is consistent with a continuing negative estimate of that identity. Both of these would seem concessions too far for Galeotti.

We seem then to have a choice. We can call for the unmediated recognition of specific identities, which seems inescapably to entail calling, in some form, for the approval or endorsement or validation of each specific identity that we wish to be recognized. But, in that case, it is hard to see what room is left for the disapproval that would make these acts of recognition exercises in toleration. Alternatively, we can recognize someone under a description other than, and more general than, their specific identity, and that general form of recognition can gives us reason to show respect and consideration for a specific identity, even though it is an identity of which we disapprove. But, in that case, our recognition is directed first and foremost not at the specific identity but at a more general identity and it is the generality of that recognition that gives us reason to tolerate the specific identity of which we disapprove.

The question of whether there can be 'toleration as recognition' and, if so, what form it can take, is not merely one that concerns the compatibility of the concepts of toleration and recognition. More importantly, it is a question about what we can reasonably demand of people who live in diverse societies and who take exception to one another's identities. The problem involved in demanding that we recognize identities of which we disapprove is well illustrated by the two groups that serve as Galeotti's primary examples: Muslims and gays. For much of the time, Galeotti seems to think of recognition as a unilateral act: it is the majority that must recognize the minority. Because the majority dominates the society and defines itself as legitimate and normal, it does not stand in need of the recognition sought by marginalized minorities. But the model of recognition more commonly proposed is one of *mutual* or *reciprocal* recognition: everyone should accord recognition to everyone else.

If we seek mutual recognition of identities and if Muslims and gays are present in the same society, what must we demand? We must demand that

Muslims accord recognition to gays as gays. But is that reasonable? Given the way in which homosexuality is regarded within orthodox Islam, how can we expect Muslims as Muslims to accord recognition to gays as gays? And that is not the only dissonance. It is sometimes observed that recognition works only if the recognized esteems the recognizer. If group X despises group Y, group X will gain nothing psychically from its recognition by group Y. If Muslims deprecate homosexuals, recognition directed at them by the gay constituency will be valueless for them. And if gays find themselves unrecognized or 'misrecognized' by Muslims, they may reciprocate by refusing to accord recognition to Muslims—a reaction perfectly exemplified in the stance of the late Dutch politician, Pym Fortune.

SHOULD WE TOLERATE IDENTITIES?

I want to conclude with some general observations on the relationship between toleration and identity and, in particular, to suggest that toleration fits uncomfortably into a world constructed in terms of identity and difference rather than belief and value. There are a number of reasons for this discomfort.

One is that the language of identity sinks people's particularities into their very being. Their particularities become hallmarks of who they *are* rather than merely manifestations of what they believe or what they do. Thus tolerating someone's identity becomes tantamount to tolerating their very existence. But that someone's mere existence should be the object of our toleration is a proposition that we rightly find disconcerting.

Moreover, for some sorts of identity, toleration is arguably nonsensical. We can tolerate only what might be otherwise. If things cannot be but as they are, it makes no sense to say that we tolerate them.[37] Thus Richard Bellamy observes, 'whilst one can tolerate someone's weird dress sense, odd behaviour, strange views and the like, to claim to tolerate the fact someone is black is as nonsensical as saying one tolerates that the sun rises in the morning and sets at night'.[38] Whether Galeotti is right to regard identities such as Muslim and gay as ascriptive is obviously open to a certain amount of argument. But, if someone's identity really is ascriptive, if they cannot be but as they are, 'toleration' of their identity seems misplaced.

A further reason why toleration sits uncomfortably alongside identity and difference is of a rather different sort. The language of identity and difference is not politically innocent. It is commonly part of an agenda that seeks to persuade us to see difference as *mere* difference. The differences that people manifest have often been occasions for conflict, oppression, and unequal treatment. But, if we can be persuaded to see these differences as *mere* differences, we shall come to see the irrationality or unreasonableness of the hostility they often encounter and the injustice of visiting disadvantage and discrimination upon people simply because they are different. In other words, the vocabulary of identity and difference is associated with an agenda of acceptance: rather than viewing difference negatively, we should accept it and, more positively, cherish and celebrate it. That is why toleration can seem the wrong response to differences of identity. If we encounter hostility to an identity, the right strategy, if it is a feasible strategy, is to remove the hostility, rather than to leave it respectfully in place while trying to persuade the hostile to be tolerant.

Indeed, this is the strategy most obviously associated with recognition. Galeotti's majority starts out by regarding the minority as illegitimate, abnormal, deviant, alien, pejoratively 'different', and threatening. In according recognition to the minority, the majority must, if its recognition is genuine, shed those negative attitudes and come to regard the minority as no inferior in status to itself. So does its recognition leave it with anything to tolerate? One obvious possibility is that there will remain a conflict of beliefs between majority and minority but, since Galeotti consigns belief-based conflict to the past, she presumably does not see that as generating a pressing contemporary need for toleration. Perhaps all that is left is a brute dislike of the majority for the minority.[39] But, if that is all that remains, it would seem best if the majority could be induced to shed that too. In fact, it is likely that their dislike will be caught up with their misrecognition of the minority, so that the dissipation or diminution of their dislike will accompany their coming to recognize the minority.

If we turn to the traditional terrain of toleration—beliefs and belief-based practices—things appear very differently. There is a simple reason for that and I shall use the standard case of different and conflicting religious beliefs to indicate what it is. Suppose I am a Protestant and, because I am a Protestant, I take exception to Roman Catholicism. To require me to shed my objection to Roman Catholicism is to require me to give up my Protestantism and that seems a step too far. Similarly, if I am a Muslim, I have reason to object to Christianity and Judaism and even more reason to object to Hinduism, Zoroastrianism, and atheism. The only way I can cease to have these objections is to cease to be a Muslim, but to demand that I should give up my own beliefs, simply so that I shall cease to object to the beliefs of others, is unreasonable. Different beliefs (on the same subject) are conflicting beliefs and that is why, if we think it acceptable that people should continue to hold different beliefs, mutual toleration seems the right policy. Different identities are not, in the same necessary fashion, conflicting identities and that is why a policy of eradicating rather than tolerating conflict can seem the better option when conflict arises in relation to identities.[40]

All of this is, of course, too simple, if only because beliefs and identities are not as separable as my remarks imply. In some instances, such as religious identities, beliefs are constitutive of identity. People's religious identities often owe more to sociological factors than to self-propelled acts of faith, but belief and dogma remain inescapable elements of a religious identity. Beliefs also commonly contribute, very significantly, to ethnic and cultural identities. Even when an identity is not itself obviously belief-based, as for example in the case of a gay identity, it may find itself the object of other people's censorious beliefs. Still other identities incorporate beliefs that are conflictual in very immediate ways; consider, for example, the beliefs constitutive of loyalist or nationalist or republican identities in Northern Ireland. These examples serve notice that generalization across identities is not easy and that the notion of 'mere difference' risks oversimplifying complex social phenomena: different identities/differences are different in nature, raise different issues and invite different responses.

Even so, objections to and toleration of an identity still seem more acceptable if they are directed at the belief- and practice-dimensions of the identity. If people's objections to an identity are targeted at the beliefs and practices intrinsic to the identity and if their objections are rooted in their own deeply held beliefs, we have reason to hesitate before demanding that they give up their objections. As I have indicated, that demand requires the objectors to sacrifice their own beliefs and that may be an unreasonable demand to make.[41] If it is, toleration is likely to emerge as the best policy. If, on the other hand, 'mere' identity is at stake and objection to an identity is fuelled only by hatred or some other form of brute dislike, the best policy, if it is practicable, would seem to be one directed at removing the hatred. Urging toleration of the hated identity will emerge as a second-best strategy, to be fallen back on only if we cannot remove the hatred. I do not pretend that these distinctions will be easy to maintain but neither are they without substance. Consider the terms 'Islamophobia' and 'homophobia', both of which, I suggest, are acceptable only if understood in light of the distinction I am making here. Islamophobia and homophobia describe irrational fears or dislikes directed at Muslims and gays which, because they are irrational, would ideally be overcome. Better to remove a phobia than to indulge it. But it would be absurd to class all objections to Islam as 'Islamophobia', as though any and every challenge to Islam must manifest a psychological disorder that should be corrected therapeutically. The term 'homophobia' is similarly open to overextended use. Doubtless, an unreflective dislike motivates much of the negativity that homosexuals encounter, but sometimes those who voice beliefs that regard homosexual practices or lifestyles unfavourably should be countered by argument rather than by suggestions that they are in the grip of a phobic disorder.

Does, then, toleration have a future? If it does, that is not because it can be easily transferred from a world of beliefs to a world of identities. It is because different and conflicting beliefs and values are still very much a part of our world and because beliefs and values should treated *as* beliefs and values and not as mere markers of identity. If we re-present beliefs and values as nothing more than markers of identity, we misrecognize both them and their holders.[42]

NOTES

1. Anna Elisabetta Galeotti, *Toleration as Recognition* (Cambridge: Cambridge University Press, 2002).

2. Another current issue which, Galeotti argues, calls for toleration as recognition is racist hate speech, though in this case we should accord toleration as recognition to minorities by not tolerating hate speech. I focus on her other examples since the general nature of hate speech laws means that they are less conspicuously geared to the recognition of a particular group.

3. Galeotti, *Toleration as Recognition*, 5–14, 85–109.

4. I shall not here challenge the questionable claim that people 'choose' their beliefs; on that issue, see my 'Bearing the Consequences of Belief', *Journal of Political Philosophy* 2 (1994): 24–43.

5. 'Toleration' is now sometimes used to mean a readiness to accept and positively to value difference, rather than merely a willingness to permit that to which one objects. In this sense, toleration does not entail a negative view of what is tolerated; indeed, it signifies a determination not to view difference negatively. For examples of this usage of toleration, see Karl-Otto Apel, 'Plurality of the Good? The Problem of Affirmative Tolerance in a Multicultural Society from an Ethical Point of View', *Ratio Juris*, 10 (1997): 199–212; and Michael Walzer, *Toleration* (New Haven, CT: Yale University Press, 1997). Galeotti sometimes dallies with this more positive sense of toleration (*Toleration as Recognition*, 21–22, 225) but, for the most part, she conceives toleration as something that is needed only where there is contestation, disapproval or dislike (e.g., pp. 88–94).

6. Galeotti, *Toleration as Recognition*, 133, 223, identifies the majority as male, white, Christian and heterosexual. Taken literally, that makes her 'majority' a numerical minority; but presumably membership of the relevant majority is shifting so that, on issues concerning ethnic minorities and homosexuality, straight white women are no less guilty than straight white men.

7. Recognition has not always been understood as a benign process. Sartre, for example, gave a pathological account of the recognition relation. For accounts of Sartre's thought and influence on this subject and defences of Hegelian recognition against Sartre's interpretation, see: Majid Yar, 'Recognition and the Politics of Human(e) Desire', *Theory, Culture and Society* 18 (2001): 57–76; and Axel Honneth, 'The Struggle for Recognition: On Sartre's Theory of Intersubjectivity', in his *The*

Fragmented World of the Social: Essays in Social and Political Philosophy (Albany: State University of New York Press, 1995), 158–67.

8. Cf. Patchen Markell, 'The Recognition of Politics: A Comment on Emcke and Tully', *Constellations* 7 (2000): 496–506.

9. For an analysis that problematizes 'political toleration' in this way, see Glen Newey, *Virtue, Reason and Toleration* (Edinburgh: Edinburgh University Press, 1999), especially chapters 4 and 5.

10. I argue for the compatibility of neutrality and toleration at greater length in chapter 2.

11. Jonathan Seglow marks the difference between these two sorts of recognition by distinguishing between 'narrow' recognition, which consists in being recognized in measures instituted by the state, and 'wide' recognition, which resides in the affirmative attitudes and sensibilities of a population; 'Theorizing Recognition', *Multiculturalism, Identity and Rights*, ed. Bruce Haddock and Peter Sutch (London: Routledge, 2003), 78–93. In Seglow's terminology, Galeotti's goal is to secure wide recognition; narrow recognition has value if and because it manifests wide recognition.

12. Galeotti, *Toleration as Recognition*, 8–9, 12, 96–99, 100–05, 112–13.

13. Axel Honneth, 'Invisibility—On the Epistemology of Recognition', *Aristotelian Society Supplement* 75 (2001): 111–26 at 115.

14. Galeotti, *Toleration as Recognition*, 8, 16, 101.

15. Axel Honneth, *The Struggle for Recognition: The Moral Grammar of Social Conflicts* (Cambridge: Polity, 1995), 107–21.

16. Honneth, *The Struggle for Recognition*, 122.

17. Honneth, *The Struggle for Recognition*, 121.

18. Honneth, *The Struggle for Recognition*, 121.

19. Honneth, *The Struggle for Recognition*, 126.

20. Honneth, *The Struggle for Recognition*, 122.

21. Honneth allows that there will be conflict over the specific way in which a society's value-horizon should be interpreted, as different groups try to raise the value ascribed to their particularities (*The Struggle for Recognition*, 126–27). That is part of the struggle for recognition. But that struggle, as Honneth conceives it, is not a struggle for toleration. It is a struggle for a new social consensus, or 'solidarity', that will accord positive value, and therefore recognition, to the struggling group (pp. 127–29).

22. Honneth's idea of a population's esteeming one another's particularities is most plausible when those particularities consist in individuals' different functional contributions to their society's common good. It becomes much less plausible when he extends those particularities to include people's different 'ways of life' (*The Struggle for Recognition*, 134) and their 'self-chosen life-goals' (p. 174). He suggests that people with different and conflicting conceptions of the good may be able to esteem one another's conceptions by way of a formal conception of ethical life lodged midway between Kantian moral theory and communitarian ethics (pp. 171–79). That formal conception would be concerned with 'the structural elements of ethical life, which . . . can be normatively extracted from the plurality of all forms of life' (p. 172).

But that is a wholly unconvincing proposal—why should we suppose that there can be any such common 'formal conception' and, even if there could, how could anything so pale and thin do anything for anyone's esteem? More recently, Honneth has limited the particularized recognition he proposes to an achievement principle that recognizes people's different contributions to their society's goals, principally through work. See Nancy Fraser and Axel Honneth, *Redistribution or Recognition? A Political-Philosophical Exchange* (London: Verso, 2003), 135–59. In that volume he addresses issues of identity politics more explicitly than previously and rejects the demands of those who call for specific recognition of different identities (pp. 160–70). In part that is because he believes that many of those demands are really complaints about discrimination and disadvantage and are properly dealt with under the equality principle of legal recognition. But he also observes that the publicly shared value-horizon that would be needed to satisfy those who seek positive endorsement for the practices, ways of life, and value orientations of particular identity groups, simply does not exist (pp. 168–70). I comment on Honneth's thinking on recognition in greater detail in 'Equality, Recognition, and Difference', *Critical Review of International, Social and Political Philosophy* 9 (2006): 23–46.

23. Charles Taylor, *The Ethics of Authenticity* (Cambridge, MA: Harvard University Press, 1992), 51.

24. Taylor, *The Ethics of Authenticity*, 52.

25. Charles Taylor, 'The Politics of Recognition', in Amy Gutman, ed., *Multiculturalism: Examining the Politics of Recognition* (Princeton, NJ: Princeton University Press, 1994), 25–73 at 64 (emphases in the original).

26. Taylor, 'The Politics of Recognition', 70.

27. Taylor, 'The Politics of Recognition', 66.

28. For a different reading of Taylor's position on this point, see Jean Bethke Elshtain, 'Toleration, Proselytizing, and the Politics of Recognition: The Self Contested', *Charles Taylor*, ed. Ruth Abbey (Cambridge: Cambridge University Press, 2004), 127–39. Taylor himself does not juxtapose toleration and recognition in the way I describe here, but I take a dissonance between tolerating and recognizing to be implied in what he does say. The focus of his concern is rather different from mine. The issue to which he addresses his remarks is not how we should respond to conflicts amongst cultures but how we should assess the value of each culture and what might be the result of that assessment. Even if we judge one culture inferior to another (because, for example, it has yielded an inferior literature or no literature), that need not imply a conflict between cultures of a sort that raises issues of toleration. I examine Taylor's approach to recognition more critically in 'Equality, Recognition, and Difference'.

29. For example, Galeotti, *Toleration as Recognition*, 96–99.

30. A further issue is that the specific identities under which people should be recognized and the manner in which they should be recognized may be controversial amongst those at whom recognition is targeted. See Carolin Emcke, 'Between Choice and Coercion: Identities, Injuries, and Different Forms of Recognition', *Constellations* 7 (2000): 483–95. Galeotti, *Toleration as Recognition*, 180–84, notices this as an issue in relation to same-sex marriage.

31. Galeotti, *Toleration as Recognition*, 14–15.

32. Galeotti, *Toleration as Recognition*, 15; also pp. 103, 108, 176, 194–95, 207–08.

33. Galeotti, *Toleration as Recognition*, 14, 73. An intermediate possibility is that, rather than giving either full endorsement or no endorsement to a specific identity, we might give it partial or limited endorsement. Thus, if we take the case of Islam again, those who are not Muslims might recognize value in some features of Islam and Islamic culture. Similarly, Muslims are able to give limited recognition to other 'peoples of the book'. But the demand that we should give limited recognition to the intrinsic value of different ways of life does not avoid the difficulties associated with a demand for full endorsement and Galeotti rejects it (p. 104).

34. Galeotti, *Toleration as Recognition*, 15; also p. 104.

35. Galeotti, *Toleration as Recognition*, 15.

36. At one point (Galeotti, *Toleration as Recognition*, 104), Galeotti goes so far as to say that recognition of a group can be 'content-independent', but it is hard to reconcile that with her repeated assertion that recognition must be recognition of difference. 'Content-independence' implies that we should look past or through difference rather than at it and begins to sound like the difference blindness of which she is so critical.

37. Colloquially, this is not quite true. I might say, for example, that I 'tolerate' a hot climate even though I can do nothing to change it. That could be consistent with what I say in the text—I may choose to remain in an unpleasantly hot climate rather than move to a cooler location. But the 'toleration' I affirm could also be no more than my adopting an attitude of stoical resignation to something I cannot avoid. The Stoic ideal of tolerance was, in part, 'a cultivated indifference toward uncontrollable externalities'; Andrew Fiala, 'Stoic Tolerance', *Res Publica* 9 (2003): 149–68 at 154.

38. Richard Bellamy, 'Toleration, Liberalism and Democracy: A Comment on Leader and Garzön Valdés', *Ratio Juris* 10 (1997): 177–86 at 177. See also Susan Mendus, *Toleration and the Limits of Liberalism* (Basingstoke: Macmillan, 1989), 16–17, 149–51.

39. Galeotti is much more inclined to characterize the negative disposition of the majority towards the minority as 'dislike' rather than 'disapproval'; e.g., *Toleration as Recognition*, 91–94. That presumably reflects her view that contemporary difference concerns identity rather than belief and value. If identity supplants belief and value as the principal marker of difference, antagonism will take the form of dislike rather than disapproval.

40. For a rather different argument against transferring the language of toleration from beliefs to identities, see Wendy Brown, 'Reflections on Tolerance in the Age of Identity', *Democracy and Vision: Sheldon Wolin and the Vicissitudes of the Political*, ed. Aryeh Botwinick and William E Connolly (Princeton, NJ: Princeton University Press, 2001), 99–117. Although there is some overlap between Brown's argument and my own, her view rests upon a decidedly jaundiced analysis of 'tolerance' that forms no part of my argument.

41. I phrase this tentatively because, even if we look favourably upon diversity of belief, there may be some beliefs that we think should be dropped. The classic example is, of course, racist belief. Our thinking about the appropriateness of toleration

will depend partly upon our view of which objections are reasonable (assuming that we can recognize an objection as reasonable even though it is one that we do not share). If we think an objection is unreasonable, we shall think that it should be dropped rather than be retained but provide occasion for toleration. But given that toleration becomes relevant only in contexts of conflicting belief and value, it may very well be that those conflicts will infect the question of which beliefs and values are reasonable and which unreasonable, and therefore the question of when toleration is virtuous and when it is not. Cf. John Horton, 'Toleration as a Virtue', *Toleration: An Elusive Virtue*, ed. David Heyd (Princeton, NJ: Princeton University Press, 1996), 28–43.

42. I argue against reinterpreting beliefs as identities in chapter 5.

Chapter 8

Liberalism, Belief, and Doubt[*]

The relationship between liberalism and scepticism has long been a contro-versial one. Does the liberals' commitment to freedom of belief derive from their own uncertainties about the true, the right, and the good or does their liberalism stand foursquare upon a view of what is indeed true, right, and good? Some contemporary exponents of liberalism, such as Bruce Acker-man,[1] find a significant place for scepticism in the foundations of liberalism. Others, such as John Rawls and Ronald Dworkin, will have no truck with it and have reacted sharply to suggestions that their own positions owe anything to scepticism.[2]

The anti-sceptics are probably in the majority amongst contemporary lib-eral writers and there is good reason why that should be so. First, most liber-als take a firm stand on what is right and what is wrong in political life and the firmness of that stand is at odds with the uncertainties of scepticism. Sec-ondly, a liberalism founded upon scepticism is in danger of being engulfed by its own foundations; why should liberalism be the only belief to escape the corrosive consequences of scepticism? Thirdly, scepticism may seem to offer too many hostages to fortune. Should our commitment to what is right in political life really be contingent upon the vagaries of human knowledge? Will not scepticism result in ambivalence, indifference, or withdrawal leav-ing liberals ill-equipped to fend off the confident claims of their opponents?

In this chapter I shall argue that, in spite of these reservations, doubt may have a significant role to play in liberal argument. I shall argue neither that liberalism necessarily entails scepticism nor that scepticism must issue in

* Earlier versions of this chapter were presented to seminars at LSE and at the Universities of New-castle, Oxford, Pavia, and Stirling. I am grateful to participants in those seminars for making me think harder and particularly to Andrea Baumeister, Susan Mendus, Monica Mookherjee, and *The Journal of Political Philosophy*'s anonymous referees for their detailed comments.

liberalism. Rather, more modestly, I shall argue that some sorts of liberalism are plausible only given certain background epistemological assumptions and that 'reasonable doubt' may often be amongst those assumptions.

Liberalism comes in a variety of forms and has been supported by a variety of arguments, not all of which are compatible with one another. I cite that as a feature, not as a failing, of liberalism, and it is no more a feature of liberalism than it is of other ideologies such as conservatism and socialism. Thus freedom of belief has been defended on a variety of grounds. Among those are that it is conducive to social peace and harmony, that it facilitates the progress of knowledge, that coercion is inefficacious in the case of (certain sorts of) belief, and that governments cannot be trusted not to abuse power over beliefs. These are strong arguments and nothing I say will challenge them. The defence that I want to examine is that individuals should be free to form, to promote, and to live according to their own beliefs because they have an interest in so doing. On this view, freedom of belief is to be respected not because of desirable consequences that flow from it, such as social harmony and progress towards truth, nor because of the ineptitude and corruptibility of those who wield political power, but because of the interest individuals have in having their beliefs respected simply because those are *their* beliefs. I shall examine this notion as it occurs in two sorts of liberal philosophy: first, the deontological liberalism of writers such as Rawls and Dworkin which seeks to establish principles for a just society while remaining neutral between competing conceptions of the good, and second, the perfectionist liberalism of writers such as Vinit Haksar and Joseph Raz which gives a central place to the value of autonomy.[3]

I

Before turning to either I shall say something about the distinction between the two things that the liberal may be liberal about: wants and beliefs. Suppose that we confront a number of people each of whom expresses a want and (if this is not pleonastic) each of whom wishes that want to be satisfied. Suppose too that those wants conflict in some way. That might be because they are wants for incompatible states of affairs or because, while they are not inherently conflicting wants, their satisfaction demands resources which are in scarce supply. We shall then need some principle or principles to determine whose wants should be satisfied and in what measure. If we give each individual equal standing and if we view the conflict simply as one of competing wants, it is easy to see how a liberal solution to that conflict might be justified. Equal standing requires that no individual's wants should be considered of greater significance than any other's. And if the matter to be settled is construed as purely one of conflicting wants, there is no case for censoring or preferring certain wants in the name of the true, the right, or the good. There need be nothing especially 'sceptical' in such a view; it may be simply that, in so far as a conflict of wants is viewed as merely that, no epistemic issues are thought to arise.

Now suppose that we confront a body of individuals each of whom proffers different beliefs. The 'different beliefs' that are the concern of liberalism are, of course, not beliefs about different things but different beliefs about the same things and therefore, of necessity, conflicting beliefs. Beliefs are clearly different from wants. Beliefs are about what is true or right or prudent or efficacious or whatever. It is in the nature of beliefs that they are either correct or incorrect (or perhaps a mixture of the two) even though in many cases we may be unable to establish which particular beliefs are correct. People hold the beliefs they do either because they think that they are correct or because, given their current state of information, they think they are more likely to be correct than any of the alternatives. If they had adequate reason to think that their current beliefs were false, they would, of course, cease to hold them. Moreover, beliefs are not person-centred in the same way as wants. If my claim to something is grounded simply in my wanting it, then it is relevant not only that I *want* it but also that *I* want it. My claim to having that want satisfied relies, in part, on my being a person whose wants merit attention. Beliefs are not similarly person-centred. My claim that so-and-so is the case need not be a claim about myself or for myself and it is a claim the merits of which are independent of the individual who puts it forward. This contrast in the relevance of person-centredness can also be seen in that, while it would be absurd for a group to seek to satisfy a want that no one possessed, it would not be similarly absurd for a group to consider and evaluate a belief that none of its members currently held.

Two things seem to follow from these contrasts. First, people who hold conflicting beliefs do not have conflicting interests in the straightforward way in which those with conflicting wants have conflicting interests. On the contrary, *prima facie*, there would seem to be no conflict of interests in the case of beliefs. All individuals have an interest in holding and acting upon those beliefs which are, in fact, true or right or judicious, and they themselves are committed to their current beliefs only because they hold them to be true or right or judicious. Consider the position of two people both of whom want international peace. One of them believes that unilateral nuclear disarmament is the strategy most likely to promote peace, the other does not. It would seem bizarre to hold that one of them has an interest in the adoption of a policy of unilateral nuclear disarmament while the other does not merely because that accords with the beliefs of each. Rather, the interest of both lies in that policy's being adopted which will actually do most to promote peace, whichever policy that turns out to be and with whoever's belief that happens to coincide. Consider now a quite different example. The Christian and the Muslim in presenting their different systems of belief to the world are not simply confronting the world with their different wants. Each is advancing a claim about the one true god and the one true religion and, because they hold those beliefs to be true, they also hold it to be in the interests of all, and not just of themselves, to embrace and act upon those beliefs. By the same token, if those beliefs were false, it would be contrary to the interests of all, including those who currently hold them, to embrace and act upon them.[4]

Secondly, and consequentially, it is not at all obvious that the appropriate response to a conflict of belief is the liberal response. Rather than giving everyone equal scope to pursue their own beliefs as one might give each equal scope to satisfy their own wants, it might be more appropriate for a group of individuals to seek to resolve their differences by attempting to establish which, if any, of their different beliefs are correct. That, after all, should be their primary concern *qua* believers. It is only if there is no satisfactory way of determining which beliefs are correct that it would seem necessary or desirable to cast around for other ways of dealing with conflicting beliefs such as providing for individuals to each follow those beliefs which they themselves have come adopt.

Before proceeding, two complications must be mentioned. One is the obvious point that, in reality, wants and beliefs are more intricately related than my simple dichotomy suggests. Wants will often be nested in beliefs so that it will be difficult to assign differences amongst individuals simply to one or other category. For the same reason we may hesitate to accept that individuals have an interest in having their wants satisfied whatever the nature or origin of those wants. An individual may want x rather than y because that individual wants z and because he or she believes, mistakenly, that x will, and y will not, secure z. In that case we may say simply that this person's interest lies in having (or even that his or her 'real want' is for) y rather than x. Again, an individual may want something for its own sake, such as a ride on a roller-coaster or a career in medicine, but this want may be mistaken in that it relies upon a misapprehension of what that ride or that career will really be like. However, the significance of the distinction between wants and beliefs is not destroyed by the complicated truth about their inter-relation. The different characters of conflicts of want and conflicts of belief remain obvious and important even though establishing to which category a conflict ultimately belongs may require a good deal of unravelling.

A second complication is that what matters fall within the province of want and what within the province of belief is not simply given in the nature of the case for all to see. Where that line falls (if it falls anywhere) is itself a possible matter of contention. Thus A, being an Aristotelian, may believe that there is a good for humanity which is objectively identifiable, independently of the expressed wants of particular individuals. For A, therefore, what is good for someone falls within the province of belief and is not merely a matter of satisfying the wants that people happen to have. B, being a Hobbesian, thinks differently. B rejects any notion that humanity has an objectively identifiable *telos*. What is good for people is simply a matter of what they want. Human beings have similar make-ups and that is why they often exhibit similar wants so that what is good for one will sometimes be good for all. But that does not indicate that there is an objectively identifiable good for humanity but merely a coincidence of wants. Thus, on B's view of the world, there is no case for disregarding or censoring an individual's wants in the name of some good discerned independently of that individual's wants because there is no such independently discernible good. In other words, what is an epistemic matter for A is not for B. (B might allow a certain amount of 'correction' of an individual's wants in so far as they have been formed on the basis of false information but ultimately, B's view of an individual's good, unlike A's, would have to remain tied to the individual's actual wants.)

Thus what areas of life are susceptible to knowledge and what are not is itself a disputable matter. It is unlikely that anyone would make no place for both areas. However cosmic and comprehensive one's system of belief, it is unlikely that there will remain no area in which wants can be simply innocent or 'indifferent' (in the old theological sense of that term). Equally, those who give maximum scope to the sphere of wants would still have to recognize the distinction between wants and beliefs and that some questions are questions of belief. Nevertheless, there is still considerable room for disagreement over what is, and what is not, an epistemic matter. And clearly one tactic that liberals can and have used in meeting their opponents is to deny that there is any objectively given order of norms which justifies imposing a particular form of life upon individuals. That is, the liberal may argue that each should be allowed to follow his own path on a certain matter simply by characterizing that matter as one of want rather than belief.

In so far as one assigns a matter to the realm of wants, issues of scepticism simply do not arise for the matter is thereby rendered nonepistemic. One simple reason therefore why liberalism cannot be comprehensively underpinned by scepticism is that, on many matters which are of concern to the liberal, scepticism will not be at issue. It may be that, if B assigns to the realm of wants what A insists belongs in the realm of beliefs, B's view will be described as sceptical simply because B rejects what A asserts. More generally, the assignment of a matter to the realm of wants itself involves a sort of epistemic judgement if only a negative one. For that reason too, a largely want-regarding view may be labelled sceptical. I do not want to become entangled here in what we should understand by 'scepticism'. My interest is in the question of how far doubt and uncertainty have a role to play within liberalism and the only point I want to make now is that, in so far as one confidently treats a conflict as purely one of wants, issues of doubt and uncertainty do not arise. Thus my concern henceforth will be almost entirely with how the liberal should respond to conflicts of belief.

II

In considering that question, I want to begin by looking at the neutralist liberalism of writers such as Rawls, Dworkin, and Ackerman. Simple and crude the distinction between wants and beliefs may be, but the conceptual apparatus used by those writers is ill-equipped to recognize it or to give it any significance. Neutralist liberals hold, amongst other things, that the state should function as a neutral arbiter amongst individuals who possess different and competing 'conceptions of the good'. The phrase 'conception of the good' would seem to incorporate both of what I have described as wants and beliefs. As the phrase stands it might suggest something essentially epistemic in character (it is, after all, a 'conception') and certainly Rawls, particularly in his recent writings, seems inclined to view it primarily in that way. Dworkin and Ackerman, on the other hand, clearly intend it to take in what we would ordinarily describe as wants or preferences and it is difficult to see how a comprehensively neutralist theory could do otherwise. Indeed, there is some justification, within neutralism itself, for overlooking the wants/beliefs distinction. To characterize the good either as a matter of want or as a matter of belief would be to prejudge the nature of the good in a way that would violate the very neutrality which is at the heart of the doctrine. On the other hand, ignoring the distinction also brings problems in its train. I have already indicated that, given the different natures of wants and beliefs, reasons for respecting individuals' wants might not also be reasons for respecting their beliefs. Different sorts of conceptions of the good may have to be handled in different ways. The blurring of that distinction might also explain why these authors seem overready to treat conflicts of belief either as, or as if they were, simply conflicts of want or preference.

The force of the neutralist's argument is, I think, clear within the realm of wants. But can we suppose that identical reasoning will apply with identical force in the case of beliefs? Would, for example, rational individuals in Rawls's 'original position' respond to differences of belief in the same way as to differences of want? Would their response in no way depend upon the epistemic status of the beliefs with which they were confronted? In Rawls's original position, individuals know that they possess different beliefs but they do not know which particular beliefs each of them holds and they are no more able to assess which beliefs are correct than they are in ordinary life. Now let us reverse that last circumstance. Suppose that individuals in the original position remain behind a veil of ignorance so that they still do not know which particular beliefs will turn out to be theirs, but suppose that in one respect they are uniquely informed. They have revealed to them 'the truth'. They are enabled to know with certainty whether there is one right way to live, and if so, what that one right way is, whether there is a God, and if so, what God requires of us, and so on. They are therefore in a position to know which beliefs are true and which false even though they continue to remain ignorant of whether their own beliefs will turn out to be true or false. However, this shared knowledge of the truth is temporary. As the veil of ignorance is lifted, so the shutters will descend upon their vision of the truth and they will forget what that truth is and even that there is such a truth. What would individuals agree to under these conditions? Surely they would attempt to establish an order of things which would ensure that, as far as possible, they lived in accordance with the truth. What possible wish could anyone have now to live in accordance with his or her future, independently formed beliefs if it were clear, beyond doubt, that those future beliefs would be false? Establishing such an order of things would, of course, present all manner of practical difficulties. Given that a substantial number of future citizens would not be able to recognize the truth for what it was, they might be too recalcitrant to enable such a society to exist. Even if it could, the costs in coercion might be adjudged too great to be acceptable. In other words, we would encounter problems of what Rawls calls 'the strains of commitment'. But these would be merely practical obstacles which stood in the way of their shared aspiration not to live lives based upon falsehoods. They do not show that individuals would have a readymade incentive to opt for a society which allowed or encouraged each to live in accordance with his or her own independently formed beliefs irrespective of the character of their content.

The point of my rendering Rawls's thought experiment still more fanciful in this way is to suggest that how it is rational for individuals to handle conflicting beliefs is not entirely independent of the epistemic status of those beliefs. If there were some authority to whom people could refer and in whom they could have complete confidence, it would seem rational for them to defer to his or her or its pronouncements rather than to stick with their own independently formed beliefs. The same would apply if there were some decision-procedure, such as Rousseau contemplated, which could be relied upon to come up with the right answers or which had a greater probability of lighting upon the right answers than any particular individual.

Even when we insert the assumption of reasonable doubt into the original position, the reasoning by which rationally self-interested individuals arrive at freedom of belief might still be quite different from that suggested by Rawls. If conflicting beliefs constitute *bona fide* endeavours to discern a single truth, the rational individual might approach those not as so many conflicting interests calling for a distributive solution but as a state of affairs in which all share a common interest. If his reasonings about the conditions most propitious for the pursuit and the emergence of the truth lead him to thoughts similar to those found in chapter 2 of Mill's *On Liberty* (which, in spite of the criticisms they have received, still strike me as immensely powerful arguments), then he may conclude that all individuals have a common interest in allowing the propagation of as wide a variety of beliefs as possible. In other words, each will think not so much in terms of an interest each has in propagating his own beliefs, but rather in terms of the interest all have in the free espousal of every individual's belief. Indeed, given the impartial view individuals are forced to adopt in the original position, they are peculiarly well-situated to look at beliefs in that way.

How then might we get beyond this common interest in the free exchange of ideas to the view that each has an interest in being able to propagate and to live according to his or her own beliefs? Can we hold that view without paying any regard to the epistemic status of those beliefs? In considering Rawls's answers to these questions I want to draw upon his more recent writings since those seem to provide a more direct treatment of these issues than his *Theory of Justice*.[5] In those writings, Rawls offers a view and a defence of a liberal society that is more narrowly based than his *Theory of Justice*. He now stresses that justice as fairness is a theory designed only for a constitutional democracy under modern conditions and that it is intended simply to articulate and to organize the principles implicit in the public culture of a modern constitutional democracy.[6] This makes it difficult to know quite what is a premise and what is a conclusion in his argument, or even if it is right to view his theory in those terms.[7]

Setting aside that problem of interpretation, Rawls's position now seems to rest more fully than in his *Theory of Justice* upon a certain conception of the person. That conception sees persons as moral agents possessed of two moral powers: (1) 'the capacity for an effective sense of justice, that is, the capacity to understand, to apply and to act from (and not merely in accordance with) the principles of justice', and (2) 'the capacity to form, to revise, and rationally to pursue a conception of the good'. Persons so conceived are deemed to possess highest-order interests in the realization and the exercise of those two moral powers.[8] Thus individuals in the original position are now to be conceived not merely as human beings motivated by typically human concerns but as moral beings who see themselves as having an overriding interest in the realization and exercise of their moral powers. Similarly, primary goods are to be understood as goods which are instrumental to the realization and exercise of those powers. Thus, in the original position, individuals would be concerned to reach an agreement upon the distribution of primary goods which maximized their opportunities for realizing their moral powers. In particular, they would agree to an equal distribution of basic liberties, including freedom of thought and liberty of conscience.[9]

Clearly, in relation to the issue that I am concerned with, the burden of Rawls's view is carried by his notion that individuals have a highest-order interest in being able to form, revise, and rationally to pursue a conception of the good. But why should individuals be deemed to have a highest-order interest in that capacity? One possible answer would be that what *is* good for each individual is simply the development and pursuit of a plan of life that she has devised for herself. There simply is no objectively identifiable good or right way of living for individuals. Good living consists only in the pursuit of one's self-chosen goals and projects. But that cannot be Rawls's view for two related reasons. First, it would involve his taking a stand upon the nature of the good whereas his theory is intended to remain scrupulously neutral upon that question.[10] Second, Rawls is quite clear that conceptions of the good can be, and perhaps normally are, nested in philosophical, religious, or moral beliefs. That is, his view is meant to accommodate conceptions of the good which are regarded by their holders as objectively right or true (rather than merely as chosen or even as matters in which there is scope for choice) and Rawls does not intend to challenge the epistemic foundations of conceptions of the good so conceived. On the contrary, his theory is intended to provide a just way of dealing with those conflicting beliefs as well as with the conceptions of the good which result from them.[11]

A second possible answer as to why we should give such pre-eminence to the capacity to form and pursue a conception of the good is that there is no clear way of establishing which of the conflicting beliefs involved are correct and which are incorrect. Nor is there good reason for supposing that the beliefs held by a particular group in a society are true merely because they are held by that group. Were there a clearly correct set of beliefs, or a set of Platonic philosophers whose pronouncements could be accepted as authoritative, individuals would have an overriding interest in having their lives shaped to accord with those true beliefs or pronouncements. But, since there is room for reasonable doubt and difference of view, there is also room for taking account of the fact that people can think for themselves and can arrive at their own conclusions about what they should do with their lives. Of course, the absence of manifest truths in these matters does not, of itself, entail that individuals should be left to decide for themselves. That inference also requires some view of the capacities of individuals and the significance of those capacities in their lives. But, without the possibility of reasonable disagreement over conceptions of the good, there would not seem to be scope for the value Rawls gives to individuals' being free to form and to pursue conceptions of the good based upon the philosophical, religious, or moral beliefs that they themselves have come to adopt.

Rawls himself is extremely reluctant to make any room for epistemological considerations of this sort. However, some of his remarks on the nature of justice as fairness imply a similar train of thought. Justice, as it occurs in his theory, presupposes that there is no objectively set order of justice which individuals have to discover.

> The search for reasonable grounds for reaching agreement rooted in our conception of ourselves and in our relation to society replaces the search for moral truth interpreted as fixed by a prior and independent order of objects and relations, whether natural or divine, an order apart and distinct from how we conceive of ourselves.[12]

The absence of any such antecedently given principles of right and justice is presupposed both by the conception of individuals in the original position as autonomous agents of construction and by the evolution of principles of justice via the technique of pure procedural justice.[13] Presumably if there were such a given moral order we could hardly give value, let alone overriding value, to a different conception of justice that individuals had (incorrectly) settled upon merely because they had settled upon it. Similarly, if there were a determinate and discoverable good, we could hardly think of individuals as being morally at liberty to ignore it and to pursue some other self-chosen form of life.

Yet, as I have already remarked, Rawls fights shy of giving any weight to this sort of consideration in dealing with conceptions of the good. His own approach to the phenomenon of rival beliefs focusses not upon beliefs and their epistemic status but upon believers and their inability to agree. Much of the impetus behind his argument derives from his conviction that principles of justice need to be mutually acceptable to all of the members of the society which they are to order, even though those members are deeply divided over philosophical, religious or moral matters and even though there seems no prospect of their ever reaching agreement on those matters.[14] Rawls's stress upon this need for mutually acceptable and practically workable principles might suggest that his theory of justice is ultimately inspired by a pragmatic concern for the attainment of social peace and stability rather than by high moral ideals. Thus freedom of belief might seem no more than an expedient for social harmony. In fact Rawls is anxious to deny that what he is proposing is a mere *modus vivendi*.[15] Although his conception of justice is a specifically 'political' conception in that it is intended not as a comprehensive moral theory but as a theory of justice specifically for the basic structure of a state, it is still a 'moral' conception: a conception of what constitutes a fair system of cooperation between free and equal moral persons.[16] Thus, we are not being told that the designer of a constitution for a pluralistic society has to operate merely *as if* individuals possessed an interest in forming and pursuing their own beliefs and conceptions of the good because, for all practical purposes, that mimics the social reality that the constitution designer has to cope with. Rather, we are asked to accept that individuals do indeed have an interest in being able to form and to pursue their own beliefs and conceptions of the good. In other words, Rawls's conception of the just society remains grounded not upon what, as a matter of fact, is necessary to secure consensus but upon what, as a matter of right, is owing to each individual as the possessor of a system of beliefs including a conception of the good.

Under certain assumptions, of course, the status of rival beliefs may be built into the standing given to rival believers. At one point Rawls remarks that 'the basic intuitive idea' behind his conception of citizens as free and equal persons is that 'in virtue of what we may call their moral powers, and *the powers of reason, thought and judgement connected with those powers,* we say that persons are free. *And in virtue of their having these powers to the requisite degree* to be fully cooperating members of a society, we say that persons are equal'.[17] It is difficult to know just how much intellectual competence is being attributed to individuals here. But, if part of the idea is that each individual has sufficient competence to develop a 'reasonable' set of beliefs upon which to found a conception of the good, it follows that disagreements amongst such individuals about their beliefs and their related conceptions of the good must themselves be reasonable. In other words, if reasonable people can disagree over such matters, those matters must themselves be ones over which there can be reasonable disagreement and reasonable doubt. To that extent, therefore, the epistemic latitude necessary to make Rawls's view plausible may be implicit in his conception of citizens as persons.[18]

Before leaving Rawls, I want to point to one other feature of his theory which illustrates both his tendency to assimilate beliefs to wants and the difficulty involved in ignoring the epistemic standing of certain sorts of belief. Rawls, as we have seen, thinks that if a conception of justice is to perform its social role it must be mutually acceptable to all members of the society that it is to order. The principles of justice must be such that, if individuals encounter a conflict between those principles and their conception of the good, they are willing to see that conception give way to the principles of justice. Those principles limit the conceptions of the good that are 'permissible' and, in that sense, Rawls asserts the priority of the right over the good.[19] Thus, although he uses a model in which individuals are assumed to possess specific conceptions of the good of which they are ignorant in the original position (rather than one in which they have yet to form conceptions of the good),[20] he is careful to argue that each is not tied inescapably to any particular conception of the good.[21] That is, individuals are capable of revising their conceptions of the good if these turn out to be at odds with the principles of justice. Moral persons may have '*higher-order* interests' in their being able to pursue the *particular* conception of the good that they hold at a given time, but they have '*highest-order* interests' in developing and exercising the capacity for a sense of justice and their *capacity* for forming, *revising*, and rationally pursuing *a* conception of the good.[22] Since their highest-order interests prevail over their higher-order interests, they should be willing to revise their conception of the good if it does not conform to the principles of justice.

Now, once again, this view is far more plausible if we model conceptions of the good upon wants rather than upon beliefs. In advance of there being settled rules allocating rights, liberties, and material resources, I may entertain goals and aspirations which turn out to be unsustainable once those rules have been established. The fulfilment of my initial aspirations may demand more than my fair share of resources or may be attainable only at the expense of other people's allotted liberties. I should therefore revise or moderate my aspirations to fit with what justice allows. But if we interpret conceptions of the good as beliefs, or as critically linked to beliefs, this notion of revision in the light of the principles of justice is much less plausible. If I hold a philosophical or religious or moral belief that turns out to be at odds with the principles of justice, why should I give it up? It might be convenient for me to do so, but convenience hardly ranks as a reason for ceasing to believe that something is right or true. This question is particularly pressing given that Rawls's constructivist account of justice issues in principles which are 'most reasonable' rather than 'true'.[23] Thus, that my beliefs conflict with Rawls's principles of justice is not obvious evidence of their falsity. It would seem reasonable to require that sacrifice only if my beliefs were not securely grounded enough to warrant their continued assertion in opposition to the principles of justice.[24]

Without that assumption the viability of Rawls's theory seems to depend upon there being few or no beliefs which will challenge his conception of justice. That may be why Rawls has recently stressed the significance of 'overlapping consensus'.[25] The idea of an overlapping consensus is of a consensus that can be found amongst opposing religious, philosophical, and moral doctrines, in spite of their opposition, because they each contain within themselves reasons (albeit different reasons) for supporting the political conception of justice as fairness. A society will be more stable to the extent that it is supported by such an overlapping consensus. The general direction of that idea is quite contrary to the rest of Rawls's theory. Most of what Rawls has to say on justice seeks to found it upon reasons that people can acknowledge quite independently of any particular conception of the good and which they can therefore support whatever conception of the good they hold. However, overlapping consensus puts things the other way round; it is the idea of a society's finding support for its principles of justice from *within* the conceptions of the good held by its members. It therefore relies upon individuals already possessing a commitment to freedom of belief and liberty of conscience as part of their particular conceptions of the good rather than finding reasons for acknowledging those freedoms independently of their particular conceptions.

The terms in which Dworkin deals with fundamental questions of liberty also invite us to conflate wants and beliefs. Much of his argument is cast in the language of 'preferences'.[26] Thus the imposition of the beliefs of some upon others is represented as merely the imposition of the (external) preferences of some upon others, whereas those who are actually demanding that liberty be curtailed in the name of what is right or true would protest that this has nothing to do with their 'preferences'. However, Dworkin might well reply that his use of the language of preference is simply a concession to the utilitarianism that he takes on board purely for purposes of argument. He himself is not necessarily committed to that utilitarianism or the reduction of beliefs to preferences.[27]

The principle to which Dworkin is committed is that of equal concern and respect. It is upon that principle that his liberalism is based. In particular, he understands the obligation of a government to treat its citizens with 'equal respect' to require that it treat them 'as human beings who are capable of forming and acting on intelligent conceptions of how their lives should be lived'.[28] It is therefore a central tenet of liberalism for Dworkin that a government must remain neutral as between different conceptions of the good so that 'political decisions must be, so far as is possible, independent of any particular conception of the good life, or of what gives value to life'.[29]

Why should we be bound by the principle of equal concern and respect in this form? Does the notion of respecting citizens equally entail, without further assumption, that we should treat their beliefs as of equal merit or as if they were of equal merit? Dworkin seems implicitly to accept that it does not in allowing the possibility of a nonliberal interpretation of the principle of equal concern and respect. A nonliberal equipped with a specific theory of what is good for people might also embrace that principle and go on to hold that it requires a government to treat each of its citizens as 'the good or truly wise person would wish to be treated'. On this view, 'good government consists in fostering or at least recognising good lives; treatment as an equal consists in treating each person as if he were desirous of leading the life that is in fact good, at least so far as this is possible'.[30] Indeed, Dworkin does not merely recognize that possibility, he goes on to give an account of a conservative position of just this sort, viz. a position which embraces the principle of equal concern and respect but which interprets that principle in the light of the conservative's conception of the good person and the virtuous society.[31]

Now Dworkin does not accuse his conservative of any simple error of logic or understanding in relation to his use of the principle of equal concern and respect. So wherein lies the difference between the conservative and the liberal? The most obvious answer is that liberals believe that conservatives claim an authority for their conception of the good person and the virtuous society that is quite unwarranted. What conservatives present as simply 'the good' and 'the virtuous' are really no more than their contestable interpretations of those notions. Consequently, conservatives, in imposing their conception of the good upon a society, are really doing no more than imposing their views upon others whose own views on these matters are no less deserving of respect. That is why the conservative's position really constitutes a violation of the principle of equal concern and respect.

Dworkin himself is reluctant to accept that the liberal's position owes anything to scepticism.

> Liberalism cannot be based on skepticism. Its constitutive morality provides that human beings must be treated as equals by their government, not because there is no right and wrong in political morality, but because that is what is right.[32]

That may be so. But Dworkin's bold statement of the liberal conception of right still leaves room for reasonable doubt and reasonable disagreement to play some part in explaining why a government's treating people equally should entail its not preferring some conceptions of the good over others. If we do not accept that and we continue to hold that the imperative of neutrality is a matter of principle rather than of practical caution, we seem to be left with only two possibilities. One is that conceptions of the good really are reducible to preferences so that epistemic questions of doubt and certainty simply do not arise. The other is that individuals should be accorded a fundamental right to determine the course of their lives however ill-founded are their beliefs. That right is most immediately intelligible as a sort of irreducible right of ownership of each over his own life—'irreducible' because it does not stand upon some more fundamental claim concerning an individual's interests. 'My life is *mine* and that, of itself, entitles me, and only me, to decide upon its disposition'. I concede that, if it is that sort of proprietorial claim that lies at the heart of a liberal theory, the soundness of an individual's beliefs is ultimately irrelevant to how she should be treated. (Although, if it is that right that lies at the heart of the liberal principle of equal concern and respect, Dworkin's liberal and conservative would be better understood as subscribing to different ultimate principles rather than merely offering different interpretations of the same principle.) The only other obvious interpretation that can be placed upon the assertion of a fundamental right of self-determination is that it is a right grounded upon the claim that each has an overriding interest in his autonomy[33]—a possibility that I consider in the next section.

III

I want now to consider a variety of liberalism of a quite different sort: perfectionist liberalism. 'Perfectionism' is a general label for doctrines which incorporate an ideal or standard of human excellence.[34] That perfectionist ideal might be the leading idea of a doctrine or it might simply figure in the doctrine as one value alongside others. A perfectionist liberalism is therefore one grounded upon some ideal of the person and of the form of life we should lead. It therefore stands in stark contrast to neutralist liberalism. Whereas neutralist liberals seek to expound a form of liberalism which owes nothing to any particular conception of the good, perfectionist liberals do the opposite and take their stand upon a specific conception of the good person and the good life. The perfectionist ideal that has been most prominent within the liberal tradition is that of autonomy, although that is certainly not the only form of perfectionism to be found within the liberal tradition.

The ideal of the autonomous individual is that of the person who takes control of her own life and whose form of life is in large measure her own creation. Obviously there are limits to how far an individual's life can be self-made, but an autonomous individual is conceived as one who is, in significant measure, the author of her own life. The term 'autonomy' is used to refer to a condition as well as to an ideal. Internally, autonomous individuals must possess the capacities essential to making choices which are authentically their own and, externally, they must have adequate scope to act upon those choices. But autonomy as an ideal consists not merely in the presence of those conditions but in their being taken advantage of in living an autonomous life. That autonomous life may be valued intrinsically or instrumentally or both. Instrumentally it may be valued because it is believed to promote some desirable social consequence such as a diversity of forms of life or progress in human understanding, or because it is thought essential to some other perfectionist ideal focussed upon the individual such as self-realization or self-development. But, within the perfectionist liberalism that I want to examine, the ideal of autonomy is valued wholly or partly as something of intrinsic worth. An autonomous life is simply better than one which is unthinking, manipulated, or servile.[35]

The question I want to take up is how the value of autonomy figures in relation to beliefs and their verity. But I shall begin by saying a little about autonomy and wants. In so far as we construe a matter as one in which nothing is at stake but what people want, there is a clear case for respecting their autonomy as wanters. If nothing is at issue amongst a community of individuals except that each of them wants something then, *ex hypothesi*, there is no case for censoring or overriding their wants by subjecting the content of those wants to some independent test of the good. There may of course be a case for subjecting the satisfaction of conflicting or competing wants to a system of rules simply because the conflict or competition has to be resolved in some way. But on the 'pure wants' view that should be a matter of adjudicating among rival wanters rather than one of evaluating the content of their wants.

An appeal to autonomy might seem superfluous if we take this purely want-regarding view of the world. Does it not reduce the good of autonomy to the good of want-satisfaction? In fact, respect for autonomy might have an independent role to play within such a view. It might, for example, be used to explain why we should respect the wants that people happen to have rather than establish a Brave New World in which, for reasons of social convenience, people are transformed into beings with different sorts of wants. Even so, autonomy theorists do not normally regard human lives as concerned with nothing but wants and their satisfaction. The capacity for autonomy is typically conceived as a uniquely human one rooted in our ability to make informed and reasoned choices. Those choices will, of course, manifest wants but, in at least some cases, those wants will not be 'mere' wants but will be rooted in beliefs and values to which individuals subscribe independently of their wants. The ideal of autonomy is therefore unlikely to be concerned solely, or even primarily, with wants and their satisfaction.

Suppose then that the choices with which we are concerned are choices on (what I have labelled) matters of belief. How would the value of autonomy stand in relation to those matters? Consider first an extreme version of the ideal of autonomy. According to that version, nothing would be of value but an individual's being the author of his own life. On this view we should be entirely indifferent to the substance of the ends that people pursue, to the content of their chosen form of life; all that would be of value in those ends or forms of life would be that they were self-chosen. There are two things to be said about this exclusive commitment to autonomy. The first is that such a thorough-going indifference to the content of people's choices is hard to swallow. The position described here is significantly different from the neutralism of theorists such as Rawls and Dworkin. Their version of liberal political theory refrains from evaluating the content of people's conceptions of the good not because they suppose that nothing is of value in a person's conception of the good except that it is the adopted conception of its holder. On the contrary, they would accept that some forms of life can be held of greater value than others and that people can therefore sensibly argue about the value of different forms of life.[36] Their neutralism is simply a political neutralism; they contend only that it is not the proper business of the state to concern itself with the internal merits of people's conceptions of the good. But the extreme perfectionist view that we are considering here does not remain aloof from questions of the good life in that way. On the contrary, it asserts that all that is of value in a person's conception of the good is that it is self-chosen. But if the content of an individual's aims in life is of so little consequence, it becomes puzzling why her choice over those aims should be of such all-consuming importance. Moreover, this view seems to remove any foundation for choice itself. If nothing is of value but my choosing, what I choose becomes an entirely arbitrary matter.

A second feature of this extreme view is that it entails some strong negative assumptions about the content of beliefs. In particular it must reject any conception of the ends of life as given, for any such conception would introduce values other than choice. It is at odds, for example, with any religious vision of the world in which a good or right form of life is already prescribed for individuals. The extreme view might allow that people can choose to believe in such given ends if they wish and structure their lives accordingly, but it would still value the consequent chosen forms of life only as chosen. This way of viewing and of valuing people's lives would be odd in two ways. First, it sets up an opposition between the reasons why the individual values his ends and those why the autonomy theorist values those ends. For the believer, his ends are valued as true rather than as chosen while, for the autonomy theorist, they are valued as chosen rather than as true. Secondly, it entails the autonomy theorist's giving value to a chosen form of life which he is logically bound to regard as mistaken for it is based upon a view of the world which the extreme autonomy theorist must suppose is false. Thus it seems impossible to apply the extreme version of the ideal of autonomy to matters of belief without its becoming seriously incoherent.

How else then might the value of autonomy stand in relation to beliefs so that it has greater plausibility and appeal? One possibility is that we should think neither of there being no standard of value other than autonomy nor of there being only one such standard, but of there being a multiplicity of valuable forms of life. A significantly autonomous life is possible only under certain conditions and amongst those conditions is that an agent must have available to him an adequate range of options. Those options must be 'available' not only in that the human and nonhuman environment of the agent must be such as to render them genuinely possible and eligible options. They must also be morally available. That is, if there is to be scope for the ideal of autonomy in people's lives, they must have available to them an adequate range of morally acceptable options. Given such a multiplicity of valuable forms of life, autonomy can be valued when it is exercised within that range of good forms of life and there need therefore be no conflict or tension between the autonomous life and other constituents of the good life. That is not to say that, on this view, autonomy will be valued only as instrumental to some other good or goods. Autonomy may still be viewed as a distinct ideal possessing intrinsic value but it would be attributed with that value only within the morally permitted range. Although people may autonomously opt for wrong or bad ends, no value need be attached to autonomy when it is so used. This is the sort of view argued for skilfully and persuasively by Joseph Raz.[37] He defends both moral pluralism and the ideal of personal autonomy as well as their combination in a unified theory of freedom. Moral pluralism does indeed have great appeal given the broad sense of 'moral' that Raz employs. But it seems neither designed for, nor capable of accommodating, the sort of radical conflict of belief that is my concern. We may indeed recognize the value of quite diverse forms of life and we may therefore cherish a society which makes available to its members a wide variety of occupations and pursuits all of which have value. But can we similarly value a diversity of beliefs each of which claims to be right or true and each of which claims that its rivals are wrong or false? Consider the diversity of religious beliefs. It is not unusual to find people also celebrating that diversity as part of the rich and complex mosaic of human existence. Yet that celebration comes close to not taking those conflicting beliefs seriously as beliefs. Each religion offers a system of beliefs which it holds to be true. One of those systems of belief may indeed be wholly true or some may each be partly true or all of them may be wholly false; but they cannot all be wholly true. And it seems a matter for lamentation rather than delight that humanity should be smitten with disputes over something so fundamental to the nature of human existence and how it ought to be lived. Anyone who takes religious belief seriously cannot applaud the proliferation of different brands of faith (all or most of which are erroneous) merely because that makes for greater choice in the supermarket of life.

Is there then any scope for the ideal of personal autonomy when what people are confronted with are competing views of the truth? While the notion of a diversity of goods is perfectly intelligible, the parallel notion of a diversity of truths makes no sense at all. How then can we find room for the value of autonomy when what people are confronted with is a number of competing beliefs all of which claim to be true rather than a range of alternative forms of life all of which claim to be good? How can that sort of diversity constitute a range of options all of which have value?

One way of linking autonomy and truth is to present one as the instrument of the other. We may respect autonomy in relation to belief not because the truth of belief is of no consequence but because, as Mill argued, the society whose members are afforded autonomy of belief is also the society that is most likely to ferret out the truth.[38] I want to place that argument on one side, not because it is of no merit, but only because the sort of perfectionist view that I am concerned with presents autonomy as an ideal in its own right and not as something to be valued only instrumentally.

For some, autonomy and truth are necessarily associated, for a person can be considered to have acted autonomously only if the beliefs upon which that person acted were indeed true. However, that way of foreclosing the issue involves an exceptionally severe view of what autonomy requires and I (along with most contemporary autonomy theorists) would want to allow that there can be circumstances in which an individual acts autonomously but mistakenly. A different possibility would be to hold that, although an individual can act autonomously even though he acts mistakenly, autonomous action has value only when it conforms to truth. Both of these ways of viewing and valuing autonomy are open to two objections. One is that, as Raz argues, autonomy requires that individuals should have an adequate range of options before them. If the only option (of value) open to them is the single path of truth that does not seem to provide adequate 'space' for the ideal of autonomy to function. Secondly, and more practically, if we tie autonomy to truth but we are uncertain or in dispute about what is true, the ideal of autonomy can contribute nothing to our response to that uncertainty.

At the other extreme, it might be argued that the value of autonomy is unaffected by questions of truth and that the ideal of autonomy can and should be ranked above truth. I am not sure that it is possible simply to refute this view, but it is one that I cannot find persuasive for it is at odds with the very point of belief. Beliefs have content and the point of holding a belief is to hold a correct belief. Generally, people place a value upon their beliefs not merely because they are, in some sense, *their* beliefs; rather, they value their beliefs because they hold them to be *true* beliefs. Truth is what beliefs are about. It therefore seems strangely at variance with the whole nature, the whole *telos*, of beliefs that we should be required to give greater significance to their autonomy than to their truth. Consider people who have committed their whole lives to a religion, their belief in which was crucially based upon a number of ancient documents. Research has now disclosed that those documents were forgeries and there is therefore no reason for taking their content seriously. Is it of no consequence that a person's chosen form of life was founded upon beliefs which are now demonstrably false? Can the value of a person's choice be so utterly independent of its content? What seems perverse about answering yes to this question is that that is not how it can appear to believers themselves whose interest in autonomy is being prized so highly. They valued their beliefs not because those beliefs simply happened to be those that they had chosen. Indeed, from their point of view, these beliefs were not 'chosen' at all. They committed their lives to those beliefs only because they thought that those beliefs were true.

If there is scope for the ideal of autonomy in these sorts of matters it must surely fall somewhere in between simply identifying autonomy with truth and treating truth as of no consequence in relation to autonomy. That is, there seems more scope for giving intrinsic value to the ideal of autonomy in matters where the truth is either undetermined or undeterminable. It is not surprising therefore that religious, moral, and political beliefs should have been at the forefront of liberal concerns, for, although those belong to the province of belief, they are also subjects on which it is extremely difficult, if not inherently impossible, to present uncontestable truths. Not only does that, in itself, provide reason for objecting to some seeking to impose their beliefs upon others in the name of truth, it also permits the necessary scope for giving independent value to individuals' arriving at, and living in accordance with, their own beliefs. Of course, that there is scope for reasonable disagreement and reasonable doubt does not, of itself, establish the value of autonomy but it does provide a context within which the value of autonomy is more intelligible. The more manifest and indisputable the truth, the harder it becomes to value forms of life which ignore it or fly in the face of it. Remember that the value with which we are concerned here is not merely that of autonomy as a condition but that of autonomy as a form of life in which an individual plays a significant role as the creator of that life. The more a matter is one of undoubtable truth, the less scope there is for that creativity or, at the very least, the more one is obliged to regard a life 'created' in opposition to that truth as the pursuit of an illusion.

IV

In conclusion I want to make a few remarks on coercion, mainly to justify my having given it so little direct attention. Can an individual's interest in freedom of belief be viewed simply as his or her interest in not being coerced? Is not there something odd about the very idea of coercing beliefs as opposed to actions?

The immediate answer to the second question is, of course, that phrases such as 'freedom of belief' and 'liberty of conscience' refer to the ability to act upon one's beliefs as well as merely to hold them. It is sometimes argued that coercion is inefficacious in this area because coerced action is of no value if those who are coerced do not genuinely subscribe to the beliefs to which they are made to conform. For example, the worthlessness of religious rites unaccompanied by sincere belief has often been pleaded by advocates of toleration.[39] But, although this argument is of considerable force, it will not see off all the opponents of toleration. Calvin, for example, held that the state which permitted public idolatry and blasphemy was failing in its duty towards

God.[40] Even if belief, as distinct from action, cannot be reached by coercion narrowly understood as force or the threat of force, freedom of belief can be undermined in other ways such as (the misuse of) education, control over the ideas and information to which people have access, or even the general social milieu. That point hardly needs making in the twenty-first century.

How far then can a person's interest in freedom of belief be represented as simply her interest in not being coerced? What has just been said indicates that coercion cannot provide the whole of the explanation, for freedom of belief can be at stake even when coercion is not. What about cases where coercion is the instrument in question? Given the association of pain and frustration with coercion one can present coercion as being, in any circumstances, *prima facie* undesirable. But if there is, all things considered, reason to object to the use of coercion in some cases but not in others, the intrinsic undesirability of coercion cannot explain how and why we make that distinction. If there is something especially objectionable about coercing people in matters of belief, that has to be explained by the special importance of freedom of belief rather than by the intrinsic undesirability of coercion alone.

Finally, let me briefly restate what I have, and also what I have not, tried to argue in this chapter. I have argued not only and obviously that there is a difference between wants and beliefs but also that the different characters of wants and beliefs should not be ignored when we consider how we should respond to conflicts amongst people. It matters greatly whether we construe what is at issue in a dispute as merely conflicting wants or different beliefs about a single truth. Where a conflict is one of beliefs, the epistemic status of those beliefs may well be relevant to how we view people's interests in relation to the beliefs that they hold. However, I have not argued that the claim that there is scope for reasonable doubt and reasonable disagreement must, of itself, translate into an assertion of liberalism. Much less have I argued that liberalism either requires or must issue from a more general and more profound scepticism. I have argued only that, where they encounter competing views of the true or the right, certain sorts of liberalism, such as the ideal of personal autonomy or Rawls's notion of individuals' possessing a highest-order interest in forming and pursuing their own conceptions of the good, are more plausible against a background of reasonable doubt and reasonable disagreement. I have not claimed that doubt must figure in every liberal argument. Just as importantly, I am not holding that, where certainty begins, freedom of belief should end. Even if we are justifiably certain that someone would be better off holding different beliefs, we may have no effective or acceptable way of changing those beliefs. And even if we could effect that change by resort to political power, there are a host of reasons why we should not. Many reasons have been advanced for cherishing freedom of belief; we do not have to embrace all of them but neither need we subscribe to only one.

NOTES

1. Bruce A. Ackerman, *Social Justice in the Liberal State* (New Haven, CT, and London: Yale University Press, 1980), 365–69.

2. John Rawls, *A Theory of Justice* (London: Oxford University Press, 1972), 214–15; John Rawls, 'Kantian Constructivism in Moral Theory', *Journal of Philosophy* 77 (1980): 542; John Rawls, 'The Idea of an Overlapping Consensus', *Oxford Journal of Legal Studies* 22 (1987): 12–15; Ronald Dworkin, *A Matter of Principle* (Oxford: Clarendon Press, 1986), 203; Ronald Dworkin, 'What Liberalism Isn't', *New York Review of Books* 29, no. 21 (1983): 47.

3. Joseph Raz, *The Morality of Freedom* (Oxford: Clarendon Press, 1986); Vinit Haksar, *Equality, Liberty and Perfectionism* (Oxford: Oxford University Press, 1979).

4. I take this to be generally rather than invariably true. There may be occasions on which a person has an interest in coming to hold a false belief; e.g., when this prompts the person to achieve some good result that he or she would not otherwise have been motivated to achieve. There may also be occasions when someone is better off not being disabused of a false belief; e.g., if someone has devoted most of his or her life to the promotion of a cause that, we come to realize, is falsely grounded, we may still conclude that such a person is better off continuing with these false beliefs than being disabused of them at the eleventh hour and spending the remainder of his or her life in a state of disillusion and despondency. However, these can be regarded as exceptions to the general rule that people are better off holding and acting upon true rather than false beliefs. Certainly, the claim that people have an interest in holding false beliefs is not conspicuous in liberal arguments for freedom of belief.

5. Rawls, 'Kantian Constructivism in Moral Theory', 515–72; John Rawls, 'The Basic Liberties and Their Priority', *The Tanner Lectures on Human Values*, vol. 3 (Cambridge: Cambridge University Press, 1982), 3–87; John Rawls, 'Justice as Fairness: Political Not Metaphysical', *Philosophy and Public Affairs* 14 (1985): 223, 251; John Rawls, 'The Idea of an Overlapping Consensus', *Oxford Journal of Legal Studies* 7 (1987): 1–25. This chapter originally appeared before the publication of Rawls's *Political Liberalism* (New York: Columbia University Press, 1993).

6. Rawls, 'Kantian Constructivism', 518; Rawls, 'Justice as Fairness; Political Not Metaphysical', passim.

7. Thus, for example, it is unclear whether he would see himself as justifying religious liberty or simply taking that as a 'settled conviction' in a modern democratic society and articulating, generalizing, and providing a coherent account of what is implicit in that conviction. Cf. Rawls, 'Kantian Constructivism', 540; Rawls, 'Justice as Fairness; Political Not Metaphysical', 228.

8. Rawls, 'Kantian Constructivism', 525.

9. Rawls, 'Kantian Constructivism', 525–27; Rawls, 'The Basic Liberties', 22–23.

10. Whether Rawls's theory is in fact neutral between competing conceptions of the good is disputed. See, for example, Thomas Nagel, 'Rawls on Justice', in

Norman Daniels, ed., *Reading Rawls* (Oxford: Blackwell, 1975); Adina Schwartz, 'Moral Neutrality and Primary Goods', *Ethics* 83 (1973): 294–307; William Galston, 'Defending Liberalism', *American Political Science Review* 76 (1982): 621–29; Raz, *The Morality of Freedom*, chapter 5; Haksar, *Equality, Liberty and Perfectionism*, chapters 10 and 11; and my 'The Ideal of the Neutral State', in R. Goodin and A. Reeve, eds., *Liberal Neutrality* (London: Routledge, 1989). While I do not myself accept that all of the doubts expressed about Rawls's neutrality are well-founded, it is difficult to see how his theory can remain comprehensively neutral with respect to the good given the view of individuals' highest-order interests to which he is now committed.

11. Rawls sometimes seems inclined to include philosophical, religious, and moral beliefs within the compass of conceptions of the good, while at other times he describes a conception of the good as a scheme of final ends which may therefore be distinguished from the totality of philosophical, religious, or moral beliefs upon which those ends are founded. But this seems to be of no great importance since, in justice as fairness, conflicting philosophical, religious, and moral beliefs are regarded and treated in exactly the same way as conflicting conceptions of the good. Cf. Rawls, 'Kantian Constructivism', 542–43, 544–45; Rawls, 'Justice as Fairness: Political Not Metaphysical', 234, 240n23; Rawls, 'The Basic Liberties', 16, 25.

12. Rawls, 'Kantian Constructivism', 519. Most of Rawls's third lecture (pp. 554–72) is given over to developing this contrast.

13. Rawls, 'Kantian Constructivism', 523–24, 527–28, 551–52.

14. Rawls, 'Kantian Constructivism', 517, 536–43, 560–61. For another statement of the view that liberalism requires that a society's arrangements should be acceptable, or be capable of being made acceptable, to all members of that society, see Jeremy Waldron, 'The Theoretical Foundations of Liberalism', *Philosophical Quarterly* 37 (1987): 127–50.

15. Rawls, 'Justice as Fairness: Political Not Metaphysical', 247; 'Overlapping Consensus', 9–12.

16. Rawls, 'Justice as Fairness: Political Not Metaphysical', passim.

17. Rawls, 'Justice as Fairness: Political Not Metaphysical', 233 (my emphases); cf. p. 244.

18. Although this could again be seen as raising the issue of whether Rawls is *really* attributing this intellectual competence to all (normal) adults or whether he is simply holding that this is the sort of 'as if' *assumption* that we have to make about citizens in a pluralistic society if we are to arrive at arrangements that will be acceptable to all of them. Cf. Rawls, 'The Basic Liberties', 16.

19. Rawls, *Theory of Justice*, 30–32, 446–52; Rawls, 'Justice as Fairness: Political Not Metaphysical', 249–50; Rawls, 'Kantian Constructivism', 532, 540–41; Rawls, 'Fairness to Goodness', *Philosophical Review* 84 (1975): 536–54.

20. See, e.g., Rawls, 'The Basic Liberties', 25.

21. Rawls, 'Kantian Constructivism', 521, 544; Rawls, 'Justice as Fairness: Political Not Metaphysical', 240–41.

22. Rawls, 'Kantian Constructivism', 525.

23. Rawls, 'Kantian Constructivism', 519, 554 ff.

24. For a reading of Rawls which argues that his position implicitly relies upon a form of scepticism, see Gerald Dworkin, 'Non-Neutral Principles', in Norman Daniels, ed., *Reading Rawls* (Oxford: Basil Blackwell, 1975), 124–40; and for an attempt to defend the sort of position that Rawls adopts while rejecting scepticism but still making some appeal to ideas of reasonable doubt and disagreement, see Thomas Nagel, 'Moral Conflict and Political Legitimacy', *Philosophy and Public Affairs* 17 (1987): 215–40.

25. Rawls, 'The Idea of Overlapping Consensus', passim. This idea is not entirely new to Rawls's theory; cf. Rawls, *Theory of Justice*, 387–88.

26. E.g., Ronald Dworkin, *Taking Rights Seriously* (London: Duckworth, 1978), chapter 12; Dworkin, *A Matter of Principle*, chapter 17.

27. Dworkin, *Taking Rights Seriously*, 357; *A Matter of Principle*, 370.

28. Dworkin, *Taking Rights Seriously*, 272.

29. Dworkin, *A Matter of Principle*, 191.

30. Dworkin, *A Matter of Principle*, 191.

31. Dworkin, *A Matter of Principle*, 198–201.

32. Dworkin, *A Matter of Principle*, 203.

33. This would not appear to be Dworkin's position. Cf. Dworkin, 'What Liberalism Isn't', 47: 'Some philosophers appeal to the idea of autonomy to justify neutrality. But this cannot advance the argument. Autonomy is a notoriously ambiguous idea; in its only pertinent form it is simply another name for neutrality—that is, for the idea that government should not seek to impose any way of life on individuals—and so cannot provide any argument for that idea'. For a different view, see Ackerman, *Social Justice in the Liberal State*, 367–68.

34. On perfectionism, see Rawls, *Theory of Justice*, 325–32; Haksar, *Equality, Liberty and Perfectionism*, 1–8.

35. For excellent accounts of the ideal of autonomy, on which I have drawn here, see Raz, *The Morality of Freedom*, chapter 14; Richard Lindley, *Autonomy* (London: Macmillan, 1986); Robert Young, *Personal Autonomy: Beyond Negative and Positive Liberty* (New York: St. Martin's Press, 1986).

36. See, e.g. Rawls, *Theory of Justice*, 328–29.

37. Raz, *The Morality of Freedom*, especially chapters 14 and 15.

38. That is not to say that Mill valued autonomy only instrumentally; cf. John Gray, *Mill on Liberty: A Defence* (London: Routledge and Kegan Paul, 1983).

39. See, for example, John Locke, *A Letter on Toleration*, R. Klibansky, ed. (Oxford: Clarendon Press, 1968), 99–101.

40. Jean Calvin, *Institutes of the Christian Religion*, book 4, chapter 20, s. 3.

Chapter 9

Toleration, Value-Pluralism, and the Fact of Pluralism

In his *Two Faces of Liberalism*, John Gray distinguishes two traditions of liberal thinking about toleration. One conceives toleration as a route to rational consensus on the best way of life; the other holds that there is no single best way of life but rather many ways of life in which human beings can flourish. Gray argues that the first tradition has come to dominate liberal thinking and that it encompasses the work of contemporary liberals as diverse as Rawls, Dworkin, Hayek, and Nozick. It has become so dominant that Gray sometimes describes it simply as 'liberal toleration'. He believes that this tradition, with its aspiration to secure rational consensus on how we should live, is fundamentally misconceived. It has always been mistaken, but its error has been made more conspicuous by the sheer range of the different ways of life that toleration has to encompass in the late modern world. Gray argues that liberal thinking needs to relocate itself in the second tradition which recognizes the goodness of many different ways of life, none of which is better than the rest.

This second tradition constitutes Gray's second 'face' of liberalism, but it actually belongs to a broader way of thinking that he calls 'pluralism'. Pluralism can endorse liberalism as a form of life that is good for some societies, but it does not accept that a liberal order is the best or the uniquely legitimate form of life for all humanity. Rather, for the pluralist, liberalism describes merely one of many good forms of life and one that can make no claim to be intrinsically better than those other forms. That is why Gray gives only limited applause to liberals whom he locates in this second tradition, such as Berlin and Raz. Although they have broken free of the dominant liberal tradition, they still give liberalism a special status to which it has no claim. To be a pluralist liberal is to accept that, while a liberal way of life may be contingently good for some societies given their histories and circumstances, it is not the only good way of life or the best for all societies in all circumstances.[1]

Gray's characterization of the dominant liberal tradition of toleration is extremely broad-brush. Even those whom he identifies as its leading spokesmen, such as Locke and Rawls, cannot be easily represented as pursuing 'the ideal of a rational consensus on the best way of life' (2000a, 1). However, I shall not stop to examine the accuracy of Gray's representation of liberal thinking on toleration. Rather, I shall focus on the sort of thinking on toleration that he does endorse. I want to examine what the role of toleration might be in the world as Gray sees it and whether his value-pluralism can justify that role. More specifically, I want to ask: given the fact of pluralism, can Gray's value-pluralism provide a case for the toleration needed to secure a *modus vivendi*? I begin by saying something about each of the four constituents of that question.

TERMS OF REFERENCE

Value-Pluralism

Gray understands value-pluralism to hold 'that ultimate human values are objective but irreducibly diverse, that they are conflicting and often uncombinable, and that sometimes when they come into conflict with one another they are incommensurable; that is, they are not comparable by any rational measure' (1995b, 1). I follow Gray in taking the essential claims of value-pluralism to be that values are irreducibly plural and, in significant measure, uncombinable and incommensurable. Value-pluralism therefore stands opposed to the claim that there is a single master value, such as utility, or a set hierarchy of values. Applied to forms of life, value-pluralism holds that there are many good forms of life, none of which can claim to be the single best form. Because goods are frequently uncombinable, it also holds that not all goods can be realized fully in the life of one individual or one community. Although it emphasizes the diverse and conflictual nature of values, value-pluralism entails neither relativism nor subjectivism. Value-pluralists, including Gray, understand human values to be objective in that they are rooted in objective human needs and interests.

As a general position, value-pluralism admits of degree. We may recognize that values can be uncombinable and incommensurable but hold that they exhibit these properties only rarely. Alternatively, we might hold that conflict, uncombinability, and incommensurability are ubiquitous features of value, features that must shape our understanding of the entire nature of ethical and political life. Although Gray (1995a, 68) claims only that values are 'often' uncombinable and 'sometimes' incommensurable, his value-pluralism stands at the more comprehensive end of the spectrum.[2] It may be less than fully comprehensive, but it is sufficiently comprehensive to be a major factor, perhaps *the* major factor, that should guide our ethical and political thinking.

The Fact of Pluralism

Value-pluralism is both a meta-ethical and an ethical theory. The 'fact of pluralism' is neither; its claim is empirical. It describes the fact that people live different sorts of life whether as individuals or groups or communities. However, in conformity with the meaning given to this phrase by writers such as Rawls (1993) and Larmore (1996), I use 'the fact of pluralism' to describe more than the mere existence of diverse modes of life. It also describes the fact that people hold different and conflicting beliefs and values so that they possess different views about how we should live and make different assessments of how people actually live. Thus people disagree as well as differ. This makes for an asymmetry between value-pluralism and the fact of pluralism. Whereas the plurality noticed by value-pluralism is a plurality of different and conflicting *goods*, the plurality noticed in the fact of pluralism is a plurality of different and conflicting *conceptions* of the good.

That is not to say that value-pluralism and the fact of pluralism are wholly independent. Gray suggests two ways in which they are related. First, the truth of value-pluralism can help to explain the fact of pluralism. One reason why people are committed to different sorts of life is that conflicts of value can be settled in different and incompatible ways no one of which is uniquely good or right (Gray 2000a, 8; see also Crowder 2002: 65). Value-pluralism therefore helps us to make sense of the fact of pluralism. Secondly, the fact of pluralism provides evidence of the truth of value-pluralism. For Gray (2000a, 41, 46–47, 64; cf. 1995b, 63; 1997, 95–96; see also Galston 2002, 33–34), it is experience that provides the test of the 'truth' of our ethical beliefs. The fact that people live diverse modes of life and evidently flourish in those many different modes provides evidence for the truth of value-pluralism. Indeed, he claims the experience of late modern societies has made value-pluralism a matter of 'common knowledge' (2000b, 325).

Despite these possible links, value-pluralism and the fact of pluralism make importantly different claims. Gray (2000b, 332) recognizes the fact of pluralism as I have described it. Indeed, he complains that others have recognized it insufficiently. One of the failings of current liberal theories of toleration is, he argues, that they draw on a tradition of thinking that was evolved for a monocultural society whose disagreements were contained within a shared religious and moral outlook. These liberal theories have not adjusted to the breadth and depth of differences of belief and value to be found in our world (Gray 2000a, chap.1; 2000b, 323–325).

Modus Vivendi

For Gray, '*modus vivendi*' describes a condition of peaceful coexistence. *Modus vivendi* is a goal that we should pursue both within societies and between them. It describes a settlement secured amongst people who subscribe to different and possibly conflicting values and ways of life. However, it is an altogether more contingently based arrangement than the just societies sought by deontological liberals. Because conflicts of value afflict considerations of justice as much as other values, the aspiration to ground a plural society on a consensus concerning principles of right is, for Gray, misguided. A *modus vivendi* is something that must be achieved without the benefit of consensus upon values. In any particular case, it must also be geared to the particular circumstances and ways of life that characterize the parties to the *modus vivendi* and to the compromises they are able and willing to make. We cannot therefore set out a universal pattern to which each *modus vivendi* must conform.

At the same time, a *modus vivendi* is not, for Gray (2000a, 133), just any condition that falls short of open conflict. It is more than a cold war and more than the mere absence of war. It is also more than a mere balance of power. It connotes an established arrangement, even though it may be one that is fragile and shifting, that enables people to live together in spite of their differences. As I have said, it does not presuppose a consensus upon values, but it does entail a population's possessing and recognizing common institutions through which they can negotiate compromises between their different values and interests. The more successfully these institutions provide for negotiation and compromise, the better the *modus vivendi*.

Gray sometimes draws the link between value-pluralism and *modus vivendi* very close. He remarks, for example, that '*modus vivendi* expresses the belief that there are many forms of life in which humans can thrive', and that 'the ethical theory underpinning *modus vivendi* is value-pluralism' (2000a, 5, 6, 25). However, I understand these statements to describe the value-pluralist's commitment to *modus vivendi* rather than beliefs and commitments that are essential for a *modus vivendi*. As I have already remarked, *modus vivendi* is peaceful coexistence secured without the benefit of a consensus on value and we need not suppose that all or any of the parties to a *modus vivendi* are value-pluralists (Gray, 2000a: 25).

Toleration

I shall use the term 'toleration' in its orthodox sense, according to which we tolerate when we object to something yet do not seek to prevent it. Thus reasons for toleration are reasons for not seeking to suppress or otherwise prevent beliefs and practices even though we believe them to be wrong or objectionable in some other way. As Gray himself has observed, 'the objects of toleration are what we judge to be evils. When we tolerate a practice, a belief or a character trait, we let something be that we judge to be undesirable, false or at least inferior; our toleration expresses the conviction that, despite its badness, the object of toleration should be left alone' (1995a, 18).

The terms 'tolerate', 'tolerance', and 'toleration' are sometimes used nowadays in more relaxed senses which make the presence of disapproval or dislike inessential. I shall refer to some of these alternative senses, but in general I shall keep faith with the orthodox meaning of toleration.

Toleration is not coextensive with liberalism. There are reasons for being tolerant that are not distinctively liberal, and we may tolerate practices and ways of life that the liberal would have us not tolerate. More to the point here, liberalism need not entail toleration. Most obviously, it does not when liberalism takes the form of a theory that applauds the pursuit of a wide range of forms of life because it endorses the goodness of each of those many forms. Prima facie, a liberal theory grounded in value-pluralism looks likely to take that generously approving, and therefore nontolerant, form. Argument over whether value-pluralism does or does not entail liberalism is not then coextensive with the issues I shall examine.

The link between the fact of pluralism, *modus vivendi* and toleration is fairly obvious. If the members of a population, either societal or global, possess different and conflicting conceptions of the good, they will be able to coexist peacefully only if they are ready to tolerate one another's different and conflicting conceptions and the ways of life, individual or collective, that derive from these. I turn then to the question of whether value-pluralism can deliver the toleration necessary for a *modus vivendi*.

I examine that question in two parts. I begin by looking at the world as the value-pluralist sees it and consider whether value-pluralism itself generates a need for and a case for toleration. However, the value-pluralist has to recognize—and Gray does recognize—that the world in which he has to operate (a world characterized by the fact of pluralism) is one in which many people hold beliefs and values that are incompatible with his own. Thus, in the second part of this article, I consider what Gray might say to induce those who reject value-pluralism to participate in a *modus vivendi*.

TOLERATION AND THE DEMANDS
OF VALUE-PLURALISM

Value-pluralism insists that values conflict and, when they do, we have to sacrifice the achievement of some for the sake of others. In some cases, goods may be absolutely uncombinable so that we have to sacrifice one wholly for the sake of another. In other cases, they may conflict in ways that permit trade-offs, but more of one will still entail less of the other. No individual or community can therefore expect to realize the good fully and uncompromisingly; there are goods that they will simply have to forego. Moreover, just as we are obliged to make choices or compromises between goods, so we shall often have to choose amongst or trade-off evils; evils will not be entirely avoidable or removable. In addition, in Gray's version of value-pluralism, as in Berlin's, it is not merely that good competes with good and bad with bad. Some goods may be achievable only if accompanied by evils and some right actions may unavoidably involve an element of wrong (Gray 1995a, 162; 1995b, 35–36, 53–57; 2000a, 10, 46, 138).

A world in which we are obliged to forego goods and to put up with evils looks like just the sort of world in which toleration will be at a premium. But what sort of toleration does it call for? It is not toleration in its orthodox sense—toleration of other people and of the values they pursue. It is toleration of the way things are—a readiness to recognize the impossibility of perfection and to accept the limitations upon the achievement of goodness that value-pluralism explains are inescapable. This 'toleration' is little more than resignation to an unalterable fact about the world. It resembles stoic toleration: 'a cultivated indifference toward uncontrollable externalities' (Fiala 2003, 154).

If we move from the conflicting nature of values to the diverse forms of life they generate, how should the value-pluralist view these? Let's put aside evil for the moment. People either find themselves living, or commit themselves to living, various forms of life each of which embodies some goods and each of which, of necessity, excludes or diminishes others. Because the goods at issue are in conflict and cannot be realized fully together, Gray (e.g., 2000a, 5, 20, 34) describes them as 'rivalrous' and then goes on to describe the ways of life based upon them as 'rivals'. But are these different forms of life rivalrous in ways that could require toleration amongst those who live them? Must agonism amongst values yield agonism amongst ways of life (cf. Gray 1995a, 84)? From the vantage point of the value-pluralist, it would seem not. Each form of life is on balance good, each of necessity does not encompass every good, and in so far as the goods manifested or pursued in different forms of life are incommensurable, no form can be held inferior or superior to another. Thus, although a world in which everyone was fully apprised of value-pluralism might be highly diverse, the value-pluralists who inhabited that world would not, if they remained true to their value-pluralism, find themselves objecting to and having to tolerate one another's ways of life.

Although this is how the value-pluralist would have us see the world, it might be less easy for those who find themselves in the world to view its diversity with quite such indifference and equanimity. Can someone who is genuinely committed to a particular form of life readily accept that other forms, to which he feels no similar allegiance, are no less good? If those other forms of life are incommensurable with his own, that is indeed what he should accept. To hold that goods or forms of life are incommensurable is to hold that they are not rationally comparable. Thus, when we face a choice between such goods or ways of life, all we can do is to make a 'radical choice'. Radical choice is choice that is groundless rather than reason-based (Gray 1995a, 70; 1995b, 23). 'Such groundless and criterionless choice is', Gray observes, 'the stuff of moral and political life, in so far as it is pervaded by incommensurabilities' (1995b, 71). Radical choices that are forced by incommensurability must be themselves incommensurable; hence the radical chooser who condemns another's radical choice mistakes the nature of his own choice and of the choice he condemns. The only sort of tolerance appropriate to radical choice is what Gray describes as 'the radical tolerance of indifference' (1995a, 28–29; 2000a, 25).[3]

Gray does say that, even when conflicts are between incommensurables, some resolutions can be better than others. However, I take that to encompass two possibilities, neither of which frees incommensurability from the need for radical choice. First, it may be that, when we confront issues beset by incommensurability, the scope of that incommensurability is limited such that answers that are incommensurably right, or solutions that are incommensurably good, form a limited set. We can then say that any answer drawn from that set of right or good answers is better than any that falls outside it. Thus, the absence of a single right answer does not mean that no answer is better than any other, but the right or best answers will still be incommensurable with respect to one another (Gray 2000a, 6–7, 42, 62–68).

The second possibility that Gray (2000a, 36, 42–43, 55–56; 1995b, 154–55) points to is that a conflict between values may, at a general level, admit of no rational resolution, yet may do so when conflict arises in a specific context. But if that is so, the specifics of the context must in some way remove or diminish the incommensurability and that is why we can make a choice that is more than merely radical.[4]

It is difficult then to see how the value-pluralist could object to, and could experience a need to tolerate, differences that arise from the uncombinability and incommensurability of values. Equally, there need be little about the make-up of a *modus vivendi* that he need regret or tolerate. He may take a positive view of the great majority of forms of life that are accommodated in a *modus vivendi*. Establishing a *modus vivendi* will require the bearers of different forms of life to enter into compromises with one another and that may well tax their tolerance. But it will not tax the tolerance of value-pluralists, whether they are participants in or merely observers of the *modus vivendi* since, from their synoptic perspective, such compromises will appear inevitable and necessary and wholly positive in consequence.

It may be, however, that the world can appear so unchallenging for value-pluralism only so long as we view it in a simple abstract fashion. Even if we are value-pluralists, we cannot be only value-pluralists. Each of us must also live a way of life that is particular. Perhaps the world viewed from inside a way of life will appear differently from the way it appears from outside. Affirming a way of life entails committing ourselves to, or discovering that we are committed to, a specific set of values and perhaps also a set of beliefs. The beliefs and values that are fundamental to our way of life may require us not merely to set aside other ways of life as uncombinable with our own. They may be such that we must view some, if not all, other ways of life as bad or inferior or falsely grounded. Thus differences, that may be matters of indifference when viewed from the Olympian heights of value-pluralism, may assume a quite different character when observed from the vantage point of a particular way of life. The toleration that is otiose as long as we remain outside our caves may be essential when we return to them.

One feature of Gray's pluralism that makes this a significant consideration is his recognition that lives can be good even if they are based upon beliefs that are at odds with value-pluralism. What matters for Gray is the objective goodness (or badness) of lives, rather than people's own conception of their lives or their reasons for living as they do. Thus, his value-pluralism is not a doctrine that can recognize as good only lives that are predicated upon its own truth. He is willing to accept that there are good forms of life that are based upon illusion and that can be lived only so long as the illusion is maintained.[5] That is why he believes that a world in which everyone was persuaded of value-pluralism might not be a better world (Gray 2000a, 136–37).

How then should the value-pluralist respond to the possibility that ways of life that he identifies as good may be ways of life that find one another unacceptable? His most obvious option, qua value-pluralist, is to disabuse the bearers of those ways of life of their objections to one another. In other words, his most obvious recourse is to lead them out of their caves and inform or remind them of what the world is really like. Once they are dragged into the external world of value-pluralism, they will see that their condemnation of others' forms of life is misplaced. That will solve by dissolving the problem of toleration, or it will if people can be induced to take their corrected conceptions of the world with them when they return to their particular ways of life.

The trouble is, of course, that this may mean that the form of life to which they return is not the form of life that they previously led. Some ways of life may be able to survive an encounter with the truth of value-pluralism but others may be transformed or destroyed by it. Their adherents, having seen the world from outside their cave, must find their conception of life within their cave forever altered. That will be most obviously so for those whose form of life rested upon a belief in its unique rightness. How, for example, can those whose way of life was predicated upon the belief that it was uniquely ordained by God continue living as if the falsity of their foundational belief made no difference to their way of life?

Value-pluralism might seek to avoid this transformative effect by inviting us to adopt a split-level view of the world, analogous to the two-level view proposed by the indirect utilitarian, R. M. Hare (1981). Hare distinguishes between a critical and an intuitive level of moral thinking. At the critical level, our moral thinking should be utilitarian while, at the intuitive level, it will consist of everyday 'common-sense' morality according to which it is simply right that we should keep our promises, treat people justly, and so on. The truth of morality really lies at the critical level and our thinking at that level should recognize utility as the single value that subsumes all others. Nevertheless, Hare argues, we are right to conduct our ordinary lives according to the rules of intuitive morality because, in so doing, we shall more successfully promote utility than if we attempted its direct pursuit, given our limited knowledge, foresight, impartiality, and the like.

In a similar fashion, the value-pluralist might enjoin us to live forms of life on their own terms rather than only under the aegis of value-pluralism. That may enable us to live forms of life that value-pluralism recognizes as good but that it would render unlivable if people were to take it fully to heart. By keeping value-pluralism at arm's length, people may be able to live a greater range of good forms of life, including lives based on illusions, than they would if they were overly conscious of the truth of value-pluralism.

Whether people could really perform this trick of double consciousness is highly doubtful. One criticism that has been levelled at Hare's split-level theory is that it may not be feasible for people to keep the two levels of moral thinking as separate as his indirect utilitarianism requires. That sort of criticism would seem to apply even more forcefully to the split-level value-pluralism that I contemplate here. It would require people to conduct their lives as though value-pluralism were false, even though they know it to be true. One way of dealing with that conundrum would be to keep the truth of value-pluralism under wraps. The analogue would then be not merely indirect utilitarianism but a form of 'government house' utilitarianism in which a governing elite keep people, for their own good and perhaps for the good of others, ignorant of the full moral truth.[6] That subterfuge would be morally unappealing and difficult to execute but, even if it could be carried off, it would leave the value-pluralist having to provide those who live good but benighted lives with something other than value-pluralism as their reason for toleration.

Before turning to the general question of how value-pluralists might cope with those who do not share their beliefs, I want to suggest that value-pluralists are likely to encounter a phenomenon that will create the circumstances for toleration even within their own ranks: the phenomenon of reasonable disagreement.

VALUE-PLURALISM AND REASONABLE DISAGREEMENT

Generally, Gray views the idea of reasonable disagreement unsympathetically. That is because the notion that people disagree implies that they are in dispute about one right answer and also that there is one right answer to be had. But value-pluralism shows that, when we encounter value conflict, frequently no single right answer is available but rather many right answers, no one of which can properly claim to be better than the others. Thus, when people come up with different answers to value conflict, we should conceive their answers as merely different rather than as authentic expressions of disagreement. People may, of course, conceive themselves as engaged in disagreement but they mistake the nature of their differences (Gray 2000a, 5, 8, 9, 21, 35).

George Crowder, by contrast, ties the idea of reasonable disagreement into value-pluralism and uses it to link pluralism with liberalism. He argues that the idea of reasonable disagreement presupposes the truth of value-pluralism since it is that pluralism that explains how there can be reasonable disagreement on moral and practical questions (Crowder 2002, chap. 7, especially pp. 165–72).

Despite Crowder's efforts to embed reasonable disagreement within value-pluralism, it seems to me that Gray is right to distinguish between the differences generated by value-pluralism and disagreement properly so-called.[7] In one case, differences amongst people are grounded in the plurality, uncombinability and incommensurability of values. Differences have their origins in objects rather than in subjects, in goods rather than in conceptions of the good, and, if those differences generate disagreement, that disagreement is apparent rather than real. In the other case, differences are grounded in subjects rather than objects, in the different judgments people make about the good rather than in the nature of the good itself, and the disagreement to which these differences give rise is real rather than apparent. In the first case, value-pluralism generates many possible 'right answers', no one of which is uniquely right. In the second case, a right answer is, in principle, available even though people can reasonably disagree about what it is.[8]

If we accept that distinction, we then have to ask how comprehensively value-pluralism can account for the value differences that we find amongst people. Can value conflict, uncombinability, and incommensurability together swallow up the entire domain of value-disagreement? That seems wholly implausible. It may be that many apparently conflicting conceptions of value each recognize something of real value and that, where others see only disagreement, the value-pluralist can expose the reality of value conflict. But we cannot plausibly dismiss every value disagreement as merely value conflict misrecognized. Nor should we expect differences that arise amongst value-pluralists themselves to be explicable wholly in terms of value-pluralism.

For one thing, agreement on value-pluralism need not entail agreement on the values that should figure in that pluralism. Consider, for example, the many different conceptions of distributive justice that people have proposed. There may be merit in more than one of these but a value-pluralism that tried to honour all of them would collapse into incoherence. Nor, if we think that justice encompasses a plurality of different and conflicting considerations, need we suppose that each value-pluralist will find value in the same range of considerations. Incommensurability itself may be a focus of dispute: will we always agree on when goods are incommensurable and when they are not? Moreover, even in the world of the value-pluralist, not all values (or not all values all of the time) are uncombinable and incommensurable. Sometimes there will be, in principle, a combination of values that is right, or best judged, but opinion can be reasonably divided on what that is. Another matter that figures prominently in Gray's thinking is the ethical significance of circumstance and context. His hostility to universalism stems not only from his belief in the incommensurability of different cultural forms but also from his acute sense that the good must always be attuned to contingencies of time and place. But that too calls for judgement and what calls for judgement will, experience shows, frequently elicit conflicting judgements.

Even a value-pluralist like Gray, therefore, has reason to take disagreement seriously. Indeed, the complex circumstances and hard cases that abound in Gray's world make not merely for disagreement but also for reasonable disagreement. In fact, Gray himself frequently moves from the language of difference to that of disagreement, from conflicts of value to conflicting conceptions or judgements or views of value.[9] The ease with which he moves between these languages suggests that he sees their distinction as of little consequence, perhaps because he believes that diverse conceptions of the good are little more than the epiphenomena of diverse goods.

In fact, goods and conceptions of the good are really two quite distinct phenomena. That goods or values are irreducibly plural and conflicting is a central claim of value-pluralism. That people arrive at different conceptions of the good, which they reasonably regard as conflicting and mutually exclusive conceptions of what is good, is no part of it. Yet we have good reason to suppose that a world of value-pluralists would be a world characterized by reasonable disagreement. That, in turn, means that it would be characterized by the circumstances of toleration. How then should value-pluralism respond to that disagreement? Does it yield a case for toleration? I consider how value-pluralism might respond to the broad fact of pluralism in the next section. Here the question is more limited in scope: how should value-pluralists respond to disagreement within their own ranks?

The short answer is that value-pluralism, in and of itself, has no answer. Value-pluralism is a theory about the nature of the good that we should pursue and about the way in which we should pursue the good given its nature. It is not a theory that tells us how we should respond to conceptions of the good that we reckon to be erroneous or to genuine disagreement, whether reasonable or unreasonable.

There are features of value-pluralism that might intimate an answer. One is its acceptance of imperfection. But the imperfection it accepts is not the imperfection we are considering here, which has its origins in limited human capacities, but an imperfection that is forced by the conflicting nature of values (Gray 2000a, 10, 39).

A more obvious tactic for Gray is to resort to his argument for a *modus vivendi*. For Gray, the principal virtue of a *modus vivendi* consists in its creating circumstances in which many good forms of life can flourish. If the reality is that we have to achieve a *modus vivendi* in a context of (genuine) disagreement as well as difference, extending toleration to conceptions of the good that we believe to be erroneous may be a price we have to pay to secure a *modus vivendi*. In that case, toleration can be justified as a means to the end of peaceful coexistence—or it can if, in this instance, means and end are commensurable.

I shall consider the limits of this case for toleration in a moment. There are other more immediate ways in which the reasonableness of disagreement might be used to argue for toleration but these have no evident connection with value-pluralism.

One points to the epistemic modesty that reasonable disagreement should induce. If we recognize that we are parties to a disagreement that is reasonable, that is not usually understood to require us to forsake our own beliefs and to accept that all views that figure in the disagreement are of equal merit. We can continue to hold our own beliefs while recognizing that they are subject to reasonable disagreement. Even so, the reasonableness of the disagreement can give us reason to allow that our beliefs could be wrong and those of others right, even though, as things stand, we reckon otherwise. The risk that we ourselves could be mistaken becomes a reason why we should tolerate the apparent error of others.

The other way in which reasonable disagreement can be deployed to argue for toleration is associated with liberals like Rawls. We are justified in coercing others and suppressing their ways of life only if we can justify our coercion and suppression to them. If the value of the ways of life at issue is subject to reasonable disagreement, we cannot justify our intolerance in that way. To that extent, we must tolerate conceptions of the good to which we object.

Both of these are, by my reckoning, imposing arguments for taking reasonable disagreement seriously and both provide a significant case for toleration. But neither can be generated by value-pluralism itself. Value-pluralism may therefore need more that itself to cope with a diverse world, even if that world were one in which everyone embraced value-pluralism.

VALUE-PLURALISM AND THE FACT OF PLURALISM

Up to now, I have considered value-pluralism mainly in relation to forms of life that it identifies as good or whose goodness is controversial amongst value-pluralists themselves. But value-pluralism is a discriminating moral position and there are forms of life that it will identify simply as bad—most obviously forms of life that are impoverished or marked by evils that unnecessarily impede human flourishing.

There is a further sort of 'bad' that preoccupies Gray: the error of moral theories, political ideologies, religions, and other systems of belief that are at odds with the central claims of value-pluralism itself. He does not seek to diminish the presence or significance of these beliefs in the fact of pluralism. He repeatedly berates the sponsors and heirs of the so-called Enlightenment project for their folly and naivety in supposing that, with the passage of time, human thought would converge on a rational consensus and he points insistently to the recrudescence and persistence of a multiplicity of dissonant beliefs and allegiances that confound the Enlightenment's optimism (e.g., Gray 1995a, 13, 65, 145–46). The downside of that for Gray himself is that he too has to cope with a world of diverse beliefs, many of which are at odds with value-pluralism. He is unambiguous in affirming that universalist religions, in so far as they hold that one way of life or a small family of ways of life is best or right for all humanity, are incompatible with the truth of value-pluralism (Gray 2000a, 21; 2000c, 90–91; 1995b, 42–43).[10] Clearly, Christianity and Islam, especially in their more fundamentalist forms, cannot live comfortably with value-pluralism, particularly not with Gray's version of it. Nor can Judaism, although Gray finds that faith less problematic since its claims are mostly directed at one people rather than at humanity at large. He is better disposed towards polytheistic religions, for the simple untheistic reason that they are more compatible with a diversity of good forms of life (Gray 1995b, 151; 2000a, 4; 2002, 125–27). But, polytheism is still very different from value-pluralism and Hinduism, as Gray notices (2002: 174), has its fundamentalists. Liberalism is also very much a problem for Gray in so far as it sees itself as the foundation for the uniquely legitimate social order rather than merely one way of life amongst many. So too are other doctrines and ideologies that have universalist aspirations. For Gray, all of these are 'illusions' (2000a, 20–21, 135; 1995a, 155).

Despite his intellectual dismissal of these systems of belief and their associated conceptions of the good, Gray wishes them to be part of a mutually tolerant *modus vivendi*, so that people are able to live the many different forms of life in which they can flourish. Can he offer his own conception of value as a reason why they should tolerate diverse forms of life? Of course, for the value-pluralist himself that is precisely why others should tolerate a plurality of lives. But that cannot function as a reason for those whose beliefs are at odds with value-pluralism. That I am right and you are wrong is, for me, a good reason why you should tolerate what I applaud and you condemn; but it cannot be a good reason for you. Reasons for toleration need to be reasons that people can embrace along with, not in place of, their other beliefs and values.[11] Value-pluralism remains a conception of the good and, for those who conceive the good differently, it cannot provide reason to be tolerant. Gray himself describes value-pluralism as a 'subversive doctrine' that 'does not leave everything as it is', but which 'undermines all claims about the best life for the species' (2000a, 22; see also 1993, 292; 2000c, 101). It does not therefore provide a way of seeing the world that adherents of other systems of belief can easily graft on to, or hold alongside, their own 'comprehensive doctrines'.

That verdict may seem too quick and too harsh. Value-pluralism might be conceived as a purely formal theory of value. It might be conceived, that is, as a theory that tells us certain things about the nature of values, such as their frequent uncombinability and incommensurability, but that does not, or need not, tell us what actually is valuable (cf. Crowder 2002, 177–78). In fact, Gray and other proponents of the theory give value-pluralism substance as well as form. Yet that substance is of a limited sort, partly because the core tenets of value-pluralism dictate that it must be. Gray therefore does not see the practical application of his value-pluralism as the imposition of a comprehensive doctrine (1995a, 78; 2000a, 134).

Keeping the content of value-pluralism largely formal may seem one way of making it more congruent with the fact of pluralism. In so far as it remains merely formal, it will be compatible with, and will be able to accommodate, a variety of substantive conceptions of the good. But actually that will not help at all. If value-pluralism is merely a formal type of which there can be different substantive tokens, value-pluralists will then present different and conflicting conceptions of what is valuable (as they do). The mere fact that these different conceptions are all versions of value-pluralism will not legitimate them for all value-pluralists, nor will it do anything to resolve or ameliorate the conflicts amongst them. Value-pluralism will be even more evidently part of the problem posed by the fact of pluralism, rather than its solution.

Gray invests his hope for the toleration needed for a *modus vivendi* mainly in people's ability and willingness to recognize peace as a shared good. He does not present peaceful coexistence as an a priori value or transcendent good that can escape the conflicts and incommensurability that characterize other values and that must be overridingly valuable for all. His more modest claim is that most ways of life have an interest in peace: 'all or nearly all ways of life have interests that make peaceful coexistence worth pursuing' (2000a, 135). Thus it is to people's overlapping interests in peace, rather than to any more ambitious consensus on value, that we should look for the foundation of a *modus vivendi*.

This appeal to peace as a shared good has very considerable force. It once figured prominently in arguments for toleration but has been unjustifiably sidelined in more recent defences of toleration which have preferred philosophy to pragmatism. We should remember that, as Gray points out, people's interest in peace consists not only in their being spared suffering and bloodshed, but also in their enjoying the many positive goods for which peace is a practical precondition.

Nevertheless, while the appeal to peace can contribute powerfully to a general case for toleration, as an isolated justification it has its limits. One reason why many advocates of toleration fight shy of resting their case on that appeal is that, as Gray concedes, peace may not figure as an overriding value for everyone. Clearly, in our world that remains much more than a theoretical possibility. Another limitation of the appeal to peace, and one that may be more significant, is that peace may be attainable without toleration. If power is distributed sufficiently unequally, ways of life can be suppressed with little hint of open conflict.[12] The last twenty years have provided ample evidence that repressive regimes can be instruments of peace, while more tolerant regimes can be catalysts for conflict and bloodshed. That is merely a dark instance of two of Gray's core claims: that good cannot always be freed from evil and that there is no necessary harmony amongst goods.

Moreover, the sort of intolerance that should and does worry Gray need be neither bloody nor repressive. It may consist in the active promotion of one way of life by proponents who (wrongly) believe it to be morally superior or uniquely legitimate, and their active erosion of rival ways of life that they deem illegitimate or inferior. Ironically, it is regimes and cultures committed to liberalism that Gray sees as presenting the greatest contemporary threat of that sort. The creeping dominance of one culture over others may provoke a violent reaction, but it may also confront nothing more than resignation and a sense of helplessness.

Might there be other values to which the pluralist might look for an overlapping consensus? One whose acceptance would facilitate a *modus vivendi* is the value of diversity itself. That is a good that is closely associated with value-pluralism and one whose recognition is not confined to value-pluralism. But that good is also problematic as the foundation for a *modus vivendi*. The problem is not merely that too few doctrines would acknowledge the good of diversity or that those which do might dispute what sort of diversity is good. It is also that value-pluralism itself is not unambiguously committed to diversity as a good.

Because value-pluralism recognizes goods as irreducibly plural, it is often supposed that it must favour a world in which many different values are realized over one which realizes fewer. Or, to apply the same point to ways of life, because value-pluralism holds that good ways of life can take many different forms, it is commonly thought that the value-pluralist will regard a world in which people live many diverse good ways of life as better than one in which everyone lives pretty much the same sort of life. But, in so far as different values or different ways of life are incommensurable, that cannot be so. If values X, Y, and Z are incommensurable, we cannot say that a world in which X is realized fully and Y and Z not at all is inferior to one in which X, Y, and Z are all realized in some measure. We cannot say, for example, that a world in which justice is realized fully without concession to mercy or social utility is inferior to one in which justice is sacrificed in some measure for the sake of mercy and social utility. The same holds true if X, Y, and Z represent ways of life. If lives X, Y, and Z are incommensurable, we cannot say that a world in which everyone lives life X is less good than one in which some live life X, some life Y and some life Z. Thus, in so far as he insists that different ways of life are incommensurable, Gray has no reason to lament—even though he clearly would lament—a world in which the range of different ways of life diminishes or one in which a single way of life supplants all others.[13]

In a similar fashion, it might be supposed that, in so far as diverse lives are incommensurably good, a government would be acting wrongly if it sought to diminish their diversity. But, as an inference from incommensurability alone, that is too strong. In so far as diverse lives are incommensurable and we take account of nothing but their incommensurability, a government does indeed have no reason to diminish their diversity, but it also has no reason not to diminish their diversity.

Even if goods are incommensurable, we may be able to apply a Pareto test to compare the relative value of different combinations of good. If X, Y, and Z are each positive values, we can say that a world in which X alone is realized, and realized to a specific degree, is less good than a world in which X is realized to the same degree and some of Y is realized as well. Similarly, we can say that a world in which X and Y are each realized to a specific degree is inferior to one in which X and Y are realized to the same degree and some of Z is realized as well. In these cases, we can say that more diversity is better than less. But those comparisons will be possible only so long as the worlds we compare are identical except that one has something that the other does not. If worlds differ in other ways, as they usually do, they are not open to Pareto comparison. Notice that the Pareto test does not imply that a world in which different people live different good lives is better than one in which everyone lives one of those lives. If, as before, X, Y, and Z are incommensurable, a world in which everyone lives life X is not necessarily inferior to one in which some live life X, some life Y and some life Z; three Xs are not obviously inferior to one each of X, Y, and Z. At least, that is so if we evaluate the goodness of a world by assessing the goodness of the life of each individual or each community in that world. It would not be so if what mattered to us was the mere presence of X, Y, and Z in the world.[14]

There are reasons other than incommensurability that lead Gray to favour more diversity over less, the most prominent of which is his particularism. But even particularism does not claim that a world in which there are many different good ways of life must be better than one in which there are fewer. It claims only that what is good for particular communities or individuals must take account of their particular histories and circumstances. For particularism, diversity as such is not a good; it is merely a byproduct of the way in which the good needs to be realized in a world in which people's lives are embedded in different contexts.

The attempt to find a reason that can be a reason for tolerating conceptions of the good or forms of life that we believe to be mistaken is most associated nowadays with deontological liberals who distinguish between the right and the good. If we accept that distinction, we can be duty-bound not to prevent ways of life, even though we judge them bad. Gray (e.g., 1995a, 1–10, 75–80; 1997, 51–54; 2002a, 69–104) has absolutely no sympathy with those who seek to distinguish the right from the good and he reserves some of his most withering and dismissive criticism for liberal theories built upon that distinction. Even so, I want to suggest that Gray, qua value-pluralist, has reason to rethink his wholesale subordination of the right to the good.

The relation of the right and the good is obviously a complex and highly controversial matter and my comments here can be only brief and suggestive. Gray is adamant that the right must always be subordinate to the good and so gives no independent role to the right.[15] More generally, he seems to subsume all values relating to human beings within an idea of well-being or human flourishing. For a value-pluralist, well-being cannot be the super-value that gives value to all other values. Presumably Gray conceives it as an inclusive general notion that encompasses all that is of value in human lives, including all values that others assign to the right rather than to the good.[16]

Gray's claims about which values are, and which are not, subordinate or reducible to others are independent of value-pluralism as such. What is incompatible with value-pluralism, assuming that its reach extends to all values, is the claim that the right will escape the uncombinability and incommensurability that afflicts the good. Conflicts do arise in what we think of as the sphere of the right and, if we accept that goods conflict in ways that make them uncombinable and incommensurable, it seems reasonable to suppose that the same properties will occur in relation to the right. In addition, if we extend the idea of incommensurability to conflicts between the good and the right, we cannot say that the right must always be prior to the good.

All of that is, however, entirely consistent with the claim that the 'right' describes a different type of value from the 'good'. So, for example, the wrong of subjecting someone to an unfair trial is categorically different from the bad of failing to maximize their well-being. Similarly, the issue of how much responsibility we should take for one another's well-being is a different kind of issue from the question of what constitutes our well-being. A theory of value-*pluralism* might be expected to be sensitive to, rather than dismissive of, these different types of value.[17] Of course, with various twists and turns, we might try to recast every aspect of the right into a form of good, but I respond to that as Gray (1995b, 63–64; 2000a, 45; 2000c, 93) does to the reductivism of the utilitarian: it misrepresents the reality of our moral lives. I do not want to deny that the right is often geared to the good. If the right takes the form of rights, it will often be the significance of a good that explains why we think of it as a matter of right. Indeed, while rights-thinking and consequentialism are frequently counterposed as rival forms of morality, the best arguments for some rights, such as freedom of expression, are the goods that they deliver. But that is not to concede that the right can always be cashed out as the good.

Consider the following case. We reach an all-things-considered judgement that the form of life someone is living is bad and that it is possible for us through our intervention to make the way that person lives good or, at least, less bad—again, all things considered. Could it be wrong for us to intervene even so, assuming that our intervention would be uninvited and unwanted? If it could, would the wrong be a wrong to the person in whose life we intervene? If we answer 'yes' to these questions, we seem bound to accept that the right cannot always be reduced to the good. (My use of the phrase 'all things considered' in relation to the good is designed to exclude all possibility that it might be some good not already taken into consideration, such as the alleged 'good' of autonomy, that tips the scales against intervention.) Our affirmative answer might be only a logical affirmation, or it might be both a logical and an ethical affirmation. We might concede only that, if it were wrong to intervene in the circumstances I describe, logically the right could not be wholly reducible to the good; but we might still insist that, morally, it would never be wrong to intervene in those circumstances. Alternatively, we might accept (as I do) both that, logically, the right can sometimes be conceived independently of the good and that, morally, there is indeed a right of self-determination that makes uninvited intervention wrong, at least prima facie, even though, all things considered, intervention would make someone's life go better.[18]

I insert the qualification 'prima facie' because we may believe that what we should do in the case I describe will depend upon how bad a person's life is and on how much better our intervention can make it. If someone's life is very bad and our intervention could make it go very much better, we may think that the good of a better life should trump deontic objections to uninvited intervention. Alternatively, if someone's life is bad but not too bad and if our intervention would improve it only marginally, we may think it wrong to intervene. In so far as the right and the good are incommensurable, these trade-offs will not be easily made. But even though the right may conflict with and compete with the good in this way, rather than be simply 'prior' to the good, it must, in so far as it can conflict with and compete with the good, be independent of the good.

I see no reason then why value-pluralism should not recognize a distinction between the good and the right. If it does not, it betrays its mission to respond to the plurality of values by embracing the reality of value conflict rather than by engaging in value reductivism. Without acknowledging self-determination, individual or collective, as a matter of right independent of the good, value-pluralism will be hard put to cope with the fact of pluralism. Merely invoking 'well-being' as a catch-all good will not do the job. According to value-pluralism, the potential constituents of well-being must be diverse and in significant measure uncombinable and incommensurable, but that of itself is not a problem—or at least, for the value-pluralist, not a problem that should raise questions of toleration. What will present problems is disagreement amongst value-pluralists about which of the many ways of life that people do live and might live satisfy the internally diverse criterion of well-being. What presents a further problem is the different and conflicting conceptions of well-being possessed by those who are not value-pluralists, and perhaps also their rejection of well-being as the standard by which the goodness of human lives should be judged. If, in the face of doubts over the content and status of well-being, we still believe there is reason to allow people to live the way of life to which they are committed, we seem driven to a conception of right that is not reducible to a conception of the good. The status of those who are committed to a way of life should be factored into our response to it, as well as our estimate of its goodness.[19]

I remain deeply suspicious of claims that we should allow people to pursue their ways of life only because and in so far as we reckon them to be (commensurably or incommensurably) good. There is especial reason for suspicion if the range of lives we are enjoined to recognize or tolerate is as diverse and inclusive as Gray evidently intends. Frequently, we will not know enough about particular forms of life to make any worthwhile assessment of their goodness. We may also be unable fully to appreciate the nature of lives that we ourselves have not experienced from the inside, particularly when we address human diversity on a global scale. Yet, our limited understanding of others' ways of life does not prevent our accepting that we would be wrong, at least prima facie, to prevent people living ways of life that are distinctively their own. The driving thought behind that acceptance is not a judgement that their way of life is good or the best open to them—how could we know that in these circumstances? Rather, it is the deontological thought that people should be able to pursue their way of life because it is *theirs*. The moral standing of those who are committed to a way of life should matter independently of our conception of the goodness of that way of life. In so far as Gray rejects any such conception of the right, he deprives himself of a moral resource that could contribute (and, I would argue, already does contribute) significantly to securing a *modus vivendi* in a world characterized by the fact of pluralism.

ACKNOWLEDGEMENTS

I am grateful to the participants in the Workshop on the Political Thought of John Gray held at Manchester Metropolitan University and to my colleagues in the Newcastle Political Philosophy Research Group for helpful comment on an earlier version of this chapter. Special thanks to John Horton. Much of the work for this chapter was conducted during my tenure of a Leverhulme Research Fellowship; I am very grateful to the Leverhulme Trust for their support.

NOTES

1. Gray (1995a, 155–57, 177–78) suggests that liberalism's giving up its self-conception as a universalist philosophy and reconceptualizing itself as merely one tradition amongst others must entail its undergoing a 'profound cultural metamorphosis' and one that threatens its continuance.

2. Commenting on Berlin, but in a way that indicates his own thinking, Gray writes, 'Berlin's pluralism is not the claim that there are occasional pockets of incommensurability, such that utilitarian maximization is not always a possibility: it is the more radical claim—but also the more defensible claim, if human experience is to be our guide—that incommensurability is pretty pervasive in human life and so in practical reasoning' (1995b, 59).

3. In *Two Faces of Liberalism*, Gray seems to give a more limited remit to radical choice than he does in *Enlightenment's Wake* and *Berlin*. In the last two works, radical choice appears as a regular feature of our lives, and Gray presents it as a central feature of agonistic liberalism. But in *Two Faces of Liberalism* he remarks that 'radical choices occur as crises in ethical life, not as normal episodes within it' (2000a, 65). That may be because he has become even more convinced than formerly that the most significant incommensurabilities arise among communal ways of life rather than within them (Gray 2000a, 12–13, 121; 2000b, 329–31). In so far as people find themselves already embedded within a way of life, rather than having to choose amongst several ways of life, they are spared a major occasion for radical choice. The need for radical choice will arise most frequently amongst those who are heirs to different ways of life and who therefore have to choose between the conflicting demands of those different ways of life. Yet Gray also observes that nowadays 'nearly all of us belong in several ways of life' (2000a, 52) and that 'as more people come to belong to several ways of life, choices of this far-reaching kind tend to become more frequent' (2000a, 65). Although a radical choice looks as though it must be a mere act of will, Gray (1995b, 158–160; 2000a, 54–55) suggests that it may be more than that.

4. Pressed to its full conclusion, the view that a particular context will provide us with grounds for favouring one value over another, or for opting for a particular balance of values, could mean that we never, in reality, have to wrestle with incommensurability. Values that are incommensurable and that confront us with radical choices when considered in the abstract will be rendered commensurable and objects of rational choice by the specific circumstances of any real-life situation. For an optimistic account of how we can reasonably resolve conflicts arising from incommensurability and incompatibility by reference to traditions and conceptions of the good grounded in them, see Kekes (1993), especially chap. 5. Kekes's (1993, 94) view is not that a particular tradition and an associated conception of the good will remove incommensurability and incompatibility as causes of conflict but that they can provide us with reasons for responding to those conflicts in specific ways. Gray (2000a, 53–54; 1997, 86–90) is more sceptical than Kekes of the determinacy of traditions in late modern societies, but he too emphasizes that 'the context of my history and circumstances' can render my choice between conflicting incommensurable goods either right or wrong (2000a, 43).

5. More generally, though in a different context, Gray has observed that 'Humans cannot live without illusions' and that 'Illusion is our natural condition' (2002, 29, 81, see also 82–83). In contrast with Gray's willingness to indulge illusion, Bernard Williams, commenting on the value-pluralism of Isaiah Berlin, suggests that recognition of the truth of value-pluralism is itself valuable: 'the consciousness of the plurality of competing values is itself a good, as constituting knowledge of an absolute and

fundamental truth' (1980, xviii). He goes on to suggest that Berlin 'finds value in knowledge and true understanding themselves, and regards it as itself an argument for the liberal society that that society expresses more than any other does a true understanding of the pluralistic nature of values' (1980, xviii). Crowder also argues that a life that recognizes 'the true nature of human values, including their pluralism' is better for that reason (2002, 181–82). Galston, on the other hand, asserts, like Gray, that a life can be good even though based on illusion: 'There are some genuine goods whose instantiation in ways of life allows or even requires illusion. . . . While self-aware value-pluralists cannot lead such lives, they must recognize their value. To demand that every acceptable way of life reflect a conscious awareness of value-pluralism is to affirm what value-pluralism denies—the existence of a universally dominant value' (2002, 53).

6. On this idea of 'government house utilitarianism', see Sen and Williams (1982, 16), and Williams (1973, 138–40). That term is not always used pejoratively; see, for example, Goodin (1995). I do not mean to imply that government house value-pluralism would be attractive to value-pluralists. They (like utilitarians) understand themselves to be propounding a practical rather than a merely theoretical truth and, for the most part, want it to be recognized so that people will adjust their thinking and, more especially, their conduct accordingly.

7. Crowder makes his case partly by pointing out that, of the burdens of judgement that Rawls lists to explain the phenomenon of reasonable disagreement, the two that are specific to issues of value make claims that are, in effect, formulations of value-pluralism (see also Galston 2002, 46–47). But, whatever Rawls says, we can still distinguish between (a) differences amongst people's conceptions of the good that are explicable in terms of incommensurability and conflicts amongst values and (b) differences that are grounded in people's different and conflicting judgements about what is valuable. I concede that that distinction may be easier to make in principle than in practice and that there will be cases in which both factors contribute to differences among people.

8. The disagreement could also be about what is the set of incommensurably right answers, but then the dispute would be about which answers properly belong to that set rather than, *per impossibile*, about which answer in the set is the right answer.

9. Thus, for example, throughout his discussion on rival freedoms in *Two Faces of Liberalism* (2000a, 69–104), Gray talks both of conflicting values, goods and liberties, and of conflicting judgements, views, conceptions and ideals of these, and comments (69, 72, 82) that reasonable people may differ in their judgements, views, etc.

10. William Galston (1999, 880; 2002, 25–26) disagrees. He argues that, in reality, religions are internally sufficiently complex and diverse to be compatible with value-pluralism.

11. Cf. Gray's remark (made in the course of criticizing Oakeshott for neglecting diversity and conflict amongst, and within, political traditions): 'when a society or a polity harbours diverse traditions or forms of life, with their associated worldviews, conceptions of the good and styles of political activity, political reasoning cannot be internal to any one tradition but must seek to identify human interests that are common to practitioners of different forms of life' (1997, 88).

12. Gray often describes the good that should drive us towards a *modus vivendi* as 'peaceful coexistence' rather than merely 'peace' and that would rule out securing peace through repression or the promotion of cultural uniformity. For example, 'The pluralist standard of assessment of any regime is whether it enables its subjects to coexist in a Hobbesian peace while renewing their distinctive forms of common life' (1995a, 140). 'The animating project of pluralism is that different cultures should dwell on the earth in peace, without renouncing their differences' (1995a, 180). But if they have to embrace peaceful *coexistence*, the parties to a *modus vivendi* then need to be told why coexistence has value independently of peace. For Gray, the answer lies in the goodness of each of the several ways of life at issue. But another answer will be needed for those who do not share his value-pluralism or for value-pluralists who are in dispute about which ways of life are valuable. That is why I go on to argue that, in spite of his protests to the contrary, Gray needs a conception of right that is independent of the good. Even if we are agreed on the good, that does not tell us whose good should count and in what measure.

13. Compare Williams' oft-quoted claim that 'if there are many and competing values, then the greater the extent to which a society tends to be single-valued, the more genuine values it neglects or suppresses. More, to this extent, must mean better' (1980, xvii). At one time Crowder (1994, 300–01) insisted that there was no logical link between pluralism and valuing diversity, but he too now argues that, subject to a coherence test, pluralism does imply that more diversity is better than less and that we have a duty to promote diversity (2002, 136–37). Crowder (2002, 49) adopts (what he reckons to be) a less strong conception of incommensurability than Gray, according to which incommensurable values are unrankable rather than incomparable. But that makes no difference here: if justice and mercy are unrankable, we still cannot say that a world in which there is some justice and some mercy is better than one in which there is full justice and no mercy. Crowder's argument seems to depend on his relaxing the assumptions of value-conflict and uncombinability so that, to a significant extent, opting for more or less diversity is just like choosing amongst X alone or X + Y or X + Y + Z (in which case the pluralist clearly would opt for X + Y + Z). He also claims that the pluralist must endorse all ultimate goods equally 'in the sense that they have an equal claim on us' (2002, 137). That comes very close to saying that the pluralist should attribute equal value to ultimate goods but, as Crowder himself points out, that is inconsistent with their being incommensurable. He appeals to Berlin's description of ultimate goods as 'equally ultimate', but that means no more than that they are equally irreducible.

14. One thing that may seem to make a difference here is how we suppose people benefit from ways of life. Do we benefit only from our own way of life, or do we also benefit from the existence of ways of life that we ourselves do not live? If ways of life have benign spillovers or externalities (e.g., the joy of encountering and experiencing another's culture), that may seem to provide a powerful Paretian argument for diversity. In a world in which there are ways of life X, Y and Z, people living life X will gain some external advantage from those who live life Y or Z, and the same will apply, *mutatis mutandis*, for those who live lives Y or Z. In that case, it might seem that a world in which there are ways of life X, Y, and Z must be better than one in

which there is only one of those ways of life. That, however, does not follow. It would follow if X, Y, and Z were of equal value, but we are supposing that these ways of life are incommensurable. In that case, we cannot know that a world in which all three ways of life are lived, and in which each yields benign externalities, is better than one in which only one way of life is lived. So, for example, those who live life X, and who gain benefit from others' living lives Y and Z, are better off in that diverse world than they would be in a world in which everyone lived life X; but those who live life Y or Z, and who gain some benefit from others' living life X, might be still better off if they themselves lived life X. So, even if we assume that ways of life yield benign externalities, we cannot conclude that diversity is better than uniformity, as long as the ways of life at issue remain incommensurable.

15. 'The right can never be prior to the good. Without the content that can be given it only by a conception of the good, the right is empty. A strictly political liberalism, which is dependent at no point on any view of the good, is an impossibility. The central categories of such a liberalism—"rights", "justice", and the like—have a content only insofar as they express a view of the good' (Gray 2000a, 19). Gray describes his own position as one in which 'the good has priority over the right, but in which no one view of the good has overall priority over all others' (2000a, 135).

16. 'Insofar as they have any determinate content principles of right embody substantive conceptions of the good. They express particular understandings of human interests and well-being' (Gray 2000c, 86; see also 2000a, 15–20, 47–48, 69–104, 113–14; 2000b, 326–27; 1995a, 71–72). Gray describes human well-being as 'the bottom line in moral and political reasoning' (1995a, 107; 1993, 303).

17. Contrast Nagel (1979, 128–41) who, in his version of value-pluralism, distinguishes not just between different values but between different *types* of value.

18. Doubtless some will insist, even in this case, that it simply *must* be true that the content of the right is in the interest of, or is good for, the right-holder, whether individual or group. That insistence would indicate to me that the right is being used to give content to the right-holder's good or interest, rather than vice versa.

19. I require here only that the way of life be one to which its bearers are committed and not that it must be one that they have in any meaningful sense 'chosen'. In addition, the entity that possesses the right of self-determination can be a group rather than an individual and will be where a way of life assumes a collective form. My argument here is not therefore necessarily 'liberal' as that term is ordinarily understood. Note, however, that a group right can be (though it does not have to be) conceived as a joint claim of the several individuals who make up the group rather than a claim of the group as unitary entity (see further, Jones 1999). In his determination to concede nothing to this form of valuing, Gray (1993, 306–13, especially 311) at one point seems to argue that it is forms of life, rather than the people who live them, that are the ultimate units of value and the ultimate source of rights.

REFERENCES

Crowder, G. (1994). 'Pluralism and Liberalism', *Political Studies* 42:293–305.

———. (2002). *Liberalism and Value Pluralism* (London: Continuum).

Fiala, A. (2003). 'Stoic Tolerance', *Res Publica* 9:149–68.

Galston, W. (1999). 'Expressive Liberty, Moral Pluralism, Political Pluralism: Three Sources of Liberal Theory', *William and Mary Law Review* 40:869–907.

———. (2002). *Liberal Pluralism: The Implications of Value Pluralism for Political Theory and Practice* (Cambridge: Cambridge University Press).

Goodin, R. (1995). *Utilitarianism as a Public Philosophy* (Cambridge: Cambridge University Press).

Gray, J. (1993). *Post-Liberalism: Studies in Political Thought* (London: Routledge).

———. (1995a). *Enlightenment's Wake: Politics and Culture at the Close of the Modern Age* (London: Routledge).

———. (1995b). *Isaiah Berlin* (London: Fontana).

———. (1997). *Endgames: Questions in Late Modern Political Thought* (Cambridge: Polity).

———. (2000a). *Two Faces of Liberalism* (Cambridge: Polity).

———. (2000b). 'Pluralism and Toleration in Contemporary Political Philosophy', *Political Studies* 48:23–33.

———. (2000c). 'Where Pluralists and Liberals Part Company'. In M. Baghramian and A. Ingram, eds., *Pluralism: The Philosophy and Politics of Diversity*, 85–102 (London: Routledge).

———. (2002). *Straw Dogs* (London: Granta).

Hare, R. M. (1981). *Moral Thinking: Its Levels, Method and Point* (Oxford: Clarendon Press).

Jones, P. (1999). 'Group Rights and Group Oppression', *Journal of Political Philosophy* 7:353–77.

Kekes, J. (1993). *The Morality of Pluralism* (Princeton, NJ: Princeton University Press).

Larmore, C. (1996). *The Morals of Modernity* (Cambridge: Cambridge University Press).

Rawls, J. (1993). *Political Liberalism* (New York: Columbia University Press).

Sen, A., and B. Williams, eds. (1982). *Utilitarianism and Beyond* (Cambridge: Cambridge University Press).

Williams, B. (1973). 'A Critique of Utilitarianism'. In J. Smart and B. Williams, eds., *Utilitarianism: For and Against*, 75–150 (Cambridge: Cambridge University Press).

———. (1980). 'Introduction'. In I. Berlin, *Concepts and Categories*, ed. H. Hardy, xi–xviii (Oxford: Oxford University Press).

Chapter 10

Can Speech Be Intolerant?*

Speech is frequently a candidate for toleration. We often take exception to the words of others, written or spoken, and we then have reason to ask whether their objectionable speech is tolerable. Indeed, the general case for freedom of expression is often couched in the language of toleration, as is the issue of its limits.[1] In this chapter, I want to reverse the way in which the relationship between speech and toleration is normally considered. I want to examine speech not as a possible object of toleration but as a possible instrument of intolerance. If we are committed to toleration as an ideal, does that require us to curb what we say as well as what we do? My question, therefore, is not whether speech should be tolerated but whether speech itself can be intolerant.

The most obvious way of approaching that question would be to give an account of toleration and its opposite, intolerance, and then to examine how various forms of speech stand in relation to that account. My approach will be less briskly straightforward than that because my aim, in part, is to examine some of the complications that arise when we consider what should count as toleration and intolerance in relation to speech. I shall examine a number of different sorts of speech that might attract the charge of intolerance, but I do not claim to exhaust all of the possibilities and my comments on those I do examine will inevitably leave much unsaid.

TOLERATION, INTOLERANCE, AND SPEECH

In broad terms, we tolerate when we allow something that we disapprove of or dislike even though we could prevent it. Disapproval and dislike are

* I am grateful to Graham Long and Glen Newey for their helpful comments on an earlier draft of this chapter. Some of the ideas I set out here were developed during my tenure of a Leverhulme Research Fellowship; I would also like to thank the Leverhulme Trust for its support.

essential features of toleration in its traditional sense: we have no occasion to tolerate that to which we take no exception. Nowadays 'toleration' is sometimes used more loosely to describe an absence of disapproval or dislike in circumstances in which those negative responses might arise. On this usage, the 'tolerant' person is someone who refuses to find differences objectionable rather than someone who objects to, but endures, them. In this essay, I shall keep faith with the traditional meaning of toleration. What makes toleration interesting is its combining negative appraisal with nonprevention. We often think of toleration as a virtue or an ideal. That generates the question, how can it be good or right to allow x even though we identify x as bad and even though we could prevent it? If we use 'toleration' of x to mean finding x unobjectionable, we lose that question. Hence, throughout this chapter, I shall take toleration and intolerance to incorporate disapproval or dislike of some sort.

Another basic feature of toleration is allowing when we might prevent. If we disapprove of x but are unable to prevent it, we are in no position to tolerate it. We can tolerate x only if we believe that not tolerating it is an option available to us. If we are unable to prevent x, we might still form a view on whether we should or should not allow x if we could. That is, we might adopt a tolerant or intolerant stance in relation to x, even though we are unable to influence whether x actually occurs. But, strictly, we actually tolerate x only if we believe we are able to prevent it but do not seek to do so, and we are intolerant of x only if we prevent it when we might not.

I have used the terms 'allowing' and 'preventing' in characterizing toleration and intolerance. Much of my concern will be with what should count as 'allowing' and 'preventing' for purposes of toleration and with whether toleration and intolerance might encompass more than these words describe. One factor relevant to that concern is the context in which we raise these questions. We often use the language of toleration and intolerance more generously in the context of close personal relations than in the public domain. For example, in the case of one-to-one encounters, we might describe a raised eyebrow or a reproving tone of voice as intolerant.[2] We cannot expect to replicate that degree of nuance and sensitivity in the public sphere where our concern is with the rules and norms that should govern people's conduct and relations as citizens. For public purposes, our concept of toleration has to be more robust. My discussion will focus on the public domain: I shall suppose that we ask 'can speech be intolerant?' in the context of a society whose members possess different preferences, beliefs, values, cultures, and ways of life. We might also ask that question in an international or global context.

I shall not attempt to give a precise definition of 'speech'. I take speech to encompass both the spoken and the written word. It might also include pictorial representations that have communicative content, such as cartoons.

American authors and constitutional lawyers have given a great deal of attention to what else might count as speech, given the significance of that question for interpreting and applying the First Amendment. I pass over that issue here since, for the most part, I shall focus on cases of speech whose status as 'speech' is unlikely to be controversial.

Why should it matter whether speech can be intolerant? The most obvious answer is the relevance of that question to our thinking about what we should permit or proscribe and to what we might justifiably do in the name of toleration. A commitment to toleration need not require us to tolerate the intolerant. Since intolerance is the negation of toleration, we can be intolerant of intolerance for the sake of toleration. Thus, if some forms of speech are properly identified as intolerant, we may be able to justify intolerance of those forms as an intolerance that is demanded by toleration itself.

It is not, however, uncomplicatedly true that toleration warrants intolerance of intolerance. In our personal relationships, we might find reason to tolerate the intolerant conduct of another. We might, for example, think that our tolerance is a price worth paying to maintain an amicable relationship. In public life too, there may be reason to tolerate the intolerant. A reason commonly advanced for depriving governments of the power to interfere in the sphere of speech is the risk that governments will use or misuse that power to prohibit the wrong sort of speech.[3] Thus, we may think that the safest strategy is severely to limit the power of governments to control speech of any sort, so that intolerant speech that, in principle, should be prohibited remains, in practice, unprohibited. But, while there may be cases in which the best policy is to tolerate the intolerant, identifying an act as intolerant will frequently function as a powerful reason for prohibiting it the name of toleration. In particular, those who complain of being victims of intolerance are most readily answered if the intolerance of which they complain is simply intolerance of their own intolerance.

Elsewhere I have argued that we need to rethink our understanding of political toleration—toleration secured by or through the state—to suit the changed political circumstances in which we now live.[4] In the past, political toleration has been intelligible as toleration extended by a ruler to his or her subjects. But that ruler–subject model of toleration is inappropriate to liberal democratic regimes. We should now think of a tolerant political order not as one in which a government tolerates its subjects but as one that upholds an ideal of toleration amongst its citizens. It might do that by, for example, maintaining an order of things in which citizens are prevented from using political power to impose their favoured form of life upon other citizens who are committed to other forms of life. But, if a government is to uphold an ideal of toleration, it must be able to identify what constitutes intolerant conduct amongst its citizens. That too gives practical significance to the question of whether speech can be intolerant.

In assessing this question, it is crucial to note that justified intolerance need not always be intolerance of intolerance. There are myriad instances of justified intolerance in which the object of intolerance is not itself intolerant. Murder, rape, assault, theft, fraud, and libel have, in the ordinary run of cases, nothing to do with intolerance. Probably the great majority of the acts and states of affairs that we find intolerable, and that we believe ourselves right not to tolerate, are intolerable for reasons that have nothing to do with intolerance. The intolerable should not therefore be identified with the intolerant, and the adage that we should tolerate everything except intolerance is quite misleading.

Accordingly, the question of whether speech can be intolerant should not be conflated with the question of whether it can be wrongful and justifiably limited. We might think that speech should be limited if and because it is defamatory, insulting, disrespectful, obscene, offensive, or a violation of the right to privacy. That does not entail that we must, in any of these cases, hold it to be intolerant. Intolerable speech is not necessarily intolerant speech.

Equally, intolerant speech need not be intolerable, even in principle, merely because it is intolerant. I have already indicated that we think ourselves right not to tolerate murder, rape, assault, and the like, and we would therefore reject any claim that our intolerance in these cases is intolerable simply because it is intolerant. If speech can be intolerant, it may seem less likely that it can be justifiably intolerant, but I shall indicate that there are types of intolerant speech to which virtually no one would take exception.

PREVENTION AND SPEECH

So far I have characterized intolerance as prevention. That sets the hurdle for intolerance quite high and, it may seem, too high for any sort of speech to surmount. It is commonly observed that people should enjoy greater freedom of speech than of action, because speech is less capable than action of harming, impeding, or otherwise adversely affecting the lives of others.[5] It would seem that, for the same reason, speech is much less serviceable than action as an instrument of intolerance. Yet there are occasions when speech is clearly preventative.

The simplest example is barracking or shouting down. Here the voices of the intolerant are used as instruments to frustrate the audibility of a speaker. Shouting down is clearly an exercise in prevention: it aims to prevent a speaker from communicating with his audience and an audience from hearing its speaker. So, if our criterion for intolerance is prevention, we have here a clear instance of intolerance.

A quite different instance is the speech that plays a role in the formal restriction of conduct. The paradigm case of public intolerance is legal prohibition. Speech, written or spoken, is essential to the formulation of laws, and it is also usually has an essential role in their enactment and administration. For example, declaring a defendant guilty and sentencing him or her to punishment both typically take the form of speech-acts. So, in so far as speech is intrinsic to the making and administration of law, it is clearly part of something that can be a vehicle for intolerance.

However, while there is no problem in associating both of these examples with prevention, neither is clearly an example of preventative 'speech'. Shouting down relies for its preventative effect on its volume rather than its verbal content—which may be entirely absent—and there is good reason not to describe as 'speech' just any noise that emanates from a human mouth. In the case of the enactment and application of laws, clearly much more is involved than speech. Speech is merely a medium that is used in an institutional process, legislative or judicial, and it is the process rather than the medium that is the potential instrument of intolerance. The mere fact that speech is used in the process is insufficient reason to identify speech as the source of an intolerance that the process is used to effect.

The kind of speech that we might most readily describe as intolerant is speech that articulates an intolerant point of view. If I say, for example, that public manifestations of homosexuality are disgusting and ought to be prohibited, or that Muslim modes of dress are out of place in Western societies and should not be allowed in public, my words may be described as intolerant because they express an intolerant view. In this sense, speech can obviously be 'intolerant' but, in another sense, that same speech need not be. If I merely articulate these views, for example in response to someone who solicits them, nothing need change, nor need I intend anything to change, as a consequence; homosexuals may be no less able to express their sexuality and Muslims no less free to wear their traditional modes of dress. Expressing the view that someone's conduct ought not to be tolerated does not, of itself, constitute not tolerating their conduct, any more than stating that someone ought to be punished constitutes their being punished, or proposing that someone should have their gallstones removed constitutes removing their gallstones. The intolerance I am interested in is the actual condition of not being tolerated and not merely an intolerance that someone might desire. Thus, for my purposes, intolerant speech is speech that creates or tries to create intolerance rather than speech that merely articulates an intolerant view.

But suppose now that the speech that articulates an intolerant view does more than just that. Suppose that it aims to secure legal prohibition of the conduct it condemns. It might be, for example, the speech of a legislator attempting to persuade other legislators to prohibit the offending conduct. Or it might be the speech of a public campaigner trying to persuade politicians or electors to support the introduction of a ban. This sort of speech is appropriately described as intolerant. It is clearly intolerant if it secures its aim. But it is also rightly described as intolerant in virtue of its aim, irrespective of whether it actually achieves that aim.

Of course, speech of this sort relies upon more than itself to achieve its intolerant effect. For that effect, it needs to be followed by an act that renders the offending conduct illegal. But this speech relates rather differently to a decision-making process than the case I cited earlier. In that case, speech figured as a medium used in the execution of a legislative or judicial process. In that process, a speech-act may be used to exercise authority and to pronounce decisions, but it is the act rather than the speech that is the dominant partner in effecting those decisions. In the case I am currently considering, speech is used to advocate a particular legislative outcome and is part of an endeavour to bring about that outcome. In that speech-act, speech is to the fore. That is why, in this case, speech itself can be justifiably identified as an instrument of intolerance.

My identification of speech of this sort as intolerant is unlikely to be controversial, yet this sort of speech illustrates just how commonplace and unexceptionable intolerant speech can be. Earlier I observed that we routinely accept that we should be intolerant of murder, rape, fraud, and the like. It would be odd, therefore, to object to speech that advocates intolerance of these acts. Nor would it be reasonable to limit tolerably intolerant speech to just those cases in which we think the prohibitions that it advocates would be justified. If public debate, particularly democratic debate, is to have the latitude that it needs to be real, tolerably intolerant speech must be allowed to range over a much larger set of cases.

In the remainder of this chapter, I shall focus upon cases in which the intolerance of speech is more controversial and in which 'intolerant' is likely to figure as a term of condemnation. But the principal question that I want to ask of those cases is not what makes intolerant speech wrong—supposing that it is—but rather what can justify our characterizing it as intolerant.

CRITICISM, DISAPPROVAL, AND DISLIKE

Should we describe speech as intolerant merely if and because it expresses disapproval or dislike? There are two reasons why we should not. First, I have already indicated that we can tolerate only what we disapprove of or dislike. In the absence of disapproval or dislike, there is no toleration. If criticizing or condemning were itself to constitute intolerance, we could tolerate only by remaining silent, only by objecting but not making our objection known to others, and that would seem an indefensibly severe conception of what toleration requires, at least for public life. There may be interpersonal circumstances in which we can show toleration by refraining from disclosing our disapproval, and people who bite their tongues might be said to show greater tolerance than those who gives full vent to their spleen. But, as a guide for public rules and arrangements, this 'Trappist' approach to toleration would clearly be at odds with our ordinary understanding of what toleration requires. It would also turn the demand for toleration into a form of intolerance, since those whose disapproval was silenced in the name of toleration could reasonably complain that their inability to disclose their disapproval was itself a significant form of intolerance.

That point is reinforced by a second. Many bodies of belief are, by their very nature, critical of other bodies of belief. To be a Christian is ordinarily to believe that there is one God and that Jesus Christ was His son. It is also, by implication, to reject as false, and perhaps as evil, faiths that deny the divinity of Christ or that recognize more than one god. Similarly, to be a Muslim is ordinarily to hold that Muhammad was God's Prophet and that the Koran embodies the word of God as it was revealed through His Prophet. It is also to condemn as false, and perhaps as evil, faiths that hold that Muhammad was a false prophet and that deny that the Koran is the word of God. Thus, both Christianity and Islam are, by implication, critical of one another and of other faiths and of unbelief. Unbelief is, by implication, critical of both. So it is not possible to treat holding and expressing a belief and criticizing other beliefs as if these were two independent acts, one of which should be allowed and the other not. A concept of toleration that permitted people to hold and manifest their own beliefs but debarred them from criticizing the beliefs of others would be incoherent.

For these two reasons, then, merely articulating and making known our dislike or disapproval of the conduct or beliefs of others should not count as intolerance. However, if we tell a fuller story about the context of negative comment, the compatibility of criticism with toleration may be less straightforward. Suppose person A is firmly wedded to a system of belief; person B rejects that system of belief and wishes to criticize it roundly.[6] Because A is so firmly committed to his beliefs, he does not want them to be subjected to B's critical comment. If, for example, A's beliefs are religious beliefs, he might regard B's criticisms as blasphemous. Alternatively, he might simply find challenges to his beliefs unpleasant and disconcerting and for that reason want B to desist from criticism.

Under these circumstances, we might hold that A adopts an intolerant stance towards B: A exhibits an intolerant attitude towards B in so far as he would silence her criticism if he could and is actually intolerant of B if he can and does silence her. But we might equally hold that B stands in an intolerant relation to A: B, in criticizing A's beliefs, is behaving in a manner that is intolerant of his wish that she should not do so. In that case, we seem to have a stalemate: A is intolerant of B, B is intolerant of A, and the idea of toleration favours neither party. If, for example, we are committed to upholding toleration and we have to decide upon public rules governing this sort of case, it is not clear whose intolerance we should indulge.

This simple stylized example suggests that the very circumstances in which the issue of toleration is likely to arise may be circumstances in which favouring toleration disappears as an option for third parties, such as governments, who have to arbitrate between the contending parties.[7] Yet that conclusion seems surprising. Surely there is some way of dealing with the conflict between A and B that can claim to be the more tolerant option. If there is, it suggests we need a more discriminating concept of toleration.

We can arrive at that more discriminating concept by distinguishing between agents, observers and patients. *Agents* are those who act. For my purposes, they also include those who might act but choose not to, and those who manifest a belief or identity as well as those who perform 'acts' in the ordinary sense. *Observers* are those who observe the actions or inactions of others and who may form judgements about, and wishes that relate to, those actions or inactions. *Patients* are those who are the objects of others' actions; rather than 'do', they are 'done to'.

Toleration relates most obviously to people as *agents*. Person Y acts, or refrains from acting, and those who find something to object to in Y's action or inaction can then consider whether it should be tolerated. Consider now how *observers* stand in relation to toleration. Suppose that person X stands to Y as observer to agent: X sees what Y does, disapproves, wishes that Y had not done it, and wishes her not to behave in that way in the future. Before she acted, Y knew that she would be acting contrary to X's wishes but went ahead anyway. Should we say that Y, in acting contrary to X's known wishes, has behaved intolerantly of X?

Suppose, for example, that Y wishes to have an abortion. If others, because they believe abortion to be wrong, prevent Y from having the abortion, it seems straightforwardly true that Y's would-be abortion has not been tolerated, even if we think it was rightly not tolerated. But suppose now that Y is subject to no such prevention; she goes ahead and has the abortion knowing that, in doing so, she acts contrary to the wishes of X. Should we say that Y has treated X intolerantly? I suggest not. We should hold that Y treats X intolerantly only if Y restricts X's agency. We should not hold that Y treats X intolerantly merely because Y exercises her agency in ways that X disapproves of or dislikes. If we do not restrict the concept of toleration in that way, we shall neuter it as a property that we can ascribe to public arrangements. For every Y who acts, there is likely to be an X who objects, so that, if we do not use toleration in the discriminating fashion I suggest here, preventing Y from acting will count as no less tolerant, or no more intolerant, than allowing Y to act.

If we apply the reasoning of the previous paragraph to the earlier case of A and B, A equates with X and B with Y. A cannot rightly complain that he is a victim of B's intolerance merely because B, in voicing her criticisms, fails to comply with his wishes. If we are aiming for the maximally tolerant option, it consists in A's being free to hold, express, and act according to his beliefs, and B's being be free to criticize those beliefs. That, however, may seem too easy a solution. A stands to B, it might be objected, not as an *observer* but as a *patient*. B's criticisms are directed at *A*'s beliefs so that A is the intended object of B's act and not a mere onlooker. How much difference does that make?

First, we should note that, in real-life cases involving critical speech, the question of whether A is an observer or a patient may well be disputed. Consider the Rushdie Affair. Muslims saw themselves very much as victims in that affair; it was suggested, for example, that Rushdie had subjected them to group-defamation.[8] But Rushdie conceived himself as simply writing a novel that involved references to several major historical figures within Islam. He had neither targeted Muslims nor sought to do anything *to* them. Muslims may have seen themselves as patients, but Rushdie and his defenders were more inclined to see them as observers. As a practical matter, it will frequently be difficult, if not impossible, to distinguish (i) criticism directed at beliefs as depersonalized propositions from (ii) criticism directed at beliefs as the beliefs of a particular individual or group.

Secondly, even if A is correctly characterized as B's patient, it does not follow that A suffers intolerance. I have already observed that toleration is not at issue in every interaction between people, even when one party wrongs another. The fraudster, for example, wrongs the defrauded but he is not normally guilty of intolerance simply because intolerance is not usually at issue in cases of fraud. Even if A is B's patient, A can reasonably claim to suffer intolerance in virtue of B's criticism only if that criticism in some way curtails A's agency. In the example as I have constructed it, A could complain of intolerant treatment at the hands of B only if B's criticism prevented him from holding, expressing, and living in accordance with his beliefs. But, ordinarily, B's criticism of A's belief will be compossible with A's continuing to hold and to comply with his beliefs. In what follows, I shall identify cases in which that statement needs qualification but the point that I have aimed to establish here is that we should not deem B intolerant of A merely because she acts contrary to his wishes.

OFFENSIVE SPEECH AND PERSECUTION

Suppose that B does not merely criticize A or A's beliefs but does so in a way that A finds offensive. I would use the reasoning of the previous section to resist any simple claim that to experience offence is to suffer intolerance. But I want to use the case of offence to illustrate a form of intolerance that is frequently omitted from formal analyses of toleration, including my own up to now: persecution.

'Tolerant' and 'tolerance' are frequently used as terms of commendation, just as 'intolerant' and 'intolerance' are frequently used pejoratively. The term 'persecution' has even greater emotive force. While we are unlikely to shy away from saying that, in general, we are intolerant, and rightly intolerant, of law-breakers, we are unlikely to feel comfortable affirming that we persecute, and rightly persecute, those who break the law. It is hard to escape the sense that persecution is wrong and something that we ought not to do. Despite its strongly pejorative force, I want to use the word 'persecution' to identify a particular sort of intolerance.

'Persecution', like 'intolerance', is often used as an antonym of toleration and we might therefore suppose that the terms are synonymous. I have indicated, however, that we are unlikely to describe every instance of intolerance as 'persecution', which suggests that persecution connotes something more specific. The basic meaning of 'tolerating', that has guided my argument so far, is that of allowing when we might prevent. Accordingly, intolerance, at its simplest, means preventing or not allowing. In fact, intolerance can fall short of absolute prevention. It might take the form of discouragement. For example, a society that imposes a high level of taxation on tobacco in order to discourage smoking can be described as less tolerant of smoking than one that does not, though more tolerant than one that prohibits smoking altogether. Even if we subject smoking tobacco to legal punishment, we might dispute whether that constitutes a barrier or a disincentive. As we know, legal prohibition often fails to secure actual prevention. Yet, even though toleration and intolerance can be matters of degree, the most ready sense of 'being intolerant of' is 'putting a stop to', just as the most ready meaning of 'being tolerant of' is 'putting up with'.

But suppose we do more, or other, than 'put a stop to'. Suppose that, in addition to trying to prevent, we inflict suffering on those who have wrongful thoughts and commit wrongful acts because we believe they ought to suffer. Consider, for example, the early modern monarch who, in addition to trying to suppress heresy, tortures his heretical subjects because he believes he has a God-given duty to ensure they suffer for their wrongs. Or consider a society that, while not endeavouring to stop homosexual acts, imposes disadvantages on known homosexuals, such as depriving them of the right to drive or the right to own property, merely out of dislike, disapproval, and disgust for their homosexuality. How should we describe such measures? The term 'persecution' seems justified here. I shall use it to describe acts whose primary purpose is to inflict harm, hurt, or distress, not in a serious effort to prevent objectionable activity, but to cause suffering, discomfort, or disadvantage to those whom the persecutor views negatively.

This usage accords with the pejorative ring of 'persecution', although it is not important for my purposes that it should. My usage is narrower than some past and present usage, since the mere prohibition of a practice might be described as persecution of the group with whom the practice is associated. I propose this narrower usage to highlight the distinction between preventing conduct and inflicting suffering. Of course, the two may be conflated in a single measure, but we can still usefully distinguish between preventative intolerance and persecutory intolerance.

Consider, for example, the act of tossing a severed pig's head into a synagogue. Should we place acts of that sort within the compass of intolerance? If to tolerate Judaism is to allow, or not to prevent, its practice, it is not clear that we should. Tossing a pig's head into a synagogue need in no significant way impede the ability of Jews to practise their faith, even in the synagogue into which the pig's head is tossed. Yet it would seem odd to exclude this act from the ambit of intolerance. That is because we normally take intolerance to include persecution as well as prevention and throwing a pig's head into a synagogue falls within persecution as I have defined it: the purpose of the act is to cause distress to Jews because they are Jews.

I do not suggest that to offend is to persecute. There are many reasons why that suggestion would be unsustainable. 'Offence' often describes too slight an injury to count as even mild persecution. People 'take' offence as well as give it and they may do so unreasonably. In an age in which it has become fashionable to 'be offended', those who claim offence sometimes do so in order to veto speech or conduct that they actually object to on other grounds. Perhaps most importantly, offence cannot be represented as persecutory if it is a byproduct of speech or conduct whose primary purpose lies elsewhere. But, where the primary purpose of speech is simply to cause hurt and distress, it shares the character of persecution and can reasonably be described as intolerant. That claim is more compelling when we move from offensive speech to hate speech properly so-called, a form of speech to which I shall turn in the next section.

SOCIAL DISAPPROVAL AND HATE SPEECH

I argued earlier that merely disclosing disapproval should not count as intolerance. If it were to count as intolerance, toleration would have to become an exercise in secrecy and pretence. Yet, although there is good reason not to include mere expressions of disapproval in the catalogue of intolerant acts, there are circumstances in which the manifest disapproval of others can function as an instrument of intolerance. J. S. Mill is one of the most celebrated advocates of toleration—even though he made infrequent use of that term in stating his own position—especially in the areas of thought, discussion, and expression. Yet Mill is equally well known for his concern that social disapproval can be as inimical to individual freedom as legal prohibition, and it does seem right to treat the sort of social disapproval that worried Mill as an instrument of intolerance. If we do treat public disapproval as a possible form of intolerance, it becomes much more difficult to determine what should count as toleration and intolerance. If the issue is one of legal prohibition, the combination of negative appraisal and nonprevention characteristic of toleration is both easily achieved and readily apparent. If we are legislators and we disapprove of x, we can be tolerant by refraining from using our legislative powers to ban x. If we are ordinary citizens who disapprove of x but who have no direct access to the legislative process, we can still exhibit tolerance by not pressing for the legal prohibition of x and not voting for politicians committed to banning x. But if social disapproval is the potential instrument of intolerance, it is much more difficult to characterize the combination of disapproval and nonprevention that toleration entails. We have to find some way of distinguishing manifestations of disapproval that are consistent with toleration from those that are not.

So, for example, we might place soberly reasoned objection on one side of the line and vituperative opprobrium on the other. The tolerant person will engage in the first but refrain from the second. We might similarly distinguish between the coercion of reasons and the coercion of persons. To be coerced by reasons is to recognize the force of reasons that are brought against one's position. To be coerced by persons is to be placed under pressure simply by the weight of human opposition and hostility that one encounters. Surrendering to the coercion of reasons is consistent with autonomy; surrendering to the coercion of persons is not.

Yet we cannot expect these distinctions to provide ready answers when we move into the real world. They are too simple and too easy. For one thing, we cannot reasonably require the tolerant person to shed or hide every element of affect that typically accompanies disapproval and condemnation. Indeed, if someone is entirely bereft of the feeling and emotion that we normally associate with disapproval, we might begin to question how much tolerating they are doing. Mill certainly did not believe that toleration demanded a desiccated rationalism, even when the object of toleration was the self-regarding conduct of others. He did not mean, he insisted, 'that the feeling with which a person is regarded by others ought not to be in any way affected by his self-regarding qualities or deficiencies'. That, he thought, would be neither possible nor desirable. Just as we cannot but admire those who possess good qualities, so we must deprecate those who lack them.

> There is a degree of folly, and a degree of what may be called (though the phrase is not unobjectionable) lowness or depravation of taste, which, though it cannot justify doing harm to the person who manifests it, renders him necessarily and properly a subject of distaste, or, in extreme cases, even of contempt: a person could not have the opposite qualities in due strength without entertaining these feelings.[9]

Mill therefore did not hold that the tolerated, if they were to be tolerated, must be spared every form of reproach or censure from the tolerator.[10] We cannot expect to formulate in any simple way the distinction between forms of social disapproval that are consistent with toleration and those that are not. The diversity of human interactions is too great and too nuanced for that to be possible and much will also depend on context. It is also implausible to suppose that tolerant and intolerant forms of disapproval can be sharply and precisely separated; it is much more plausible to think that they will shade into one another. But the lack of a sharp dividing line need not disable us, in very many cases, from identifying forms of disapproval as either consistent or inconsistent with toleration. A society's self-conscious commitment to toleration is one thing that should facilitate its observance of that distinction.

Hate speech properly so called is an extreme version of the sort of disapproval that concerned Mill.[11] Mill worried about the conformist pressure that could be exerted by public majorities; hate speech can speak for a majority, a minority or an individual. Nevertheless, the intimidatory and inhibitory character of hate speech would certainly have incurred Mill's disapproval.[12]

Is hate speech intolerant? That may seem a superfluous question, but there is reason to pause before affirming that it is. Toleration can incorporate dislike as well as disapproval and hatred is but an extreme form of dislike. In addition, a speaker may report his hatred in a matter of fact way that does not have, and that is not intended to have, any intolerant effect. Yet, hatred and toleration do not sit easily together. One reason is that the more dislike rises to the pitch of hatred, the less likely it is to observe the constraints of toleration. Another is the kind of speech that phrase 'hate speech' is used to describe. Typically that is not speech that merely reports an emotion or a view; it is speech that directs hatred at the object of its hate. The 'hate' in hate speech may refer only to the speaker's hatred or it may refer also to the hatred a speaker tries to arouse in others. Hate speech may aim to incite people to inflict violence or other forms of harm upon the objects of its hatred and in that case it can clearly be an instrument of intolerance. But, even if verbal or nonverbal expressions of hatred stop short of that sort of incitement, they can clearly be persecutory or preventative both in intent and in effect.

Yet, even when hate speech takes a virulent and venomous form, it may not always be best characterized in terms of toleration and intolerance. There is, of course, always an issue about whether hate speech should be tolerated, but my concern is with whether hate speech is itself intolerant. There are reasons why we might want to conceive it in other terms. For one thing, the aspiration of those who oppose hate speech is not usually that the haters should continue to hate but in a more tolerant fashion; the goal is rather that they should simply stop hating. For another, the target of hate speech may not be eligible as an object of toleration. In ordinary cases of toleration, we put up with something when we could do otherwise; we endure a state of affairs that we could change. Thus, if we cannot change something, such as a person's race, it can make little sense to think of ourselves as tolerating it.[13] Thirdly, hate speech tends to be directed at people as such, rather than at what they believe or what they do, and we are properly uncomfortable with the idea of 'tolerating' people's very existence.[14] None of these points argues that hate speech is or can be tolerant; they indicate only that, in many of its instances, toleration and intolerance may not be at issue.

The phrase 'hate speech' has been adopted for its rhetorical effect as well as its descriptive utility and, as with all such terms, people have been keen to exploit its rhetorical potential. That raises the possibility that some speech that has been labelled 'hate speech' is actually consistent with toleration, although, in so far as it is, we may question whether it should be described as hate speech. Take two terms that have recently entered the English language: 'homophobia' and 'Islamophobia'. Both have been coined as terms of condemnation designed to have the same veto effect as words such as 'racist' and 'anti-Semitic'. Now certainly these terms can describe the sort of intolerant prejudice and hatred that we have been considering in this section. But they have also been extended to encompass any comment that is critical of homosexual conduct or of Islam and its associated practices. Arguably, the attempt to stigmatize critical comment as 'phobic' is itself an exercise in intolerance, but the principal protest I want to repeat here is that critical comment should not be deemed intolerant merely because it is critical. Muslims, or the adherents of other faiths, who express theological objections to homosexual conduct but who do not seek to have that conduct coercively prevented, present a model case of toleration. So too do homosexuals and their defenders who are critical of religious faiths for their criticisms of homosexuality but who seek to silence those criticisms through no other means than argument.[15]

Is the kind of intolerant speech that I have been considering in this section always intolerable because it is intolerant? Earlier I pointed out that, since we believe we are properly legally intolerant of many things, it would be odd to regard as intolerable speech that is intolerant because it advocates legal intolerance of those things. The sanction of social disapproval, like the sanction of legal punishment, can discourage conduct that we believe ought to be discouraged. Mill, for all his fears of the oppressive potential of public opinion, was happy that it should discourage what should be discouraged. Thus, it may well be that, in the social as in the legal realm, we will welcome and applaud some instances of intolerant speech. Some American commentators, in an effort to reconcile the legal prohibition of hate speech with the First Amendment, have taken to insisting on the capacity of hate speech to 'silence' those at whom it is targeted.[16] Presumably, those commentators would be very happy to see hate speech itself silenced through the sanction of express public disapproval. To that extent, their complaints may concern not the mere fact of silencing but what it is that is silenced: it is not merely that some speech that is silenced ought not to be, but also that some currently unsilenced speech ought to be silenced.

PROSELYTISM AND CONVERSION

The forms of intolerance that I have considered so far focus on prevention and persecution. But suppose that speech is used neither to prevent nor to persecute but to change or eliminate what the speaker objects to. Does that constitute intolerance?

Imagine two societies, each of which is populated by groups holding significantly different and conflicting sets of belief. In the Separatist society, each group of believers is insistent upon living according to its own system of belief, but refrains from intervening in the lives of other groups and willingly leaves them to conduct their lives in accordance with their own beliefs. Each group is content that the criticism of others' beliefs implicit in their own should remain implicit and each refrains from any attempt to convert 'outsiders'. Contrast the Interactive society. Here people want not only to live according to their own beliefs but also to convert those who believe differently. In their zeal to promote their own beliefs, they do not resort to coercion but they engage in open and vigorous criticism of one another's beliefs, and they strive ardently to change one another's minds. Is one of these societies more tolerant than the other?

There seems no reason to find the Separatist society less tolerant than the Interactive. There would be if formal or informal sanctions were at work in the Separatist society inhibiting critical comment and conversion. But, if there are no such sanctions and if each group's conduct is explained only by its self-restraint, the society would seem to be a model of mutual toleration. The Interactive society is less straightforward. Are people tolerant if, rather than being willing to live and let live, they strive to convert others to their own way of thinking?

The issue here is more than merely academic. Members of nonevangelical faiths have long resented the proselytizing attention they have received from evangelical faiths. Jews have complained loudly about the efforts of evangelical Christians to convert members of their community to Christianity. Similarly, Muslim efforts to convert Hindus have been a significant source of tension in India.[17] Nonevangelical religions, such as Judaism and Hinduism, are inclined to conceive a properly tolerant society on the model of the Separatist society, while evangelical religions, such as Christianity and Islam, have been more willing to place the Interactive society within the compass of toleration.

Major advocates of toleration in the Western tradition have generally been happy to accept that efforts to convert are consistent with toleration.

John Locke, for example, in his *Letter on Toleration*, insisted that

> it is one thing to persuade, another to command; one thing to press with arguments, another with decrees. . . . Every man is entitled to admonish, exhort, convince another of error, and lead him by reasoning to accept his own opinion.[18]

There is a simple sense in which refraining from efforts to convert is more tolerant than seeking to convert. If I disagree with your beliefs but refrain from any effort to change them, I show a greater willingness to accept what I deprecate than if I strive to change your beliefs. We have always to bear in mind the possibility that the nonconverter simply cares less than the converter about another's beliefs, so that he exhibits greater insouciance rather than greater tolerance. But, if we posit equal levels of concern, the nonconverter seems to exhibit greater tolerance than the converter.

Why then have so many advocates of toleration not railed against attempts to convert? The answer is that they have supposed that people, confronted by argument and criticism, can genuinely make up their own minds. The issue here for toleration is very similar to that raised by social disapproval. The guiding idea has to be autonomy and what can be consistent with it. If A presents B with reasons and B changes her mind in response to those reasons, that seems entirely compatible with B's autonomy. A has not treated B intolerantly. But if A knowingly presents B with false or biased information or seeks to change B's thinking through emotional pressure or by instilling fear of social rejection, that is inconsistent with B's autonomy and with tolerance of B. Of course, when we turn to the messy complexities and ambiguities of the real world, that simple distinction will not always give us clear answers, but it is hard to know how else we might distinguish between tolerant and intolerant forms of proselytism.

CONCLUSION

The relationship between speech and intolerance is, then, far from simple. Speech can, of course, articulate intolerant opinions but, at first sight, we might suppose that mere speech cannot be an instrument that effects intolerance. Yet, we have seen that there are several ways in which it can be. The most straightforward of these is speech designed to persuade others, particularly public decision-makers, to perform intolerant acts or to adopt intolerant measures. But a separate and subsequent act of intolerance is not always necessary for speech itself to be intolerant. Expressions of disapproval can themselves assume tolerant or intolerant forms. So too can the efforts of proselytizers. And if we allow that intolerance includes persecution as well as prevention, we open up further opportunities for speech to be intolerant.

If speech is intolerant, is that a bad thing? Again, at first sight, we might suppose that it is. But I have indicated that we are likely to applaud intolerant speech that is mobilized against intolerable conduct or intolerable states of affairs. I have also indicated that speech does not have to be intolerant to be intolerable. We cannot therefore rely merely upon the tolerant or intolerant character of speech, to signal what we should applaud, condemn, allow, or proscribe. The ideal of toleration requires more than the idea of toleration. That ideal must draw upon reasons that identify a range of conduct and conditions as its rightful objects. But we need a clear idea of toleration if we are to have a clear ideal of toleration.

NOTES

1. Lee Bollinger, *The Tolerant Society* (Oxford: Clarendon Press, 1986); David Richards, *Toleration and the Constitution* (New York: Oxford University Press, 1986) and *Free Speech and the Politics of Identity* (Oxford: Oxford University Press, 1999).

2. For an analysis of toleration that pays close attention to its more private interpersonal forms, see Nicholas Fotion and Gerard Elfstrom, *Toleration* (Tuscaloosa: University of Alabama Press, 1992).

3. E.g., Frederick Schauer, *Free Speech: A Philosophical Enquiry* (Cambridge: Cambridge University Press, 1982), 80–86.

4. Chapter 1.

5. J. S. Mill, for example, commented that, for this reason, 'no one pretends that actions should be as free as opinions', although he immediately acknowledged that there could be circumstances in which the expression of an opinion constituted 'a positive instigation to some mischievous act', in which case it lost its immunity. John Stuart Mill, *On Liberty*, ed. Gertrude Himmelfarb (Harmondsworth: Penguin, 1974), 119. For a sceptical examination of the claim that speech is less capable than action

of causing harm, see Frederick Schauer, 'The Phenomenology of Speech and Harm', *Ethics* 103 (1993): 635–53.

6. To avoid a confusion of pronouns, I assume here that A is male and B female.

7. Cf. Glen Newey, *Virtue, Reason and Toleration: The Place of Toleration in Ethical and Political Philosophy* (Edinburgh: Edinburgh University Press, 1999), chapters 4 and 5, and 'Is Democratic Toleration a Rubber Duck?', *Res Publica* 7 (2001): 315–36.

8. Tariq Modood, 'Muslims, Incitement to Hatred and the Law', in John Horton, ed., *Liberalism, Multiculturalism and Toleration* (Basingstoke: Macmillan, 1993), 139–56.

9. Mill, *On Liberty*, 143.

10. It could be that, rather than describing negative attitudes that are consistent with tolerance, Mill is here describing a form of justified intolerance. But, given his insistence upon freedom in the self-regarding domain and his concern in *On Liberty* to set out the demands of that freedom, we can rule out that interpretation of his words.

11. I use the term 'hate speech' in the sense in which it is now generally used, that is, to describe speech that directs and/or arouses hatred against a particular group defined, for example, by its race or sexuality. However, honest use of this phrase must keep faith with the normal meaning of 'hate'. Not every expression of opinion or information that relates negatively to race or sexuality, for example, is justifiably described as hate speech.

12. My association of Mill with opposition to hate speech may seem to conflict with Jacobson's claims that the liberty for which Mill argued included, 'not just thought but also the expression of any opinion or sentiment, however unpopular, offensive, *or even harmful* it may be', and that Mill held 'that it is never legitimate to prohibit the expression of an opinion or sentiment'; see Daniel Jacobson, 'Mill on Liberty, Speech and the Free Society', *Philosophy and Public Affairs* 29 (2000): 276–309, at 277, 279 (emphasis in the original). Jacobson's revisionist interpretation of Mill may be correct on these and many other points. But it does raise the question of how Mill's commitment to an unqualified right to express opinions and sentiments can be reconciled with his insistence on the need for protection 'against the tyranny of the prevailing opinion and feeling, against the tendency of society to impose, by other means than civil penalties, its own ideas and practices as rules of conduct on those who dissent from them'; Mill, *On Liberty*, 63. That is too large an issue for me to take up here, but it seems unlikely that the reconciliation can be effected by representing the tyranny to which Mill objected as a form of 'action' from whose oppressive qualities expression, opinion and sentiment might be wholly disentangled.

13. Susan Mendus, *Toleration and the Limits of Liberalism* (Basingstoke: Macmillan, 1989), 149–50. But even a case involving race may be about more than mere race; the issue may be, for example, that of people of a different race coming to live in 'our' country or in 'our' neighbourhood, in which case the requirement of alterability could be met. If, moreover, we count persecution as intolerance, even the unalterable can become an object of intolerance. However, we may not want to treat persecution and prevention as wholly symmetrical with respect to toleration. Persecution and prevention may both be forms of intolerance, but does it follow that refraining from

persecution, like refraining from prevention, constitutes 'toleration'? I am reluctant to concede that it does, which may reflect the thought that, while people can have good reason to prevent, they cannot have good reason to persecute.

14. Cf. Altman's argument that the wrong committed by hate speech is 'the wrong of treating a person as having inferior moral standing'. Andrew Altman, 'Campus Hate Speech: A Philosophical Examination', *Ethics* 103 (1993): 302–17, at 309. I give greater attention to the question of what are, and are not, appropriate objects for toleration and intolerance in chapter 7.

15. Some recent writing on censorship uses that term to include virtually anything that has a limiting effect on speech. See, for example, Robert Post, ed., *Censorship and Silencing: Practices of Cultural Regulation* (Los Angeles: The Getty Research Institute, 1998), especially the essays by E. S. Burt and Frederick Schauer. That generous view of what constitutes censorship threatens to erode the very possibility of toleration since the mere expression of disapproval or dislike may have an inhibitory effect. It also begs the question of whether, in any particular instance, responsibility for the inhibition lies with the inhibitor or the inhibited. I am inclined to agree with Langton that, 'if censorship is everywhere, it might as well be nowhere'; see Rae Langton, 'Subordination, Silence, and Pornography's Authority', in Post ed., *Censorship and Silencing*, at 261.

16. For instances of this silencing argument, see Owen Fiss, *The Irony of Free Speech* (Cambridge, MA: Harvard University Press, 1996), and Frederick Schauer, 'The Ontology of Censorship', in Post, ed., *Censorship and Silencing*. For criticism of that argument, see Daniel Jacobson, 'The Academic Betrayal of Free Speech', *Social Philosophy and Policy* 21 (2004): 48–80. Perhaps surprisingly, the silencing objection has been deployed most against pornography. For statements of this objection to pornography, see Catherine MacKinnon, *Feminism Unmodified* (Cambridge, MA: Harvard University Press, 1987), 146–97 and *Only Words* (London: HarperCollins, 1995); Rae Langton, 'Speech Acts and Unspeakable Acts', *Philosophy and Public Affairs* 22:293–330 and 'Subordination, Silence, and Pornography's Authority', in Post, ed., *Censorship and Silencing*; Jennifer Hornsby, 'Speech Acts and Pornography', in Susan Dwyer, ed., *The Problem of Pornography* (Belmont, CA: Wadsworth, 1995), 220–32; Jennifer Hornsby and Rae Langton, 'Free Speech and Illocution', *Legal Theory* 4 (1998): 21–37; and Caroline West, 'The Free Speech Argument against Pornography', *Canadian Journal of Philosophy* 33 (2003): 391–422. For critical discussions of the claim that pornography silences, see Ronald Dworkin, 'Two Concepts of Liberty', in Edna Ullmann Margalit and Avishai Margalit, eds., *Isaiah Berlin: A Celebration* (London: Hogarth Press, 1991), 100–109; Daniel Jacobson 'Freedom of Speech Acts? A Response to Langton', *Philosophy and Public Affairs* 24 (1995): 64–79 and 'Speech and Action: Replies to Hornsby and Langton', *Legal Theory* 7 (2001), 179–201; Leslie Green, 'Pornography, Silence, and Pornography's Authority', in Post, ed., *Censorship and Silencing*, 285–311. I find it hard to believe that this alleged silencing effect would have assumed such prominence in objections to pornography had the Supreme Court not treated pornography as 'speech' and so created a First Amendment obstacle to its prohibition or restriction. However, I pass over that issue here, since most pornography has a poor claim to be 'speech' and the

several objections brought against it do not usually include the specific complaint of intolerance.

17. S. N. Balagangadhara and Jakob De Roover, 'The Secular State and Religious Conflict: Liberal Neutrality and the Indian Case of Pluralism', *Journal of Political Philosophy* 15 (2007): 67–92.

18. John Locke, *A Letter of Toleration*, ed. Raymond Klibansky (Oxford: Clarendon Press, 1968), 69.

Chapter 11

International Toleration and the 'War on Terror'

Terrorism and toleration do not sit easily together. Terrorism is an extreme form of intolerance of what it opposes and, for most people, terrorism is itself intolerable. Those who think otherwise usually call it something other than 'terrorism'. So an analysis of the relationship between terrorism and toleration is likely to be very brief. However, there are many issues of toleration that surround the subject of terrorism. For example, how far should we tolerate the curtailing of civil liberties by those who seek to combat terrorism, and how far should we tolerate the activities of those who, while not committing terrorist acts themselves, defend, advocate, or 'glorify' the terrorism of others?

In this chapter, I cast my net still wider. The 'war on terror' has become caught up with large issues characterized variously as conflicts between Western and non-Western values, 'wars' between cultures, and a 'clash of civilizations'. How far it is right to view the contemporary world in terms of these grand conflicts, or to conceive the 'war on terror' as symptomatic of them, is intensely disputed. However, there is no doubt that very many people, in all parts of the globe and wherever they stand on the 'war on terror', perceive it in these larger terms so that the 'war' is conceived as both embedded in and stemming from deep cultural, social, and political differences. My concern here is to investigate the idea of international toleration as it relates to those fundamental differences.

Toleration is about not preventing or impeding what we disapprove of or dislike. We have no occasion to tolerate what we find unexceptionable. The objectionable that we tolerate can include minor irritations and dislikes, but it can also include conduct to which we have serious moral objection. Normally, we might suppose that, if an act is wrong and if we can prevent it, we should. How can it be right or virtuous to fail to prevent a preventable wrong?

Yet serious instances of toleration are instances in which we willingly allow wrong to be done. Moreover, although we can use 'toleration' and 'tolerance' as neutral terms, they have generally acquired a favourable ring in our language. Thus, when we tolerate, we frequently think we are right and perhaps deserving of praise for our toleration; tolerance is commonly regarded as a virtue and toleration as a mark of the good society.

Some commentators have suggested that the way toleration conjoins the right and the wrong presents us with a paradox. But to present toleration as paradoxical is to make it seem more mysterious and puzzling than it really is. In the paradigm case of toleration, we confront conflicting reasons. If x is a possible object of our toleration, we have both (a) reason to object to x and therefore reason to prevent it and (b) reason not to prevent x. We have reason to tolerate x, all things considered, if our reason not to prevent x overrides our reason to prevent it.[1] Issues of toleration, therefore, confront us with conflicts of reason and the phenomenon of conflicting or competing reasons is ubiquitous and commonplace. Nevertheless, because toleration can entail permitting acts or events that are wrong or bad or misguided, it does prompt us to consider how it can be justified. What sort of reason can make it better to permit than to prevent the wrong or the bad?

Analyses of toleration and arguments about its justification have focused overwhelmingly on toleration as an issue within societies. Very little of the literature on toleration has turned from the domestic to the international case.[2] We need not put that down wholly to neglect or oversight. I shall suggest in a moment why an explicit concern with toleration may have seemed less pressing or appropriate in international than in domestic politics. But, in the contemporary world, there are myriad instances of issues that arise across or beyond national boundaries that are properly characterized as issues of toleration. Indeed, as humanity becomes more globally aware and interactive, we should expect issues of toleration to arise increasingly at the global level.

Toleration can be motivated by nothing other than a strategic calculation of self-interest. I may tolerate my boss's ill-mannered behaviour simply because I want to retain her favour and enhance my prospects of promotion. Similarly, a state may tolerate a regime's violations of human rights only because it wishes to retain that regime as an ally in opposing a common foe. These are quite properly described as instances of 'toleration', but they are not the sorts of case in which we puzzle over the rightness of toleration, nor will they be my concern here. Rather, I want to focus upon cases in which toleration is more than merely self-interested. Most obviously these will be cases in which toleration can claim a moral justification, though the justification may also be non-moral—it may be grounded, for example, in uncertainty about the truth and a reluctance to act on assumptions or information that may turn out to be mistaken. However, in distinguishing the moral from the merely strategic, I do not mean to suggest that the moral and the prudential must always point in different directions. There is no reason, for example, why a condition of mutual toleration cannot be both just and to the advantage of all.

I have adopted the term 'international' toleration because I am primarily interested in toleration and intolerance between societies and particularly in the reasons 'outsiders' may have for tolerating cultures and social arrangements to which they take exception. What differentiates issues of toleration in the international case is that they relate to collective units that we might label variously as states or societies or peoples. If we adopt a global perspective on toleration in which our concern is all humanity without regard to national boundaries, it would seem that issues of toleration and the arguments relevant to them will be identical with those that might arise within a single society. Certainly, the beliefs, values, and cultures that exist globally are more diverse than those that exist within any particular society, so that global issues of toleration may be more numerous, rooted in more deep-seated differences and possibly therefore less tractable than their counterparts within particular states. But it is not clear that the general considerations that militate either for or against toleration will be categorically different if the focus of our toleration is global rather than societal. However, these may well be different if we treat national boundaries as significant and take states or societies or peoples as possible subjects and objects of toleration. That is why I describe my concern with toleration and intolerance in this chapter as 'international' rather than 'global'.

THE POSSIBILITY OF INTERNATIONAL TOLERATION

I previously suggested that there might be reasons why toleration has received less attention as an international than as an intra-national issue. One such reason may be that lack of international toleration has not been the problem. Given the reluctance of governments to undertake risks and to incur costs other than for the benefit of their own nationals, the problem might be conceived as one of too much rather than too little toleration. External governments remained onlookers during the genocide in Rwanda; most remained onlookers, or little more, during the crisis in Darfur. While there have been more instances of humanitarian intervention since the end of the Cold War than formerly, we might think that governments have been unduly reluctant, rather than overly ready, to intervene in other countries for humanitarian purposes. In other words, we may think that, internationally, governments should be induced to tolerate less rather than more.

A possible explanation of a directly opposite sort lies in the dominance of the realist tradition in international relations. According to that tradition, states either will not, or should not, be concerned with more than merely strategic toleration or intolerance. We should not expect states and their governments to do any more or other than pursue their own interests.

However, there is a further consideration that relates to the viability of the very idea of international toleration. A commonly accepted possibility condition of toleration is that the tolerator must have power over the tolerated. B can tolerate A only if B is able to affect A's conduct. If B has no control over A's conduct, he is in no position either to tolerate or not to tolerate her conduct. Without that ability, he may still be tolerantly or intolerantly disposed towards A, but neither toleration nor intolerance will be real options for B.

If we adopt a simple Westphalian view of the world, in which each state is sovereign over its own affairs, toleration may seem to disappear from the international agenda. If the government and people of each state honour the sovereignty of every other state, they will regard themselves as properly powerless to interfere in the affairs of other states. They will therefore suppose that they are in no position either to tolerate or not to tolerate what happens outside their own jurisdictions and the idea of international toleration will not get off the ground.

That simple Westphalian view does not describe the world in which we live.[3] States, or their governments, interfere in one another's affairs all the time and they are not the only international actors who do so. In so far as international intervention is a matter of right or wrong rather than sheer impossibility, it is a possible subject of toleration. The intervention that is at issue in international toleration should not be limited to military intervention. It can also include measures such as economic sanctions, the setting of conditions for the receipt of aid, the passage of condemnatory resolutions in the UN, and use of propaganda and aggressive 'educational' programmes.[4]

Inequalities of power across the international system mean that toleration and intolerance are options more available to some than to others. The United States can tolerate or not tolerate what happens in Grenada, but Grenada is in no position either to tolerate or not to tolerate what happens in the United States. But the events of 9/11 and their aftermath graphically illustrate that even the most powerful states are vulnerable to the consequences of external disapproval.

REASONS FOR TOLERATION

Many different reasons have been mobilized in defence of toleration. They have varied according to the beliefs and values that people have brought to the argument and according to the specific matter at issue. In political contexts, four general types of reason have been prominent, although these by no means exhaust the field. One appeals to the adverse consequences of intolerance, such as the human suffering it may cause. Another appeals to scepticism, doubt, or reasonable disagreement in challenging the basis of intolerance. A third appeals to an idea of the human good and suggests that human well-being may be enhanced by letting people pursue their own conception of their good, even though we might think it mistaken or ill-judged. A fourth points to the status and respect that we should accord people as persons, which provides reason to allow them to take their own path even when we think it the wrong path.

Of these four general sorts of reason, that which has most ready appeal in the international context is the first. Intervention by one state in the affairs of another can result in immense human suffering, terrible bloodshed, and widespread loss of life. The bad should be tolerated if the consequences of intolerance will be even worse. Saddam Hussein's regime, for example, may have been bad for most Iraqis and a threat to the region, but if the human costs and political consequences of toppling it prove even worse, better that his regime should have been tolerated. Sometimes this sort of consequentialist defence of toleration can seem merely prudential. It is if it is motivated merely by the tolerator's self-interest, but not if the concern is to minimize human suffering and loss of life. Certainly, on this consequentialist approach, the case for toleration will be contingent upon the particularity of circumstances, but its contingency does not make it prudential rather than moral.

Any approach to political toleration or intolerance that pays no attention to consequences is not to be taken seriously. 'Let justice be done, though heaven fall' is not a good political motto, especially for the international world. However, while we must take consequences seriously, we need not place the case for toleration entirely at their mercy. Suppose that one state were so overwhelmingly powerful that it could enforce its wishes on another without either bloodshed or overt conflict. Would that put an end to the argument? We may think that intolerance can be wrong even if it does not have the dire consequences that we associate with international conflict. And even if it does have adverse consequences, we may think it wrong not only because of those consequences.

In the remainder of this chapter I want to explore the relevance to the international world of another of the four sorts of argument for toleration that I identified above: that which appeals to the status of persons and the respect they are due.

TOLERATION AND RESPECTING PERSONS

The idea of personhood is now frequently deployed in defence of toleration. To be recognized as a person is to be recognized as a being who is capable of reflection and judgement and of making decisions for oneself. It is also to be recognized as someone whose wishes and decisions about his or her own life should be respected. That respect turns not on the merit of an individual's wishes and decisions but on the status of the individual whose wishes and decisions they are.

This idea of personhood is closely associated with Kant, for whom it was integrally related with that of autonomy. Human beings were uniquely capable of autonomous conduct. They were capable of possessing and being guided by a rational will and they acted autonomously in conforming with that will. It was that capacity that distinguished them as persons. That conception of having command over one's own conduct has remained an important part of the idea of personhood but, in the hands of subsequent theorists, personhood has been loosened from the firm grip of Kant's uncompromising notion of moral autonomy. To be a person is to be capable of reflecting on and taking a view on the character of one's own life and on the life one wishes to live or believes one should live. But it does not entail the notion that one's life either can be or should be entirely self-made—that it should be chosen in a way that is independent of all external influence and indebted only to the self whose life it is. Rather than thinking of a person's life as a life that person has chosen, we do better to think of it as a life a person has 'embraced'. That is truer to the reality of people's lives and how they come to live them. People can be committed to a form of life even though their coming to live that form of life is not uniquely a consequence of their self-originated choice.

This conception of persons and the respect they are due is central to the deontological liberalism of theorists such as John Rawls, Charles Larmore, Thomas Nagel, T. M. Scanlon, and Brian Barry. But it is not unique to that school of thought and is now very widely shared. However, as a reason for toleration, it needs to be carefully distinguished from the third type of reason that I listed above, a reason that turns on a conception of the human good. An individual's well-being may be better served by allowing her to live an inferior form of life to which she is committed than by compelling her to live an intrinsically superior form of life to which she has no commitment. What does the work in this argument is not a conception of what we owe persons qua persons but a conception of how we can best promote well-being or whatever other standard we use to evaluate the quality of people's lives. We can mark the difference between these two reasons for toleration by way of the distinction between status and merit. When we appeal to the idea of personhood, we appeal to an idea of status, but when we appeal to the quality of people's lives, we appeal to an idea of merit.

Very often the practical demands of personhood and of well-being will be the same, but they need not be. If we operate purely with an idea of the good, we cannot have reason to allow someone to live an inferior form of life if, all things considered (including the impact of our intolerance), we could contrive that they should live better. But if we operate with the idea of respect for persons, we may have reason to allow someone to live a life that we evaluate as bad—and bad for that particular person all things considered. One reason why the idea of respect for persons lends itself so readily to toleration is because it entails an idea of status. Thus, even when someone's life lacks merit, the status of the person who lives it might oblige us to tolerate it. Status trumps (de)merit. That is not to say that status must always trump merit. At some point a form of life may become so bad that we think its badness is more significant than the status of the person who lives it, so that merit trumps status. All I mean to point to here is that the ideas of status and respect associated with personhood can provide a readily intelligible account of why we might think it right to tolerate ways of life, or features of ways of life, that we judge bad or inferior.

There is one sense in which the idea of personhood that I have described here is individualistic: it invests moral standing in individual persons. But there are other forms of individualism that it does not entail. In particular, it does not imply that the best form of life is individualistic. The idea that individuals are the ultimate possessors of moral status is entirely consistent with the notion that the best life (the most satisfying, the most fulfilling, the most complete life) for human beings is collective or communal in form. Nor does it imply that individuals must register their claims only as so many individuals. The ways of life embraced by persons may be collective in form so that respecting those persons will entail respecting the collective form of life to which they are committed.

RAWLS AND THE SOCIETY OF PEOPLES

Is it possible, then, to deploy this sort of reason as a reason for toleration in the international domain? One philosopher who has done so is John Rawls.[5] However, for Rawls, the parties who constitute the subjects and the objects of toleration internationally are not persons but 'Peoples'. Persons, in their role as citizens, are the actors in a liberal society; but we should view the international world as a 'Society of Peoples' and, in that society, peoples, not persons, are the relevant moral actors.[6] In his *Law of Peoples*, Rawls sets out his vision of a just international order that encompasses both liberal and decent hierarchical peoples. These two sorts of people differ fundamentally in the way they organize their societies. Nevertheless, they have reason to tolerate one another as members in good standing of the society of peoples. In a liberal society, it would be unjust for some citizens to use political power to impose their comprehensive doctrine and its associated conception of the good upon others. Analogously, in the society of peoples it would be unjust for one people to impose its conception of the best or the right society on peoples who possess different conceptions.[7] Thus, for Rawls, the form that toleration should take among peoples internationally mimics the toleration that the citizens of a liberal society should accord one another. Moreover, just as the case for toleration in a liberal society is rooted in a conception of citizens as free and equal persons, so international toleration should be rooted in a conception of peoples as free and equal.[8] Peoples should recognize and respect one another as equal members in good standing of the society of peoples. Indeed, Rawls sometimes presents that recognition and respect as what international toleration consists in, rather than as a reason for toleration.[9]

Peoples are clearly made up of individuals but for Rawls the moral standing of *peoples* seems to owe nothing to their being composed of *persons*. On the contrary, at the international level, a people stands in a strictly analogous relation to a person at the domestic level. Rather than derive its moral significance from the moral standing of its members severally, a people, for Rawls, has the same irreducibility as a moral entity as a person. We might describe peoples, on Rawls's view, as 'corporate persons',[10] although, to avoid confusion I shall continue to use 'persons' to describe only human individuals. Peoples possess equal moral standing simply as peoples and they have rights and bear duties just as peoples.

What then, for Rawls, distinguishes a people as a people? A people, he says, possesses three basic features: a common government, common sympathies, and a moral nature.[11] In ascribing a moral nature to a people, he supposes that it possesses 'a firm attachment to a political (moral) conception of right and justice'.[12] Peoples, he supposes, are capable of and committed to just relations with other peoples. Accordingly, they will offer fair terms of cooperation with other peoples and will honour those terms, provided they are assured that other peoples will do the same.[13]

Rawls is insistent that by peoples he does not mean states.[14] He distinguishes peoples from states because he wishes to emphasize the moral nature of peoples and not to ascribe to them the unconstrained sovereignty that has been traditionally ascribed to states. Is a people, then, something that has a prepolitical or nonpolitical identity; is it something that might exist in the absence of a state or a common government? Some of Rawls's remarks suggest that it might. As I have previously mentioned, he says that a people is distinguished by 'common sympathies', by which he means the sense of nationality that Mill described and attributed to factors such as common race and descent, a common language, community of religion, and a shared history.[15] He also describes peoples as possessing different cultures and traditions of thought,[16] and observes that they may exhibit a 'proper patriotism' and take pride in their histories and achievements.[17] Yet nothing he says really suggests that he means to identify peoples with anything other than the populations of states as they currently exist. In relation to the way in which humanity is currently divided for political purposes, Rawls apparently intends the concept of a 'people' to be as uncontroversial and as unchallenging an idea as it has been in the hands of the United Nations.

If a people is identical with the population of a state, it is hard to be won over to the idea that it has a strong corporate identity independently of the state, given the highly contingent origins of most state boundaries. It is also hard to accept that its nonstate identity is such that we should conceive it as a single unitary entity possessing irreducible moral standing. Rawls conceives a people as a moral, rather than a merely legal, entity and the claims that peoples can reasonably make upon one another as moral claims. His 'law of peoples' is not a 'law' in the ordinary sense. It is a set of moral principles that should govern the conduct of peoples. It aims to provide a moral foundation for international law rather than a draft of international law itself; hence his identification of the law of peoples with a 'realistic utopia'. Rawls cannot therefore rely upon law to provide the corporate identity he ascribes to a people.

More generally, the idea that we can plausibly ascribe irreducible moral standing to groups as groups is widely doubted. The idea of corporate persons has a well-established place in law. The idea that nonlegal corporate persons should occupy a similar place in our moral thinking, though sometimes canvassed, is much less readily accepted. Often the impetus behind that idea seems to be the belief that, if we do not conceive groups as moral analogues of persons, we cannot do justice to the role they play in the lives of human beings. That belief, I shall now argue, is misplaced.[18]

GROUPS: CORPORATE AND COLLECTIVE

In place of Rawls's corporate conception of peoples, we can adopt what I shall describe as a 'collective' conception. When we conceive a group claim as a collective claim, we conceive it as the joint claim of the several individuals who make up the group. If we conceive a group claim in that way, we need not ascribe to the group a moral identity or standing that is somehow separate from, and independent of, that of the individuals who make it up. On the contrary, the moral standing that underwrites the claim is that of the several individuals who constitute the group. We can therefore acknowledge group claims without having to pretend that, morally, a group constitutes a 'super-person'.[19]

Can this way of conceiving group claims cope with claims that have an intrinsically group nature? We might suspect that, while a collective conception can make sense of claims that are contingently the claims of a group, it cannot adequately characterize claims that *only* a group can make. By a contingent group claim I mean one that is registered by a group but that might also be registered by individuals severally. For example, a church may claim the freedom to practise its own forms of worship, but those forms of worship may be such that an individual adherent of the faith could intelligibly claim the same freedom as an individual. But not all group claims are like that. Sometimes they are claims to goods that can be claimed plausibly or reasonably only by a group. Consider a claim that public measures should be instituted to protect and sustain the language of a linguistic minority. Given that the language is a good that is public to the minority and given the costs involved in instituting measures to protect and sustain it, this is not a claim that a single member of the minority could reasonably make as an independent individual. Or consider the same sort of claim in respect of a culture. A culture is, by its very nature, a group phenomenon and it would seem that claims that the culture should be respected or promoted could be plausibly made only by or on behalf of the group. But, even in cases in which a good is such that it can be claimed and enjoyed only by a group, it makes perfect sense to conceive the good as one to which the members of the group have a shared or joint claim. The fact that a claim is one that the members of a group can plausibly register only as a group is quite consistent with ascribing the moral standing that underwrites their claim to the members of the group severally rather than to the group as a corporate entity.

If we conceive group claims in this collective fashion, we can appeal to the idea of persons, and to the respect they are owed, in defending group claims. In particular, just as respect for persons can be mobilized in defence of individual self-determination, so it can be mobilized in defence of collective self-determination. A claim to collective self-determination is clearly one that can be made only for a group but also one that can be conceived as a joint or shared claim of those who make up the group.[20]

The sort of shift that Rawls makes from persons to peoples in moving from the domestic to the international case would therefore seem unnecessary. I do not mean to dismiss the idea of peoples in any form. I mean only that we are neither obliged nor best advised to treat peoples rather than persons as the moral entities whose ultimate and irreducible status grounds the case for international toleration.

For my purposes, a 'people' is a section of humanity that forms a self-determining unit. A people may be an entirely contingent entity; that is, there may be a large measure of contingency in the way humanity has come to be divided up into separate societies. For my purposes, that does not matter. What matters is that a set of individuals is constituted as a collective unit that has to order its own internal affairs. Hence a 'people' in my vocabulary is primarily a political entity and it need be no more than that. I do not mean to deny that a people may sometimes be marked off from the rest of humanity by common characteristics such as a shared history, a common language, and a common culture. Those common characteristics have some bearing on my argument but, for my purposes, the only feature of a people that is crucial to its being a people is its constituting a self-governing unit. I take peoples therefore to be conterminous with states. However, I do not take states to be the fundamental objects of international toleration. If we (whoever 'we' are here) owe duties of toleration to another society, the parties to whom we owe those duties are ultimately neither states nor peoples conceived as corporate entities but the persons who make up their populations.

I do not suppose, of course, that a people will be entirely self-determining. In the contemporary world, no population's 'internal' affairs are free from external forces and influences and none is wholly self-determining. That is especially true of the economic life of societies. A society may have a greater measure of control over those of its features that are most likely to be objects of toleration or intolerance: its political structure, social organization, and way(s) of life. But I do not wish to assert any strong empirical claim to that effect. All I shall suppose is that, even after we have taken full account of the impact of globalization, supranational institutions, and other external factors, a society retains sufficient control over its own character for it to be a possible and significant object of toleration.

TOLERATING CULTURAL DIFFERENCE

Perhaps the sort of difference that is associated more than any other with the idea of international or global toleration is cultural difference. Different societies possess different cultures or ways of life, and practices that figure in one culture are sometimes condemned by another. Here I want to give substance to the general claims I have made by examining what it is that drives the thought that cultural differences between societies should be objects of toleration. In posing the issue in that way, I do not mean to suggest that, if we accept that cultures are proper objects of toleration, our toleration has to be indiscriminate. Rather my question is, if and in so far as we think that cultural differences are appropriate objects of toleration, why do we think that?

'Culture' is a problematic notion and we sometimes do better to unpack its content into other terms. It is often allowed too easily to sanctify what it describes; the rhetorical effect of describing beliefs, values, and practices as 'cultural' can be to throw a protective halo around them so that they acquire a special status and immunity merely because they are (said to be) 'cultural'. There are also well-recognized dangers of essentializing cultures and difficulties in deciding how we should individuate them. In particular, cultures do not map readily onto societies politically defined. However, I shall pursue none of those issues here. In order to get at the issue that is my concern, I shall continue to use the ideas of culture and cultural difference and to suppose that the culture that is a possible object of toleration belongs to a whole society so that the issue is one of international toleration.

Why, then, should we be tolerant in this sort of case? An answer that immediately suggests itself is: because we associate cultural diversity with relativism. 'Relativism' is another problematic and protean term. Sometimes, when it is applied to cultures, it is used to describe no more than the fact of cultural diversity, but that merely empirical observation does not help us to decide how we should respond to the fact that it describes. Alternatively, 'cultural relativism' might describe a moral doctrine: the doctrine that the right way for people to conduct their lives is in accordance with their particular culture. That is an odd doctrine. Why should we hold that view of right conduct quite irrespective of the content of any particular culture? Can a moral doctrine be quite so careless of what it endorses? If it can, it must do so in virtue of an ethical principle that undergirds its endorsement of cultural variety and it will be that principle that commands respect for cultural differences rather than the relativism it generates.

More frequently, cultural relativism expresses a form of scepticism. It expresses the belief that there is no set of norms that is properly universal in reach and that constitutes the truly correct morality for all human beings. There are merely different sets of norms that have been evolved by different segments of humanity. People may suppose that the particular morality to which they subscribe is uniquely right, but they are mistaken. They are also mistaken if they suppose that we might somehow turn up a genuinely correct set of norms that is independent of any particular culture and against which we can test the moral merit of the several cultures human beings have evolved.

In this form, cultural relativism expresses a meta-ethical rather than an ethical position, but it is a meta-ethical position that has practical implications. It implies that, if we set about imposing norms upon a community that are at variance with its own, in the belief that those norms are uniquely right or superior to the community's own norms, we act on a false assumption. We suppose our beliefs and values to be something other than, and more than, the particular beliefs and values that they really are. This sort of scepticism can be, and has been, a potent force for toleration. It undermines intolerance that is based upon a belief in the superiority of one culture over another, or that supposes that we can access a uniquely valid set of norms that is categorically different from, and that stands free of, the merely local norms evolved by particular communities. Of course, if we are concerned at all with human well-being and with right relations between people, we also have reason to resist this sort of moral scepticism as a comprehensive position, since it can corrode any sort of moral conviction and issue in a comprehensive amorality. It deprives us, for example, of the resources to say that a culture that incorporates slavery is, in that respect, worse than one that does not; and, while it may be mobilized against intercultural intolerance, it can also be mobilized in defence of cultures that are internally repressive and externally aggressive. Nevertheless, we do not have to embrace moral scepticism comprehensively to recognize that intolerance has frequently resulted from people's mistaking the local for the universal and the conventional for the absolute. The obvious way to combat intolerance of that sort is to challenge the convictions upon which it is based.

I do not wish to deny, therefore, that cultural relativism in this form can corrode intolerance. As with cultural relativism as a moral doctrine, it does not provide us with a reason for toleration strictly speaking, since it undermines intolerance by undermining the disapproval upon which it is based. Hence, in so far as it succeeds, it renders toleration unnecessary. But that may seem little more than pedantry, especially if we think that it is the absence of intolerance rather than the presence of toleration that really matters. However, even setting pedantry aside, this sceptical form of relativism does not provide us with a wholly adequate case for toleration of cultural difference. It characterizes intolerance as misguided rather than wrongful. It suggests that it is falsely based if it is grounded in a belief that another culture is wrong or morally inferior. But making a mistake is not the same as committing a wrong; we need more than an allegation of error if our toleration is to be the subject of a moral imperative. Moreover, unacceptable intolerance does not have to be the offspring of a false or questionable belief. It may be driven, for example, by a desire to dominate and by an appetite for the fruits of domination.

Where else, then, might we look for a justification of cultural toleration? Cultural diversity is frequently represented as itself a good. The fundamental thought here is that the world is richer for possessing a diversity of cultures and that it would be very much poorer if that diversity disappeared or were diminished through, for example, the erosive and homogenizing effects of globalization. The tedium and blandness of a monocultural world would compare most unfavourably with the rich cultural heterogeneity that has characterized humanity hitherto. Should we then ground the case for cultural toleration in the good of cultural diversity?

There are two reasons why that does not seem the right sort of foundation for cultural toleration. One is that, if cultural diversity presents us with a good, it ceases to be an object for toleration. In making this elementary point, I do not mean to suggest that we do better to find something objectionable so that we do not lose an opportunity for toleration. That would be absurd. Rather I mean that cultural differences do sometimes provide real occasions for toleration (or intolerance) and that to suppose that we can all find every feature of one another's cultures 'good' is not to take seriously the deep disagreements and conflicts that exist among cultures. It is one thing to celebrate differences of cuisine, dress, literature, and music. It is quite another to celebrate differences of belief concerning the relative status people should be accorded, the way they should treat one another, and the way they should treat nonhuman animals and the rest of the nonhuman world. Deep cultural differences are often founded in different religious faiths and those faiths make competing claims about truth, good, and evil. It is nonsensical to ask the adherent of one faith to celebrate the existence of a rival faith or of atheistic disbelief, which the adherent must regard as false and pernicious. Cultural differences present all of us with serious questions concerning toleration and intolerance and indiscriminately to label all diversity 'good' is not to take cultures or their adherents seriously.

There is a second reason why the 'good' of cultural diversity does not seem the most compelling reason for cultural toleration. That conception of cultural diversity presents it as a public good; that is, as a good public to humanity as a whole. Thus, if a culture is suppressed or disadvantaged, we are all the losers. But, when a culture is suppressed or disadvantaged, we do not think that we are all equally the losers. Rather, we conceive it as a wrong inflicted upon a particular section of humanity—upon those whose culture it is. The particularity of that wrong cannot be explained by the general good of cultural diversity. By the same token, if we believe we should tolerate a controversial feature of a culture, our toleration is more plausibly owed to the bearers of that culture rather than to humanity at large.[21]

So what this points to is that the case for toleration of cultural difference is most plausibly grounded in a concern and respect for those whose culture is at stake. It is not cultures themselves or their alleged relativism that drives the case for toleration. It is recognition of and respect for the status of those who bear them. Cultures do not, of themselves, possess moral standing, any more than do works of art or musical compositions or languages. Cultures matter because they matter to people, and they matter most to those whose cultures they are. We are driven back therefore to the idea of respect for persons and the claims that those persons have in respect of the culture they embrace. As I have previously argued, the collective character of a culture provides no reason why we should turn away from persons and towards peoples corporately conceived as the objects of our concern.

The idea of respect associated with personhood is not the only possible reason for grounding a concern for culture in a concern for its bearers. We might also appeal to the well-being of the people involved. We might hold that a life lived according to a culture that is in some way 'theirs' is always best for people. However, that claim will not work as a reason for toleration among people who have deeply conflicting beliefs and values and therefore deeply conflicting conceptions of what constitutes a good life and 'well-being'. More compelling are the well-documented deleterious effects upon people of efforts to eradicate their inherited way of life and to replace it with something 'better'. Thus, even when we find fault with a culture, the real alternatives may give us reason to leave it in place. I have no wish to brush aside these sorts of consideration. But, arguably, toleration is more securely based in the status of those whose way of life is at stake and our obligation to defer to their own beliefs and wishes, than in judgements of the merit of their culture and the feasibility of the alternatives.

DEMOCRACY AND POPULAR SOVEREIGNTY

Does the approach I am suggesting here imply that only democratic political systems are tolerable? After all, the idea that we should conceive adult human beings as persons, who are to be accorded equal respect, readily translates into a case for political equality, which, in turn, translates into a case for political democracy. However, the idea of democracy is not the same as that of popular sovereignty, even though those two ideas are often elided. To be committed to democracy is to be committed to the rightness or goodness of a particular form of government. To be committed to popular sovereignty is to be committed to the legitimacy of whatever form of government a society's population endorses for itself. Thus, in principle and sometimes in practice, an undemocratic form of government may pass the test of popular sovereignty. Where it does, we have reason (though not necessarily exclusive reason) to find that form of government tolerable. Of course, in the case of an undemocratic form of government, we may face empirical difficulties in knowing quite how much popular support it actually enjoys. The issue is also unlikely to be quite so simple as whether a regime does, or does not, enjoy popular support. It is more likely to involve complex assessments of the proportions of the population who either support or oppose the regime and of the relative intensities of their support or opposition. But let's pass over those issues for the moment. If people genuinely endorse an undemocratic regime, arguably we owe it to them to respect their wishes about how their collective lives should be organized and managed. In other words, in these circumstances, respecting persons does not translate into a case for democracy; it translates into a case for whatever sort of regime those persons embrace. Those who are scandalized by this conclusion might bear in mind three things. First, what I have said does not provide a case for undemocratic regimes merely because and in so far as they currently exist. It provides a case only in so far as those regimes genuinely enjoy popular support. Secondly, my argument here concerns *toleration*. Thus, it is quite consistent with the belief that democracy is always the best form of government and that a population mistakes its own interest if it opts for anything else. Thirdly, remember how 'thin' is the democracy that is urged upon those societies that do not already possess it. It is not some variant of the direct democracy of the Ancient World; the model is usually that of the United States or a Western European regime in which institutionalized popular participation is extremely limited and political equality more symbolic than real. Nor can that attenuated form of democracy be excused as the most democratic that we can enjoy under modern circumstances. If Switzerland can build referendums and the popular initiative into its political structures, so might other self-styled 'democracies'—but most choose not to. Once we take account of those realities, the contrast between *soi-disant* 'democracies' and an undemocratic but popularly supported regime appears less stark.

MORAL EQUALITY AND SOCIAL INEQUALITY

The issue of how respect for persons relates to political systems is really part of a larger issue of how morally equal status relates to social and political institutions that accord people unequal status. Normally, morally equal status argues for a similar equality of status in a society's social and political arrangements. There are, of course, all sorts of functional reasons why a society should want to create institutional structures that involve status hierarchies, such as the structures of authority normally exhibited by governments, judiciaries, and militaries. The existence of a variety of offices that are occupied by some and not others, and that give some decision-making powers not possessed by others, is still consistent with a basic institutional commitment to the equal moral standing of people.

But suppose a society's arrangements do accord fundamentally, rather than instrumentally, unequal statuses to the society's members and that all concerned accept those arrangements. How should we view that state of affairs? Does it matter that those who are treated as inferiors in an arrangement themselves endorse that arrangement? It seems to me that it does. If respect for persons entails respecting people's beliefs and wishes about how they should live, and if people are committed to a system of belief in which they occupy a lesser status than others, it would seem that we should give weight to their commitment even though we think it misplaced. There is more than a hint of paradox here, since our reason for respecting someone's commitment to their unequal status is the equal status we attribute to them. But the appearance of paradox is mitigated if the commitment we are respecting is part of a broader commitment to a system of belief, such as a religious faith, rather than mere self-deprecation. Recall, too, that the issue here is not the rightness of people's beliefs and practices but whether we have reason to tolerate them.

Men and women occupy positions of unequal standing in the Roman Catholic Church in that men are eligible for clerical office and women are not. Yet we would not ordinarily suppose that that warrants external intervention in the affairs of the Catholic Church compelling it to assign equal and identical roles to men and women. Nor do we suppose that it provides reason to find women's commitment to Roman Catholicism less tolerable than men's. The Catholic Church is, of course, nowadays a voluntary association; people have real options of entry and exit, and those options are unlikely to be similarly real for people as members of a political community. I cite the case of the Catholic Church only to indicate that people's acceptance of unequal roles can make a difference to how we respond to that inequality.

Of course, we need to be careful here. The case I describe is one in which people accept an inferiority of status for themselves, not one in which that inferiority is imposed upon them against their wishes. In addition, the perception that a society assigns different and unequal roles to its members may meet the riposte that those roles are not in fact unequal; they are merely different. That riposte is frequently given to 'outsiders' who complain about gender inequality in some non-Western societies. This is also territory in which concerns about 'adaptive preferences' are likely to arise. That is far too large an issue for me to tackle here. I shall content myself with observing that just whose preferences are adaptive and whose are not is far from straightforward; we must guard against the propensity to suppose that 'their' preferences are adaptive but 'ours' are not. Secondly, preferences or beliefs need be no less firmly and sincerely held for being adaptive and it is the fact of the preferences and beliefs that people actually embrace with which we have to deal.

SOCIAL DISSENSUS AND THE LIMITS OF INTERNATIONAL TOLERATION

Throughout this article, I have emphasized respect for persons as a reason for tolerating collective forms of life of which we disapprove but to which those who live them are committed. But we have also to confront the question of how far that respect has an opposite import. If respect for persons argues for toleration of collective forms of life, it also argues for limits on the extent to which collectivities can be intolerant of individuals or minorities who wish to live other forms of life. Internationally, this takes us into the familiar

territory of human rights, conceived as safeguards that limit what governments, groups, and other power-holders may do to (or may not do for) those
who are subject to their power. I shall not address the issue of human rights
here, but clearly the sort of ethic to which I have appealed argues strongly
for those rights.

A further complication is dissensus within societies over their basic structures. For the sake of simplicity, I have assumed that, while societies exhibit
different basic structures, each population broadly endorses the basic structure of its own society, so that, for each society, conflicts concerning the ordinary run of social and political issues are contained within a larger context
of consensus. Clearly that assumption will often be false. I have argued that
respect for persons provides a case for tolerating undemocratic and unequal
arrangements but only provided those arrangements are genuinely endorsed
by those who live under them. Thus, where conflict over a society's basic
structure takes the form of an unrepresentative elite coercively imposing
its favoured arrangements upon a dissenting population, equal respect for
persons provides no case for toleration—though others considerations, particularly calculations of cost and consequence, may still do so. But where a
population is genuinely divided amongst itself, respect for persons may give
us no steer on which side we should favour.

My principal concern has been to show the potency of the idea of respect
for persons as a reason for international toleration of different cultural, social,
and political arrangements. In particular, when we move from the domestic
to the international level, we have no need to forsake 'persons' for 'peoples'
as the ultimate objects of our concern. I have also tried to show how an idea
that is often used to argue for egalitarian social and political arrangements
can, under the right circumstances, argue for toleration of arrangements of
a quite different sort. The simple idea of respect for persons will not always
yield simple answers and it constitutes only one of many considerations that
bear upon the complicated and messy world of international politics, but it
does have something to contribute to our thinking on the larger issues that
surround the 'war on terror'.

NOTES

1. For analyses of the general idea of toleration, see Andrew Jason Cohen, 'What
Toleration Is', *Ethics* 115, no. 1 (2004): 68–95; Catriona McKinnon, *Toleration: A
Critical Introduction* (London: Routledge, 2006); Susan Mendus, *Toleration and the
Limits of Liberalism* (Basingstoke: Macmillan, 1989); Glen Newey, *Virtue, Reason
and Toleration: The Place of Toleration in Ethical and Political Philosophy* (Edin-
burgh: Edinburgh University Press, 1999); and chapter 1 of this volume.

2. Three conspicuous exceptions are John Rawls, *The Law of Peoples* (Cambridge, MA: Harvard University Press, 1999); Kok-Chor Tan, *Toleration, Diversity and Global Justice* (University Park: Pennsylvania State University Press, 2000); and Michael Walzer, *On Toleration* (New Haven: Yale University Press, 1997). Because of the latitude societies are willing to give one another through the idea of sovereignty, Walzer describes international society as 'the most tolerant of all societies' (1997, 19).

3. Stephen D. Krasner, *Sovereignty and Organized Hypocrisy* (Princeton, NJ: Princeton University Press, 1999).

4. Attempts to rationally persuade are usually deemed consistent with toleration, presumably because they do not prevent or hinder the conduct that the persuader argues against. But when such attempts move beyond giving reasons and leaving people to make up their own minds, they can be reasonably viewed as entering the realm of intolerance (which is not, of course, to say that they are necessarily wrong in any particular instance or to imply that all forms of intolerance are equally intolerant). We might even say that B, who objects to A's conduct but is content to leave it unchanged, is more tolerant than C who objects to A's conduct and tries to alter it through persuasion. Members of nonevangelical religions such as Judaism and Hinduism sometimes object in these terms to the proselytizing activities of Christians and Muslims. See further chapter 10.

5. Rawls, *The Law of Peoples*.

6. Rawls, *The Law of Peoples*, 23.

7. Rawls, *The Law of Peoples*, 11–12, 59, 84.

8. Rawls, *The Law of Peoples*, 33–34, 37, 60, 69–70.

9. For example, 'To tolerate also *means* to recognize these nonliberal societies as equal participating members in good standing of the society of Peoples, with certain rights and obligations, including the duty of civility requiring that they offer other Peoples public reasons appropriate to the Society of Peoples for their actions'; Rawls, *The Law of Peoples*, 59, my emphasis; see also pp. 63, 84.

10. Reidy describes peoples, on Rawls's view, as 'corporate moral agents' and 'as persons in the moral sense of that term'; David A. Reidy, 'Rawls on International Justice: A Defense', *Political Theory* 32 no. 3 (2004): 291–319 at 294.

11. In fact, Rawls presents these as three features of a *liberal* people and, rather than just observing that a liberal people has a 'common government', he says that they possess 'a reasonably just constitutional democratic government that serves their fundamental interests'; Rawls, *The Law of Peoples*, 23. However, I infer that Rawls regards a common government, common sympathies, and a moral nature as features common to both liberal and decent hierarchical peoples.

12. Rawls, *The Law of Peoples*, 24.

13. Rawls, *The Law of Peoples*, 25.

14. Rawls, *The Law of Peoples*, 23–30.

15. Rawls, *The Law of Peoples*, 23.

16. Rawls, *The Law of Peoples*, 11, 40.

17. Rawls, *The Law of Peoples*, 62, 111–12.

18. For a general critique of this analogical approach, though one that focuses on the analogy between persons and states rather than peoples, see Charles Beitz,

Political Theory and International Relations, second edition (Princeton, NJ: Princeton University Press, 1999), part II.

19. I examine the contrast between corporate and collective conceptions of groups in my 'Group Rights and Group Oppression', *Journal of Political Philosophy* 6, no. 4 (1999): 352–76. However, there I limit my analysis to group rights, whereas here I want to extend the implications of the collective conception beyond rights.

20. Walzer's thinking often seems in sympathy with this position; see Michael Walzer, 'The Moral Standing of States', *Philosophy and Public Affairs* 9, no. 3 (1980): 209–29. He presents himself as a defender of the standing of 'states' (1980), but, unlike Rawls, his conception of political communities as moral claimants seems to be collective rather than corporate in nature. He attributes to states rights to territorial integrity and political sovereignty, but adds that these rights 'derive ultimately from the rights of individuals, and from them they take their force' and insists that we should not conceive states as 'organic wholes' or 'mystical unions'; Michael Walzer, *Just and Unjust States*, second edition (New York: Basic Books, 1992), 53. He also observes, 'The real subject of my argument is not the state at all but the political community that (usually) underlies it . . . the idea of communal integrity derives its moral and political force from the rights of contemporary men and women to live as members of a historic community and to express their inherited culture through political forms worked out among themselves (the forms are never entirely worked out in a single generation)' (1980, 210–11).

21. It might be argued that we have to put up with particular bads if we are to retain the overall good of cultural diversity. That suggestion does have the structure of an argument for toleration. We have reason to tolerate some bad features of cultures because that it is a price we have to pay if we are to retain the overall good of cultural heterogeneity. In this argument, the badness of bad practices is not cancelled by the greater good of cultural diversity, so that it is genuinely one that calls for toleration. However, this case for toleration is highly contingent upon what is, in fact, necessary to retain the good of cultural diversity. It is frequently quite implausible to suggest that intolerance of particular practices will result in the collapse or unravelling of the larger cultures in which those practices are embedded. For example, the suppression of *sati* (or *suttee*) has not destroyed the larger Hindu culture within which it existed, and it is hard to believe that prohibition of female circumcision would trigger a domino-style collapse of the cultures in which it is currently practised.

Index

About the Author

Peter Jones is Emeritus Professor of Political Philosophy at Newcastle University, UK. Much of his work has focused on issues raised by differences of belief, culture and value. In addition to the essays that make up this volume, he has written on freedom of expression, religious accommodation, discrimination law, multiculturalism, recognition and compromise. More widely, he has examined questions relating to democracy, liberty, social policy and international justice. He has a particular interest in rights, including human rights and group rights, and is the author of *Rights* (Basingstoke: Macmillan, 1994), editor of *Group Rights* (Aldershot: Ashgate, 2009), and joint editor of *National Rights, International Obligations* (Boulder: Westview, 1996) and *Human Rights and Global Diversity* (London: Frank Cass, 2001).

www.ingramcontent.com/pod-product-compliance
Lightning Source LLC
Chambersburg PA
CBHW021139030426

R18078200001B/R180782PG42334CBX00002B/3